Best Sermons 6

CONTRIBUTING EDITORS

Best Sermons 6

James W. Cox, Editor

Kenneth M. Cox, Associate Editor

HarperSanFrancisco
A Division of HarperCollinsPublishers

Quotations from the Bible are from the Revised Standard Version, the King James Version, and the New International Version. In addition, some contributors have made their own translations and others have used a mixed text.

FIRST EDITION

Library of Congress Catalog Card Number 88–656297
ISSN 1041–6382

93 94 95 96 97 RRD(H) 10 9 8 7 6 5 4 3 2 1

Contents

110330

VI. Devotional

Preface

Much of religion, whatever faith or denomination, is a search for truth. Whether we are seeking the meaning of life, the meaning of Scripture, our place in the world, or a reason to strive and to hope, what we are really looking for is what is right, what is true. Of course, one person's quest for truth may lead to a place far from the destination of another's journey, but somehow all signs point in the same direction.

The sermon is a powerful vehicle for searching for, and sometimes finding, truth. There are nearly as many styles and forms of preaching as there are preachers, but the search for truth surely is a common thread. Someone has written that the shortest distance between a human being and truth is a story, and indeed the storytelling style of preaching can be quite meaningful. C. Welton Gaddy's sermon "Fugitives from Love," which appears in this volume, is a fine example of using story in a sermon.

Other styles and methods of preaching can be equally effective ways for us to seek and find truth through the preacher's voice, and you will find some of the best examples in these pages.

What is the process by which the sermons were chosen for this volume? First, note that twenty-two of the sermons are not a part of the competition. These sermons, for the most part, have been commissioned by the editor. Next, there are eighteen sermons—three in each of six categories—that have been chosen by six judges from the group of thirty-six finalists. Before the finalist sermons are sent to the judges, authors' names and addresses are removed to make each sermon anonymous. The editor chose the finalist sermons from all sermons submitted in accordance with the rules as defined by the publisher. Every sermon so submitted has been read and evaluated.

Requests for rules for each annual competition should be made of Best Sermons Competition, Harper San Francisco, 1160 Battery Street, San Francisco, CA 94111–1213.

Judges for the *Best Sermons 6* competition were as follows:

James W. Cox, Editor, Victor and Louise Lester Professor of Christian Preaching, The Southern Baptist Theological Seminary.

Joanna Adams, Pastor, Trinity Presbyterian Church, Atlanta, Georgia.

Daniel Aleshire, Associate Director, Association of Theological Schools, Pittsburgh, Pennsylvania.

James W. Crawford, Pastor, Old South Church in Boston (UCC), Boston, Massachusetts.

Thomas G. Long, Francis Landey Patton Professor of Preaching and Worship, Princeton Theological Seminary, Princeton, New Jersey.

Bruce Shields, Professor of Preaching and Biblical Hermeneutics, Emmanuel School of Religion, Johnson City, Tennessee.

Robert Smith, Jr., Pastor, New Mission Missionary Baptist Church, Cincinnati, Ohio.

Once again we thank all those who submitted sermons for the competition, and we encourage those and others to send us more of your best sermons.

JAMES W. COX
KENNETH M. COX

I. EVANGELISTIC

1. Fugitives from Love

C. Welton Gaddy

Mark 14:10–11, 43–46, 66–72

Why do we do things we do? What motivates us? What gets into us? How do we get out of it? Or how do we get "it" out of us? Are explanations possible?

Study two scenes. Each one is taken from the passion narratives of the New Testament.

Scene I. As the sun drops below the horizon, just as all of the beautiful pink streaks that set the heavens ablaze are being snuffed out by a bland, darkening gray, you see profiled against the sky a gnarled tree, a rope hanging from one of its limbs, and a man's body dangling on the end of that rope. You feel a sickness in your stomach. Suddenly it is night.

Scene II. As the sun's bright yellowish-orange rays begin to shoot outward to the farthest reaches of the sky, offering the first promises of a new day, you see a group of men standing around a campfire on a seashore. At first the scene makes you think of a family reunion. All present are laughing, slapping each other on the back, talking, and eating—fish as best you can tell from your vantage point. Obviously, it is daybreak.

A close look at these scenes reveals in each one the presence of at least one person who has committed a despicably evil deed—a betrayal of Christ. On the tree and on the beach are individuals who have denied the Savior. You know them both. As you think about it, you realize that the lives of these two men have paralleled each other in a remarkable manner. Many similarities exist between

C. Welton Gaddy is pastor of the Northminster Church in Monroe, Louisiana, and has served as senior minister to Mercer University and as pastor of Highland Hills Baptist Church in Macon, Georgia. He is the author of several books, including *Profile of a Christian Citizen* and *Beginning at the End.*

His most recent book is entitled *The Gift of Worship.*

their pilgrimages, their professions, and their problems. At this moment, though, one is by the seaside laughing while the other is at the end of a rope dying. What has brought about such a radical difference in their fates?

No one really knows what made Judas do what he did. Maybe he was tired of Jesus' way of doing things and ready for Jesus to follow him for a while. Giving him the benefit of the doubt, maybe Judas wanted more public recognition of Jesus' power and thought that his act would force Jesus' hand so that everyone could see his majesty and might. Of course, Judas well may have been just fed up with the whole mess and wanted it over and himself out. Perhaps Judas was jealous or even mad. There is even the outside possibility that Judas wanted to do something good. Maybe he did the wrong thing for a right reason. (That would not have been the first or the last time such a thing happened.) No one really knows what made Judas do what he did. But we do know what he did.

Betrayal! That is the word for it. A deal was struck—ill-fated to be sure, for such is the nature of any deal in which Jesus is bartered. "Jesus in your hands for thirty pieces of silver in my hands."

Be careful. Don't be too harsh in your judgment on Judas. We have sold Jesus for a lot less. And sometimes more.

Judas knew where to find Jesus. Perhaps the two of them had even prayed together in that place. For sure Jesus and Judas had broken bread together earlier that evening. After a brisk walk Judas found Jesus, quickly kissed him on his cheek, and watched the officials arrest Jesus. Then it was over. Most likely no one around knew how much it was over.

Later the whole scene exploded like a gun shot in Judas's mind. What had he done? Later still, Judas learned that Jesus was to die. It was too much for him. Judas was disoriented, hurting, reeling.

Simon Peter is easier to understand. We have good hunches about why he did what he did. A response to peer pressure, maybe. Certainly an act of reasoned fear. The disciple wanted to avoid guilt by association. Some people had recognized him. Peter had not counted on that. All he wanted was a little warmth by the evening fire. He did not intend to witness about anything. There was enough trouble already. Jesus was about to be killed. What need was there for anyone else to suffer also, Peter specifically. Peter meant to keep silent. But pressured by a questioner, he had to speak. He denied having anything to do with Jesus. Peter spoke as if he had never even known Jesus. He did precisely what many folks still do occasionally.

For Peter, as for Judas, no sooner was the deed done than he was distraught. In one sense Peter may very well have been even more upset than was Judas. He had bragged about his stamina, boasted of his spiritual strength. As Peter listened to the rooster crow, he must have remembered his own crowing, "I will never leave you, even though all the rest do!" Peter was completely undone. He bowed his head—he could not have held it up if he had tried—and wept.

Each of these men had to deal with his own sin. That is always the way it is. No one else can do that for you. Someone can dry your eyes as you cry over your sin or seek to rub away the pain caused by your sin. But no one else can settle the matter of sin for you. Each person has to face into that for herself.

Judas was sorry, desperately sorrowful, even penitent. This former follower of Jesus was willing to confess his sin. Unfortunately, he chose to make his confession to his coconspirators. Judas voiced his feelings to deaf ears. His partners had made their point and captured their prize. Judas would have to fend for himself, do the best he could with a bad conscience on his own.

I wonder what would have happened had Judas turned to the disciples. How would they have heard his penitence and reacted to his sorrow?

With deathly disgust, Judas hurled the silver pieces back at those who had bought his services, those who had bought him. As Pilate thought he could get rid of his sin by getting rid of what was on his hands, Judas tried to get rid of his sin by getting rid of what was in his hands. Judas was sorrowful. He knew of Jesus' innocence. Judas realized he was a traitor. He was frantic.

Peter also was sorrowful. The big strong fisherman cried like a disappointed little child. His tears were an outer manifestation of an inner devastation. We do not know the details of how Peter dealt with this dilemma. Ironically, in fact, we know more about Judas's response to his sin than we do about Peter's response to his sin. But the story can be pieced together.

From the biblical text, the next thing we know about Peter, the very next thing we know, Peter is with Jesus—sitting, standing, talking, laughing, fidgeting, pacing, running back and forth like a nervous little puppy that has found a caring master. From the biblical text, the next thing we know about Judas, the very next thing we know, Judas is hanging at the end of a rope. Peter is at the side of Jesus. Judas is alone.

Both men were sinners. Both men had turned on Jesus. Both men were sorry for what they had done. What made the difference between what happened to them?

What a terribly important question for all of us. Everyone of us has stood where both Peter and Judas stood in rejecting Jesus.

In a Good Friday homily by a fictional priest in one of Andrew Greeley's novels, the truth comes out. "The worst of Judas's sins was to refuse to accept the forgiveness that was offered to him."

All of us know how difficult it is to offer forgiveness. When persons close to us betray us, we swell up with disappointment, resentment, and anger. Would Jesus have been any different? Granting forgiveness is never easy. But look: Apparently, forgiveness is even more difficult to accept than to give. Peter fought it, floundering in guilt. Judas could not receive it, dying in disgrace.

Judas experienced remorse for his wrongdoing. When he threw the price of the dirty deal—the thirty pieces of silver—at the feet of Jesus' captors, Judas made a more public display of his sorrowful guilt than did Peter. At that point, why did Judas, convicted of his wrongdoing, not just head out toward Calvary and become a beneficiary of Jesus' forgiveness? Why did he remain a fugitive from love? Of course, the same questions can be asked of us.

To be offered an undeserved forgiveness is a terrifying experience. We are not accustomed to it. We balk at it, quickly step back from it. When we know that we have betrayed love—God's love or the love of another person—we find it tough to accept forgiveness. We seem to prefer the predictable guilt that is dominant within us and the scorn or rebuke that comes from the one betrayed. We can understand that. We can handle that. Forgiveness comes as a pure gift, pure mercy, pure love. We have trouble with that. We cannot envision ourselves as lovable.

As we ponder the contrast between the reactions of Judas and Peter to their sins, we begin to understand what made the difference between what happened to Judas and what happened to Peter. Judas saw himself as unlovable. He was a betrayer. Judas would not accept a love that he had not earned. Peter, too, knew dejection and despondency. Of course, he did not deserve love. Forgiveness was too good for him. But Peter accepted what Jesus offered. Peter was willing to receive that which he could never merit.

We may find ourselves squirming a bit as we continue. The subject matter is hitting close to home.

Judas sets before us that tendency within us to reject what we do not earn. Often we actually seem to prefer self-hatred and self-rejection to the acceptance of God's compassion. Peter represents another dimension of the human personality—that part of us that realizes we cannot ever earn love, we cannot merit forgiveness; that part of us that surrenders to a love beyond anything—control, manipulation, negotiation—except acceptance.

How crucial is this matter of being able to accept love, God's love? Crucial! Important beyond comprehension.

Judas could not move beyond his guilt. He saw himself as unworthy of forgiving love. So Judas went out and hanged himself with a rope. Peter bore just as much guilt as did Judas. He, too, was a betrayer—a fugitive from love. Peter knew he was not good enough to deserve forgiving love. But Peter understood that "good enough" was not the issue. Earning forgiveness was out of the question. Peter saw the truth that Greeley conveyed through his character named Father Ryan: "Love is gift, love is graceful, love is grace. And grace, needless to say, is love."

Judas did not go unforgiven because he could not be forgiven. No, God's grace is too great for that. The compassion of Jesus is too comprehensive for that. Judas turned in on himself instead of turning outward to God. The only forgiveness he could accept was what he could give. When he could not forgive himself, Judas had no one else to whom to turn.

Peter was forgiven because he turned to Jesus and accepted from Jesus what he could not give himself. Peter knew himself—the weaknesses, contradictions, and needs. Peter may not have been as strong as Judas, maybe not even as decisive. But Peter was forgiven. He accepted what he did not deserve.

The difference between what happened to Peter and what happened to Judas is as obvious as it is dramatic.

Neither sin nor guilt is a stranger to any of us. Two ways of response are possible for each of us. We can go the route of Judas—struggling with self-hatred, sensing an obligation to earn forgiveness, running fast-paced from grace, refusing to accept the wonderfully absurd love of Jesus. Or we can emulate the actions of

Peter—acknowledging our betrayals, giving up all thoughts of ever earning love, repenting honestly, and allowing ourselves to be caught up by God's pursuing compassion.

The difference between what happened to Peter and what happened to Judas is the difference between living and dying. No, not just living. Living abundantly—no longer fugitives from love but benefactors of grace. And living joyfully—recipients and celebrants of a hilarious love available to everyone.

Life in love or death as a fugitive from love. The choice is ours.

2. Go to Hell
Hal Missourie Warheim

> Then God said, "I have seen the affliction of my people who are in Egypt, and have heard their cry because of their taskmasters: I know their sufferings, and I have come to deliver them out of the hand of the Egyptians, and to bring them up out of that land to a good and broad land, a land flowing with milk and honey.... And now, behold, the cry of the people of Israel has come to me, and I have seen the oppression with which the Egyptians oppress them. Come, I will send you to Pharaoh that you may bring forth my people, the sons of Israel, out of Egypt." But Moses said to God, "Who am I that I should go to Pharaoh, and bring the sons of Israel out of Egypt?" God said, "But I will be with you; and this shall be the sign for you, that I have sent you: when you have brought forth the people out of Egypt, you shall serve God upon this mountain.
>
> —Exodus 3:7–12

There is a road in southern Italy that is born at the city of Eboli and dies in the mountain village of Gagliano. To anyone who makes that journey, it is an ascent to hell.

Gagliano is no more than a scattered cluster of white-plastered houses hanging on to barren slopes near a rocky cliff. The village has been there for centuries, and for as far back as the oldest person can remember, it has always been a place of severe poverty, unrelenting disease, frightening superstition, monotonous despair, and premature death. Oppressed and defeated by these conditions of existence, it is said that the peasants of Gagliano do not sing, and there is a saying among them that "Christ stopped at Eboli," that

---

Hal Missourie Warheim is professor of Christianity and society at Louisville Presbyterian Theological Seminary in Louisville, Kentucky. An ordained minister of the United Church of Christ and a member of the Kentucky bar, Warheim is a graduate of Elmhurst College, Eden Theological Seminary, and the University of Louisville.

Christ stopped short of their village, far away at the other end of the road, because hope and joy, the power of love, the fullness of human life that God sent to the world in Christ are not found in the hell called Gagliano.

There are some stairs in a New York City tenement that go six flights up to the apartment home of a Cuban-American family. Anyone who has climbed those stairs and been received into the intimacy of that family's life during the past year has shared in hell. Five days before Christmas, while the mother was on the first floor fetching the mail, their little boy climbed up on the gas stove, turned it on, set himself ablaze, and was taken in death only after five and a half weeks of agonizing treatment of his small, charred body. While the rest of the city sang "Joy to the World" and celebrated the New Year, these folks watched their own Bethlehem star fall out of the sky in a crimson glow of fever and entered their own new year in which every month since has been January.

There is a trail in eastern Kentucky that winds its way back into a wooded hollow where mountaineer miners have made their homes. If you were to walk that trail and visit in the camps, you would have hiked yourself into hell. Here dwell the husks of men, emptied of their germ of life by hardship and fatigue, emptied of their self-respect by exploitation and lack of opportunity, emptied of nearly everything except a bitter apathy that often erupts in violence.

Here also dwell the women of these men: frail shadows washing dishes in the polluted streams, hunting lumps of coal in the abandoned "strips," cooking skinny squirrels and cornmeal biscuits under a leaky roof, toothless at thirty-five and pregnant for the seventh time with yet another generation of condemned children.

These are the worn-out, expendable human machines that have been thoughtlessly used to rape the mountains in the quest of fabulous profits for absentee capitalists.

There is a door somewhere in America that opens into the sanctuary of a Christian church. If we were to walk through that door and understand what we see, we would recognize ourselves to be in hell. For here is a congregation that has lost the vision of its magnificent purpose, that is conformed in every way to the messed-up world around it. They have become ignorant of that God who is sovereign and righteous, and they have become insensitive to their world's most desperate needs. Its people are fearful, its leaders are cautious, and the sound of their worship together is like the rattling of dry, dusty bones.

In this so-called modern world, which is supposed to be undergoing a revolution of change in the direction of a New World Order, so many such passageways lead up, down, and into hell. Streets, corridors, elevators, superhighways, telephone lines, and pavements go to places and into situations where the forces of evil are preventing and perverting the purposes of God and impaling human lives on every imaginable form of cross, from poverty to psychosis, boredom to bigotry, loneliness to leukemia, and despair to premature death.

Paradoxically, most of these paths that lead into hell are not easy to find. Ours is a civilization in which the oppressed are ghettoed. Ours is a civilization where shocking injustices are rationalized out of our sight. Ours is a civilization where to suffer publicly is a taboo and where deeply felt torments are hidden behind the masks of smiling self-confidence.

On the other hand, you and I know where the hell is. Our own lives are occasionally dragged into it, but more especially in our everyday experiences of conversations, reading books and newspapers, and going from here to there in our own little worlds, we repeatedly stumble into it. You and I know where the hell is, and we have often felt its heat in the lives of others scorching our souls.

Furthermore, we are frightened by this hell because we instinctively sense its power. It is a universal condition of life having gigantic dimensions, bewildering complexity, and it is ancient and wise in its traditions of frustrating the maturity of human lives. It has conquered our parents, it will destroy our children, and whenever we encounter it in even its weakest forms we intuitively recognize that it is more than our match, and the moods of retreat and defeat creep into our spirits.

Yet, mysteriously, it is just in such moments when our predicament is most perilous and our hearts are most panicked that a Word is spoken to us. It is a strange Word. An unwelcome Word. An urgent Word. A demanding Word. It is the very same Word from the very same Voice that spoke to Moses in Midian, to Jesus in Nazareth, to Calvin in Strasbourg, to Rauschenbusch in New York City, to Martin Luther King, Jr., in Montgomery, and to countless other compassionate and courageous women and men through human history.

It is the Word of God, and God tells us to "go to hell!"

"I have seen the afflictions of my people," God says to us. "I know their sufferings, and I have heard their cries. I am working in this world to set them free from *all* the Pharaohs that oppress them and to give them a life that is mature and eternal. Come now," God says, "I will send you into hell, where evil is the strongest, where the need is the greatest, that you may liberate my people from their suffering and oppression."

This is the destiny to which we Christians have been called. This is the mission for which we are preparing: to go to hell, to find and walk the paths that lead to the places and conditions where evil is the strongest and the human need is greatest, and there to set people free to experience and serve the living God of righteousness who creates and loves them.

"Go to hell," says God, "and I will go with you."

We who have ears to hear, let us hear the Word of our God. Amen.

3. Changing the World from a Manger

John Killinger

Luke 2:3–7; Philippians 2:5–11

We all want power, don't we? Many psychologists list it right up there with sex and money as one of the three basic drives in human nature. The secretary wants power over the boss, so that she has job security and will not be unfairly treated. The child wants power in the family, so he will not be bullied or manipulated. The surgeon wants power with the head of staff, so her methods will be respected and her work taken seriously. The attorney wants power with the court, so that his words will be honored by the judge and the jury. The politician wants power in the statehouse, so that her constituency will see that she is influential and will continue to support her. The pastor wants power with the congregation, so that his words will be heard and his leadership assured. Power, we believe, is a necessary precondition for satisfaction and the enjoyment of life.

But is it?

I had to rethink this after a recent conversation with one of the underadministrators of the university where I work. This very attractive man in his late forties has done an exceptional job with the university. His work is praised by almost everyone. He has become so widely known for his expertise that he is constantly sought as a

John Killinger was senior minister of the First Congregational Church in Los Angeles, California, and is now Distinguished Professor of Religion and Culture at Samford University, Birmingham, Alabama. Dr. Killinger is the author of many books, including *Bread for the Wilderness/Wine for the Journey* and *The Fundamentals of Preaching*.

speaker and consultant by businesses and educational organizations around the world. He is, in other words, a man of exceptional power.

I remarked on this in our conversation and said, "Well, John, I expect you are getting offers of university presidencies right and left these days, aren't you?" "Yes," he said with modest candor, "I suppose I am. But I have decided that that is not where I would be comfortable."

"No?" I asked.

"No," he said. "You see, I fundamentally believe in servant-leadership—that one is freer to be himself and influence the world from a less conspicuous position. I do not believe I could live with the kind of compromises most executives have to make for the power to govern their institutions. I would like to return to life as a teacher and spend the rest of my days befriending students in their search for truth and meaning."

Wow! I thought, that is deep! Here was a man actually wanting to forgo the thrill and accoutrements of power to lead what he perceived as a more effective existence as a teacher of the young. It made me reassess our usual attitudes toward power and position and wonder about my own life and what I want to do with it in the years that are left to me.

I confronted in myself what I believe is a natural predisposition toward prestige and influence. I thought about the many times I have dreamed of having a prominent post from which to wield power and influence people. Oh, I rationalized the dreams, of course, by saying I didn't want the power and influence for myself but only for what I could do with them for others. But I wanted them nevertheless. I thought I would feel good letting the power flow through me. I envied the people who had it, who could speak and be heard by everyone, who could move this way or that and change the situations of others.

Then I thought about Jesus and how radically he changed the world. He never sought power over people or situations. In fact, he fled from it. When they tried to make him a king or a leader, he refused. His whole existence, I realized, was captured in those words of St. Paul in the Letter to the Philippians. He was "in the form of God" and yet disregarded this to be born in a stable and laid in a manger. He "emptied himself," Paul said, "taking the form of a servant, being born in the likeness of men" (Phil. 2:6–7). From the form of God to the form of a servant, and yet how completely he influenced human behavior and the course of history!

He could have been a king or an emperor. He could have come as the head of a great school of philosophy and been honored by all the academies of the Roman Empire. He could have appeared as a famous artist or dramatist and had everyone singing his praises in Rome and Athens and Alexandria. But he didn't. He came as the stepson of a Galilean carpenter, without a political or academic pedigree. He went about the countryside teaching and comforting the poor, befriending lepers, and praying to God. He spoke simply and honestly, from the heart. He told artless little stories and advised everyone to care more about the presence of God than they did about wealth, power, and position.

Even when the political situation had become so supercharged that he knew he was going to die, that he would be sacrificed as a miscreant and a troublemaker, he took a towel and got down on his knees and washed the feet of his troubled followers, trying to get them to understand that the way to self-fulfillment in life is not by lording it over others but by quietly serving them in love and humility. The Lord of all eternity emptied himself to become a servant!

What was it someone once said so effectively about him?

> He was born in an obscure village, the child of a
> peasant woman. He grew up in still another
> village, where he worked in a carpenter's shop
> until he was thirty. Then for three years he was an
> itinerant preacher. He never wrote a book. He
> never held an office. He never had a family or
> owned a house. He didn't go to college. He never
> visited a big city. He never traveled two hundred
> miles from the place where he was born. He did
> none of the things one usually associates with
> greatness. He had no credentials but himself. He
> was only thirty-three when the tide of public
> opinion turned against him. His friends ran away.
> He was turned over to his enemies and went
> through the mockery of a trial. He was nailed to a
> cross between two thieves. While he was dying his
> executioners gambled for his clothing, the only
> property he had on earth. When he was dead, he
> was laid in a borrowed grave through the pity of a

friend. Nineteen centuries have come and gone,
and today he is the central figure of the human
race and the leader of mankind's progress. All the
armies that ever marched, all the navies that ever
sailed, all the parliaments that ever sat, all the
kings that ever reigned, put together, have not
affected the life of man on this earth as much as
that one solitary life. (Anonymous, "One Solitary
Life")

Things began to connect up in my mind—my friend John and
his desire to return to life as a teacher; Mother Teresa and the
tremendous influence she has had by becoming a friend to "the
poorest of the poor" and bathing their sores and putting food into
their mouths; St. Francis of Assisi and his life of poverty and simplicity; Toyohiko Kagawa, electing to live in the slums of Kobe and
bringing in the sick and vermin-infested creatures of the area to
sleep with him in his tiny room; President Carter and the wonderful things he and his wife, Rosalynn, have done since leaving
the presidency, helping to build homes for the poor and campaign-
ing for human rights around the globe and now working to free
people from poverty and drug dependency in Atlanta; Bruce
Kennedy, who had been earning more than $450,000 a year as
president of Alaska Airlines and left it to go with his wife, Karleen,
as an English teacher in the little village of Wei Fang, 270 miles
southeast of Beijing, China, where his only monetary rewards are
a small house to live in and bicycles for him and Karleen to ride to
school.

It is true, isn't it, what Jesus said about real happiness. Blessed
are the poor in spirit, blessed are the meek, blessed are the peacemakers, blessed are those who are committed to righteousness in
the world, to God's ways over the ways of society and the ways of
self-promotion and power and prestige. Real happiness doesn't lie
in having power and influence. Real happiness lies in becoming
servants, in opening our lives to the healing, loving power of God
so that it flows through us and blesses everybody around us.

This is what Christmas is really about, isn't it—not getting a
new outfit of clothes and going to more parties than we've been to
all year and shopping till we drop and baking till we shake and
eating and drinking till we're all overweight. Christmas is a re-

minder that the Son of God, the Lord of the heavens, laid aside his lordship and descended to earth in the form of a servant, was born in a simple stable and laid in the clean hay of the manger to show us the way of love and peace and fulfillment. Fulfillment, not through position and power and influence, but through gentleness and lowliness and love, the qualities that are able to heal earth's fretfulness and restore us all to the presence of God.

Christmas is a time for coming home to who we really are down under all the dreams and ambitions and affectations. It is a time for change and conversion, when we, like old Ebenezer Scrooge, reassess our personal histories and trajectories and, rediscovering what it is to be human and Christlike and loving, bring ourselves into new alignment with the simple truth of God, that life was not given to us to be used selfishly, for our own aggrandizement, but to be given and shared and celebrated as the beautiful gift it truly is. It is a time to understand that we were put here not to have power but to love and to serve.

In that sense, one of the best Christmas stories I have read this year, though it was not intended as a Christmas story, is a little book by Henri Nouwen called *In the Name of Jesus*. Nouwen was asked by his friend Murray McDonnell to give a series of lectures about Christian leadership at the Center for Human Development in Washington, D.C., and these lectures form the heart of the book. But it is the circumstances surrounding the lectures that make them truly memorable.

Nouwen, as you may recall, has been a scholar at such leading universities as Notre Dame, Yale, and Harvard and has written a number of best-selling books about ministry and spiritual life, including *Reaching Out* and *The Wounded Healer*. A few years ago he became restless because he was not praying very well and was feeling burned out in the academic setting. So he sought a new kind of experience by becoming a priest at a school for the mentally handicapped, a community known as Daybreak, near Toronto. The change, he found, was staggering. For twenty years, he had been admired and respected for his academic qualifications, his books, his knowledge of the modern world. At Daybreak, no one cared about any of this. Now the only thing that mattered was how he related to the special children in the school—whether they liked him and he could communicate with them. He felt naked and powerless. It was as if he were starting his life all over again.

"This experience was and, in many ways, is still the most important experience of my new life," says Nouwen, "because it forced me to rediscover my true identity. These broken, wounded, and completely unpretentious people forced me to let go of my relevant self—the self that can do things, show things, prove things, build things—and forced me to reclaim that unadorned self in which I am completely vulnerable, open to receive and give love regardless of any accomplishments."[1]

It was in the context of this experience that Nouwen forged the lectures he gave before the Center for Human Development. The Christian leader of the future, he told those assembled in Washington, is called to be "completely irrelevant" and to stand before his or her constituents "with nothing to offer but his or her own vulnerable self."[2] This, he said, is the way Jesus came among us—not with power and position, not with a yearning to be known by all the world or to alter human destiny, but with simplicity and humility and love.

Now, there is one more thing about these lectures that makes them special. As a priest at Daybreak, Nouwen submitted himself to the same rules the children lived by. One of these rules was that no one went anywhere or did anything without discussing it with the others and receiving their input. So Nouwen talked with the group about his speaking engagements, including what he should say to the people in Washington. And another rule was that people did things in pairs; if one went somewhere, he took another person with him. So Nouwen invited young Bill Van Buren, one of the handicapped children, to accompany him to Washington.

Bill was delighted. "We are doing this together," he said on several occasions before their trip. "Yes," Nouwen would say, "we are doing this together. You and I are going to Washington to proclaim the gospel."[3]

As guests of the Center for Human Development, Nouwen and Bill were taken to the Clarendon Hotel in Crystal City, a large steel-and-glass establishment on the western side of the Potomac. They were given separate rooms with oversized beds, bathrooms full of towels, and cable TV. There was a bowl of fruit in Bill's room. He was delighted and settled in at once to check out all the cable stations with his remote-control wand.

After a delicious dinner, Nouwen was introduced and invited to the speaker's stand to give his first lecture. He had barely reached the stand when he noticed that Bill, too, had left his seat and followed him to the podium, where he took a chair at the side. Obviously, says Nouwen, Bill took the togetherness thing more literally than he had expected. Then, as Nouwen would finish a page of his lecture and lay it aside, Bill would come up and get it and lay it in a neat stack on a nearby table. When Nouwen had got over his nervousness about this, he began to feel good about it, as if he had an unusual kind of support from Bill. Lecturing wasn't the lonely business that he had sometimes experienced.

When Nouwen finished the lecture, Bill said, "Henri, can I say something now?" Nouwen was startled. His first reaction was to say no, because he knew that Bill, once he began, could talk almost interminably. But he caught himself in the presumption that Bill had nothing important to say to the audience and permitted him to speak. Bill merely thanked the center for including him, and everyone stood and gave him a round of applause. It was a wonderfully touching moment, and it had underscored as nothing else could the words of Nouwen's lecture. Real leadership, Christian leadership, is open, vulnerable, and sharing.

Do you sense the power in this? Where does it come from? Not from Nouwen, although he is the channel for it. And not from Bill, certainly. No, it is God's power—the power that will change the world. It is the kind of power we speak of when we say "for thine is the kingdom and the power and the glory." And it is what that first Christmas was about—the power of the almighty God to change all human destiny coming into the world through a servant born in a stable. It isn't any wonder those shepherds on the hillside heard an angel choir singing, "Glory to God in the highest, and on earth peace among men with whom he is pleased!" (Luke 2:14). The angels knew it was God's power being born that night and that we would all one day live to serve that power.

This, believe me, is the gospel.

Prayer

How blind we are, O Lord of glory, until you show us the light! Let your dear and holy light shine upon us once more in this Christmas season to call us back into the way of Jesus, where we will be your loving servants to all the world. For his name's sake. Amen.

NOTES

1. Henri Nouwen, *In the Name of Jesus* (New York: Crossroad Publishing, 1990), 16.
2. Ibid., 17.
3. Ibid., 6.

4. The Way, the Truth, and the Life
Chevis F. Horne

John 14:1–11

One of the most startling things Jesus ever said was "I am the way, the truth, and the life."

Note the finality of these words. He is not one way among many; he is the Way. He is not one truth among many; he is the Truth. He is not one life among many lives; he is the Life.

Thomas à Kempis had this to say about these words of Jesus:

> Without the Way there is no going; without the Truth there is no knowing; without the Life, there is no living. I am the Way which thou oughtest to follow; the Truth which thou oughtest to believe; the Life, which thou oughtest to hope for. I am the Way inviolable, the Truth infallible, the Life unending. I am the Way that is straightest, the Truth that is highest, the Life that is true, the Life blessed, the Life uncreated. If thou remain in my way, thou shalt know the Truth, and the Truth shall make you free, and thou shalt lay hold on eternal life.

Chevis F. Horne was, for his entire pastoral ministry, pastor of one congregation, the First Baptist Church, Martinsville, Virginia, after which he served as professor of preaching at Southeastern Baptist Theological Seminary, Wake Forest, North Carolina. Dr. Horne is the author of a number of books, among them *Preaching the Great Themes of the Bible, Basic Bible Sermons on Easter,* and *Basic Bible Sermons on Christmas.*

The Way

When God created us he didn't put us in revolving doors that go round and round. We never get off where we got on. Life moves forward toward an end. Jesus is the way for us travelers. He leads us to where we are to go.

The disciples of Jesus were first called Those of the Way. They had never forgotten that Jesus had said, "I am the way."

Others—saints, seers, and prophets—had gone before Jesus, but they were not the way. They were like signs and road maps pointing to the way who was Jesus Christ. But where does Jesus lead us?

First he leads us to God. Jesus in our scripture lesson said, "He who has seen me has seen the Father."

Imagine it! Standing in their midst was a carpenter from Nazareth whose hands were callused by carpenter's tools and whose face had been bronzed by wind and sun. He knew what it was to sweat in his father's carpenter shop on a hot summer day and to stand in wood shavings ankle deep. Did he really mean what he was saying? Had they been seeing the face of God in this very human face? That is what he said, and that is what the Church has been saying across these centuries. He is God's Son in whom we have seen the Father's face.

In our searching for God, ways of our own devising turn out to be blind alleys and dead-end streets. The way is in Jesus alone. He knows where the Father is and can take us to him.

Again, Jesus is the way to our neighbor and brother.

One of the great tragedies of life is that we often do not know each other. We are like ships that pass in the night. We know somebody is going there, but we are not sure who he is.

There is Bill. He is a neighbor who lives just down the street. I know the kind of car he drives. When he leaves home each morning, I probably could tell you his salary within a thousand dollars. But Bill is a virtual stranger to me. I wish I knew him, but I do not.

I have been married to Maggie for thirty years. But so often she seems elusive and far away. I wish I knew her better. And Frederick, my oldest son. I wish I knew him better, and it is painful that I do not.

Finally, Jesus is the way to myself. How often I am an enigma to myself. I can call my name, but I can't tell you who I am.

John Glenn, our first astronaut to orbit the earth, tells about taking a government test in which one of the questions was "Who am I?" At first the answers came easily: I am a man, an American citizen, a husband, a father, an astronaut. Then the answers became more difficult. Finally, it was as if his self shaded away into mystery.

Dietrich Bonhoeffer, Hitler's famous prisoner, agonized with this question. After struggling with it, he finally confessed, "Whoever I am, thou knowest, O Lord, that I am thine."

When Christ tells us who we are, he will always do it in terms of relationship. I belong to somebody. I belong supremely to God. I belong to a husband, to a wife, to a child, to a neighbor. I belong to a community. I never discover who I am by gazing at my face in a mirror. It is only as I look into your face that I can know who I am.

The Truth

Not only are we travelers, we are learners, and Jesus is the truth. We have been created for the truth, and seeking truth and learning are exciting.

Here is a child who, when speaking his first word, laughs and claps his hands. He is learning, and it is exciting.

While more books have been written about Jesus than about any other person, Jesus never wrote a book. Our records indicate that he wrote only once, and that was in the sand. A spring shower or a careless foot soon destroyed it. We may be curious about what he wrote, but we can never know.

Rather than writing the truth, Jesus lived it. His is the kind of truth you see in a person's face, hear in his voice, and feel in his touch. It is truth turned into a life-style, truth lived, truth given hands and feet and voice. It is truth incarnated.

You may learn about mercy from an essay, but it is better to learn about mercy from a merciful person. Jesus taught by living the truth.

What is the truth we learn from Jesus?

First and foremost we learn that God is a God of love. His love is not forced or contrived. It is his nature to love, and his love is free and spontaneous. We cannot merit or earn his love. No matter how broken or evil we are, he still loves us. If God should cease to love, he would cease to be God.

Abbot Damascus Winzen died when he was an old man. He had suffered much. A few months before he died he wrote, "When I look back upon seventy years of my own life, I see quite clearly that I owe my inner happiness, my peace, my confidence, and my joy essentially to one fact: I am certain that I am infinitely loved by God." This could be the testimony of many of us.

Yet, this is no tearful sentimentality. There is a terrible judgment in God's love. It is like the judgment of darkness by light. God's love judges all our lovelessness, selfishness, misuse of power, and sin.

Further, we see the truth about our world in Jesus.

Our world is not an accident, cast up by blindness and chance. It is God's world. God made it, and all the title deeds are in his hands.

Since it is God's world, it can never be ours. We are the keepers of God's creation, the stewards of his world. We are to keep his world clean, healthy, and productive.

We must confess that we have not been worthy keepers of God's good earth. We have polluted its waters, made unclean its air, poisoned its soil, marred its beauty, and exploited it for the almighty dollar. We have made earth sick with our refuse, and she now threatens to disgorge us. Nature in wrath stands to her feet with a mighty hand lifted against us.

Finally, Jesus tells us the truth about ourselves.

Jesus does not overlook the blemishes, brokenness, and sinfulness of our lives. He tells us about the tragedy of our existence. But he surprises us with the worth, value, and beauty he sees in us. He tells us that love is the great principle that should govern our lives. We are to love God, and we are to love our neighbor as we love ourselves. To be really human is to love; to be like God is to love.

The Life

These words of Jesus move in an ascending order—way, truth, life. Life is the crowning reality.

I have spoken about our being travelers, but there is no traveling without life. We are to be learners, but there is no learning without life. Without life there is nothing. It is little wonder then that the New Testament puts such a great stress on life.

John in his Gospel is rushing to tell a secret. He can't wait to tell it. So the secret is out in the fourth verse of his first chapter: "In him was life, and the life was the light of men." As John comes near the end of his book, he states his theme again: "These are written that you may believe that Jesus is the Christ, the Son of God, and that believing you may have life in his name" (John 20:31).

Jesus is the great life-giver. He once stated his mission in terms of giving life: "I came that they might have life and have it abundantly" (John 10:10).

Jesus does not give life sparingly; he gives it aboundingly. It is life full, complete, heaped up, and running over.

We may feel safe in trusting our loved ones and ourselves to the great life-giver. He will see to it that we are not like candles blown out by hostile winds and lost in darkness and nothingness. We are made for a quality of life that Jesus calls eternal life.

Robert Murray McCheyne was a great Scottish preacher. He lost an elder brother, David, by death. Years later he wrote a friend: "Pray for me that I may be holier and wiser—less like myself and more like the heavenly master; that I may not regard my life, if so be I may finish my course with joy. This day eleven years ago, I lost my beloved and loving brother, and began to seek a Brother who cannot die."

We are invited to walk in the way that is Jesus Christ, to seek the truth that is in him, and to accept the life he is able to give.

5.   Home
Kurt Schuermann

> He was in the world, and the world was made through him, yet the world knew him not. He came to his own home, and his own people received him not.
>
> —John 1:10–11

The Space Under Your Hat

I'm not exactly sure when it happened. Whenever it happened, it was a momentous event. At some point I stopped considering the two-story brick house where my parents have lived for fifty years as home. Now, home for me is where I live with my wife and two sons. This year is the first year that we actually celebrated Christmas in the house in which we are living. Before this year, we had always celebrated Christmas in someone else's house.

Now after explaining all that, it appears that this break was not complete. Not long ago, someone asked me if I was going home for Christmas, meaning to the house in which I had lived with my mother and father. I answered, "Of course." The inconsistency struck me later. I thought I *was* home. How, then, could I *go* home? I discovered that knowing exactly where home is was not always easy.

In an essay for *Time* magazine, Lance Morrow reflected on the mystery of "home."[1] He told about a man named Ernest who lived in a park outside of Phoenix. Ernest showed Lance Morrow how he had made his home out of cardboard boxes. He interlocked the boxes in an ingenious manner so that they kept out the cold Ar-

---

Kurt Schuermann is Pastor of the Cuba United Methodist Church in Cuba, Missouri. A graduate of Harvard Divinity School, Rev. Schuermann has served churches in rural Missouri for twelve years.

izona nights. Although the boxes were not a dream house, they had many of the attributes of home. The boxes were safe and warm, even cozy. Like homes everywhere, they allowed Ernest private space to keep some things secret. Lance Morrow underscored the tragedy of Ernest's story by saying that he had once been a trusted engineer for Boeing, Inc.

Ernest showed that there was another side to homelessness beyond physical hardships. Homelessness also embraced issues of emotions, hurts, and brokenness at their deepest and most basic levels.

As those who have worked with the homeless have discovered, homelessness is not just "houselessness." Ernest demonstrated this fact. Something had broken deep inside Ernest. Lance Morrow claimed that one of the things that had become dislodged in him were those instruments and charts necessary to find his way home.

It would be difficult for Ernest to find his way home. Ernest was not even at home "in his own skin." It has been said that "home is where you hang your hat." In Ernest's case, even when his hat was on his head, he was not at home. That place underneath your hat is the most basic residence. For Ernest, the space under his hat was where he was most lost.

Ghosts

It is not my purpose today to preach about the many faces and tragedies of homelessness (although that would be an important thing to do). Today my purpose is more general. How can you and I find a home "inside our own skin?" How can we dwell with grace, authenticity, meaning, and peace in that vast domain that exists beneath our hats? It is my contention that it is here, within ourselves, that we are most likely to feel out of place. Knowing ourselves like we do, how can we live with ourselves?

The folklore of our culture abounds with stories about beings who can't find a home. These characters are some of the most tragic figures in all literature. We call them ghosts. Ghosts are those beings who because of some wrong, injustice, or evil cannot rest. They spend eternity looking for a home. One only need recall Marley's ghost in Dickens's *A Christmas Carol* to get at the truth expressed in these tales. Marley was cursed to roam the earth without rest because he never showed concern beyond the profit and loss columns of his business. Caring only for himself in life, he was stuck with himself after death.

Now, I do not believe in ghosts as the disembodied spirits of the dead. What I do believe in is people whose real flesh-and-blood lives are haunting. Sometimes you can catch a glimpse of this haunting in their eyes. Maybe something they did in the past was so wrong that it continues to spook them. Perhaps a grave injustice had been done to them, tying them to the past. Whatever the actual facts of the case, these people are lost, wandering without a home.

Breaking Your Heart

Now, it would be easy here to sentimentalize home and move many people emotionally. We must travel beyond that to touch the depths of our individual homelessness. We also must remember that for some people home is not a sanctuary but a battleground where there are injuries and spiritual deaths. The hurt of not having a "real" home underscores the deep need for such a place. A person who does not experience a nurturing home as a child may search for that special place of acceptance for his whole life.

The scripture lesson today has two verses that will break your heart if you hear them truly. These verses might be overlooked in the glorious sweep of the first verses of John's Gospel. "In the beginning was the Word" begins the Gospel. This "Word" was God's means of self-expression. When God spoke, his Word had effect. What God spoke happened. God spoke, and the universe was called into existence. Everything, seen and unseen, was formed by the Word.

The highest point of all creation was the living forms called human beings. These human beings reflected the life in the Word most closely. Through the gift of language and many words, humans were able to speak to God and to each other.

The creative power of the Word did not stop at the end of the creation of the physical world. The Word also gathered a people together. It was not God's will that humans should live in solitude but in community. The Word came to form a people in the inspired speech of prophets and other leaders. History shows that these people, like people today, didn't listen very well.

Then when the time was just right, the Word took flesh and dwelt among humans. This teaching of the Scriptures is called the Incarnation by the Church. Reduced to its most basic, this means that the Word made its home in a human life—the life of Jesus of Nazareth.

The tragedy is revealed in verses 10 and 11. Let us listen to these words again: "He was in the world, and the world was made through him, yet the world knew him not. He came to his own home and his own people received him not." There can be no doubt about it. He was homeless.

Can we imagine a more tragic situation? The Word was turned away by the very world he had made. Jesus described his situation in this way: "Foxes have holes, birds of the air have nests, but the Son of man has no where to lay his head." Jesus and those who followed him led a nomadic existence on the edges of society. When Jesus finally did find a home it was a cross. It was there that he bore the full brunt of the world's rejection.

You and Me

What does this mean to us? How does this scripture help us to live inside our own skins? How does it help to save us from living like ghosts, terrorized by our own sense of homelessness?

The first thing we need to do is to bring our sense of homelessness to the One who was likewise homeless. Here we can confess our own contributions to our personal homelessness. The Word is immediately accessible to the human heart. The Word becomes active in our lives when we are able to admit our deepest needs.

Our confrontation with this homeless Word will allow us to see that human life exists in an imperfect manner that cries out for completion. To find a home in our own skins we must return to the source of our lives—the Word as made known in Jesus Christ. With Christ a new perspective on life is gained and a new beginning is offered. The past, with its ghosts of sin and terror of wrongs done to you, will lose its power over you. You will, as John proclaims in the third chapter of his Gospel, be born again.

This new starting point will mark the beginning of a journey. The journey will be a journey home. Strangely, this journey will at once bring you restlessness and peace. Yet you will be at peace because you will be at home in your own skin. You will be restless waiting for the Word to be fully formed within you. To be a follower of Christ is to be restless and at peace at the same time.

A Home—Finally

When I was first in the ministry, I attended monthly meetings with the ministers of our district. Many different topics would be discussed, but one item was almost certain to receive a hearing. One pastor, nearing retirement, wanted to set aside a section of the cemetery at a historic church as a final resting place for ministers.

When I was younger, I thought about what an odd concern this seemed to be. I don't consider it so odd anymore. In some ways the itinerancy of Methodist pastors reflects the homelessness of all people.

Jesus, knowing the depths of homelessness, sends us this assurance later in John's Gospel:

> Let not your heart be troubled; believe in God,
> believe also in me. In my Father's house are many
> dwelling places; if it were not so, I would have
> told you; for I go to prepare a place for you. And
> if I go and prepare a place for you, I will come
> again, and receive you to myself; that where I am,
> there you may be also. (John 14:1–3)

Wherever we are, with Christ we are home.

Nostalgia

Lance Morrow says in his essay that the word *nostalgia* is made up of two root words meaning "the agony of going home." Without Christ we can never find a home in our own skins. Without Christ, the loneliest spot in the world is that place beneath our hats. Have you been a displaced person long enough? Will you trust your life to the Word and finally be at home?

NOTE

1. Lance Morrow, *Time,* 24 December 1990, 78.

6.   Are You Going His Way?
David E. Sumner

John 6:53–58

Not long ago I received a letter from a friend that began, "This is typical of the way I write: one letter a year, and you are the lucky one for 1991." The same can be said for the way I preach. About one sermon a year, and you folks are the lucky ones this year. Brace yourselves.

During my one chance to preach in 1991, I felt very strongly that I should share with you what is most important in my own life, which is my faith and my relationship with Jesus Christ. I can't separate that faith from my life in the Episcopal church because it was here that Christ came to me. And so when the church is troubled, I am troubled.

A teacher sent home a report card with this note to the parents: "Alvin excels in initiative, group integration, responsiveness, and activity participation. Now if he would only learn to read and write."

This little anecdote has a sobering message for Episcopalians. We have excelled in liturgy and worship. We have attracted some sophisticated and intelligent people, and we try to make sure there are no outcasts. We've done some things very, very well. Now if we could only learn to repent and follow Jesus Christ.

Samuel Shoemaker, the great Episcopal priest and one of the founders of Alcoholics Anonymous, wrote in his book *By the Power of God,*

David E. Sumner is Assistant Professor of Journalism at Ball State University in Muncie, Indiana. A lay Episcopalian, he holds a Master of Divinity from Southeastern Baptist Theological Seminary and a Master of Sacred Theology from the University of the South. Sumner is the author of *The Episcopal Church's History*.

> To go on practicing the sacramental life of the
> church as if one has been converted to Christ,
> when all he has been converted to is the beauty or
> order or sacraments of the Anglican communion,
> is simply a form of idolatry and needs to be called
> such. Thousands of our communicants are being
> misled, not because the sacraments are not of
> tremendous importance, but because conversion
> and obedience to our Lord are also of tremendous
> importance and they are not being told these
> things.

In today's Gospel, Jesus sounds like he is talking about the Holy Communion when he says, "Whoever eats my flesh and drinks my blood abides in me." There is indeed a beauty, mystery, and grace in the sacraments that we receive nowhere else. But he is talking about more than that. He is talking about making his life, our life. He is talking about focusing our entire spiritual energy on obeying his teachings and imitating his life. As Paul says, "Look carefully then how you walk, not as unwise men but as wise, making the most of the time. Do not be foolish, but understand what the will of the Lord is."

When I was a young man, many said I had failed to reach my potential, and I had. I came from a fine family, earned football letters, graduated fourth in my class, and was president of the student government. But after college, I drifted through several jobs and never seemed to make a go of it. Life seemed meaningless because I could see nothing worth living for.

One day I accidently met an Episcopal priest who in the course of a casual conversation began to tell me about Jesus Christ. That made a deep impression on me because he seemed so humble yet so confident and assured of the meaning of life. Eventually, I was confirmed and in that process accepted Christ and developed a relationship with him. My life began to refocus, and soon I began to blossom again and use the talents that God had given me.

That's a story most of us have heard in one form or another. But the term *relationship with Jesus* is often not explained. In the years before I became a Christian, the phrase mystified me. How, I wondered, could I have a relationship with someone I couldn't hear or talk to, not to mention someone who lived twenty centuries before me? Viewed from the outside, Christianity can seem like a strange religion. Here are people who claim to have a relationship with Jesus, and furthermore, they say they drink his blood and eat his body. Is that really true?

We have many kinds of relationships: business, professional, and personal. A personal relationship is one in which we reveal our intimate feelings and thoughts. A two-way exchange of energy exists between two or more persons. The phrase *personal relationship with Jesus* is a metaphor, however. It describes the relationship, not defines it. That means that a relationship with Jesus is *like* a relationship with a friend or a spouse but not the same.

Here's another way of saying it. We find in the Jesus of Nazareth a clue to the meaning of life. And the more we examine this clue, the more compelling its power becomes over us. This image that we find in Jesus becomes so powerful that it forces us to reconsider the meaning of our lives and make some visible and concrete changes.

We've talked a lot about having an inclusive church in which there are no outcasts. But Jesus does set one condition for entry to his kingdom. Not everyone is welcome. He also said come to me all of you who are willing to turn from your sins. That means repent: The biblical word for repent is *metanoia,* which means to turn around or shift directions. Let me tell you a story about some who never made that shift and never changed directions.

In 1923, eight of the nation's top financial leaders met at Chicago's Edgewater Beach Hotel: Charles Schwab, president of the largest independent steel company; Samuel Insull, president of the largest gas company; Arthur Cotten, the richest wheat speculator; Richard Whitney, president of the New York Stock Exchange; Albert Fall, a member of the president's cabinet; Leon Fraser, president of the Bank of International Settlements; Jesse Livermore, the greatest "bear on Wall Street;" and Ivan Krueger, head of the largest monopoly.

In 1948, twenty-five years later, Charles Schwab had died in bankruptcy, having lived on borrowed money for five years before his death. Samuel Insull had died a fugitive from justice, penniless in a foreign land. Arthur Cotton died abroad, bankrupt. Richard Whitney had spent time in Sing Sing Prison. Albert Fall had been pardoned from prison so he could die at home. The three others, Jesse Livermore, Ivan Krueger, and Leon Fraser, had all died by suicide.

These men are all extreme examples of how life without Christ can end. They are examples of how a rise to the top can also be a downward spiral from the real meaning of life.

Christianity offers you this kind of choice, a choice this dramatic and visible. It offers you a choice between two kinds of lifestyles, two conditions in which your soul may live: union with God or separation from God. It isn't simply a choice between heaven and hell, between church membership or staying at home on Sunday morning. It gives you this choice about how you are going to live this life.

My change in direction took me to seminary when I was thirty years old. I arrived with two hundred dollars, no scholarship, and no knowledge of how I was going to pay for it all. Later I realized that although it was God's will for me to be there, God had better ways for me to use my talents than in parish ministry. And they have taken me mostly into writing and teaching.

But I can say the things I have this morning because I have known the pain of a soul that felt separated from God. I have known the contrast between a soul at peace with God and one that sometimes felt there was no God. I have experienced the illusion of thinking I was a Christian because I was baptized and brought up that way. But when push came to shove, my life was shallow and empty.

Again and again, when facing life's most serious questions, I am drawn back to Jesus. I have studied the great theologians and philosophers, and they have given me many insights into life. But Jesus offers a presence and a relationship I cannot define, much less describe, and never want to escape. The relationship includes my emotions but is more than my emotions. It challenges me intellectually but extends beyond my mind. That presence enables me to assert confidently that he is risen and lives today.

The point of my sermon today is not "What do you believe?" but "Which way are you traveling?" Are you moving in one direction or slipping and sliding around in different directions? Do you know where you are going, or do you succumb to the winds and temptations of each day? Do you have a purpose for living, or do you just simply exist? If you don't know where you're going, then any old road will get you there.

Robert Frost conveys the picture of the divided road in one of his most quoted verses:

> Two roads diverged in a wood, and I—
> I took the one less traveled by,
> and that has made all the difference.

I assure you that to journey with Christ, you will travel one of the least traveled roads of this world. You will be forced to make decisions that will set you apart. You will not always be popular. When I was editor of a diocesan newspaper in Cincinnati, my conscience led me to take some editorial stands that made more enemies than friends. I spoke out on social issues, and I spoke out on ecclesiastical issues in the diocese. But I have no regrets. If you journey with Christ, be sure you count the cost before you pack your bags.

Occasionally, I draw cartoons, but the only one I ever published was one that depicted a sign in front of a church. The sign read, "The Cost of Discipleship: Special, this week only—20 percent off."

The most important thing I have to say in this—my one sermon for 1991—is that Jesus Christ can make a difference in your life. There are no discount rates and no super savers. The down payment is your whole life. But that decision can make all the difference in the world and in the world to come as well.

7. Second Stanza

Mike Graves

Psalm 8

These are the words of Psalm 8. Actually though, I skipped some words in the reading. Oh, not words *of* the text; words *before* the text; words *about* the text. Do you see them there in your Bible? In mine it says, "For the choir director; on the Gittith." Other translations read, "To the chief musician; upon the Gittith tune." These words are instructions to the musicians, the conductor in particular. Psalm 8 is a song. A song written by David. A song that was to be done according to the Gittith tune.

I'm not a musician, but I do have a hunch as to what that tune might have sounded like. Surely the tune that went with this text, these words, would have been a majestic tune. Like the great hymns of our faith, the ones where the tune and the text lift you into the presence of God.

Yes, the tune to Psalm 8 would have been special, a majestic tune, one employing trumpets and timpani, no doubt. The song proclaims the majesty of God.

Can you hear it? I can. The cacophony of the symphony's warming up begins to die out. People begin to take their seats. The conductor taps his baton, and they strike up a note of majestic praise. The heavenly choir chimes in, "O Lord, our Lord, how majestic is thy name in all the earth!" It is the refrain of the song. It is the first and last line. "O Lord, our Lord, how majestic is thy name in all the earth!"

Mike Graves is Assistant Professor of Preaching at Midwestern Baptist Theological Seminary in Kansas City, Missouri. Graves received his Master of Divinity and his Ph.D. in preaching from Southwestern Baptist Theological Seminary. He is the author of *Strategies for Narrative Preaching*.

In the first stanza the whole heavenly choir bellows out the greatness of God, the God who has displayed his splendor above the heavens. The God whose greatness will be proclaimed, even by children. It is amazing, isn't it, how little children can make so clear the greatness of God? Karl Barth found that out. He was the renowned Swiss theologian who, while visiting Union Theological Seminary in Virginia, was asked what was the most profound theological truth he knew. He answered, "Jesus loves me, this I know, for the Bible tells me so." A children's song. As the psalmist writes, "From the mouth of infants and nursing babes." A simple song, yet full of majesty.

But as the song continues, we sense a tension in the music. A minor key tells us there are enemies who would overthrow this God. Still, the song reminds us that God makes the enemy and revengeful cease.

Then the string section plays a gorgeous sound of praise. The song sings of the glory of God's creation, the heavens being the work of God's fingers. He made the moon and the stars—and, oh, the stars.

When I was growing up, my parents' best friends owned a sailboat. On summer nights when the moon was full, we would go sailing out into the Gulf of Mexico, taking in the view of the heavens. It was a special treat when my grandfather went along. He was an astronomer. He would give us a tour of the stars, pointing out the better-known Big Dipper and the Little Dipper, as well as the lesser-known Orion and Pleiades. I think of those nights even now when I see the stars. And when I do, I think of God.

That's what the psalmist does. He has us out on a summer evening when the moon is full. We're lying on our backs in the grass looking at the stars while the music plays a tune of God's great creation. You hear it now, don't you?

That's the first stanza—the greatness of God. "O Lord, our Lord, how majestic is thy name in all the earth!"

Then there's the second stanza. In the quiet lull as we contemplate the greatness of God, all of a sudden the psalmist throws out this wild idea, this crazy thought, an awesome, humbling thought. We can sense it in the music. The idea? "What are human beings that thou dost take thought of them? Mortals that thou dost care for them?" In other words, why in the world would the great, majestic, creator God think anything about us?

The psalmist tells us God not only has thought of us, but the Lord has placed us in a position over all of his creation, second only to God himself. The words of the song and the music together cause us to get lost in the wonder of it all. The God who created everything, thinks highly of us. What a song! What a song! You hear it now, don't you?

I wonder what led David to write such a thing. Can you imagine him writing such a song? I picture him out among the sheep in the Judean countryside. It's a beautiful midmorning, one of those days that causes you to sing God's praises. As David takes in the beauty of God's creation, he remembers a story, a story he learned as a young boy, a story about the creation event itself. A story about God creating order out of chaos, heavens and earth out of nothing. A story about God speaking light into existence, speaking vegetation and animals into existence. And at each stage along the way, God steps back to say, "This is good." But it was when God created humanity that he said, "This is very good." Suddenly, there on that hillside, David has this wonderfully awesome thought: "The crowning achievement of God's creation is humanity."

It was a thought so wonderful that he wrote down this song, a song to the tune of Gittith, a song to be sung by all Israel in worship, a song to be sung today, a song about you and the place you hold in the heart of God.

It's an incredible song, an incredible thought. When God created the sun, that flaming ball of fire that warms our world and gives us light, and hurled it into space and told it to stay, he said, "This is good." When God dug out the Grand Canyon like a boy with his Tonka toys, he stood back and said, "This is good." When God flung the colors of the sunset onto the canvas of the western sky, he marveled at his work, saying, "This is good." And then God created you and you and you and you and you and you, and when he finished creating you, he said, "This is very good."

Next time you're on vacation, and you pull off the road at one of those scenic views, and you stand there elbow to elbow with all those people gawking at the creation of God, remember this: The God of creation is gawking back. He admires you. You are the crowning achievement of his creation.

I suppose that is something of what an author feels when he creates a character in a novel. Maybe that's how Shakespeare felt about Hamlet or any of his other characters when they began to come to life on paper. Shakespeare began to realize what a great character was coming into existence. Hamlet is a character, a character Shakespeare thought up.

And you, you are a character God thought up. You were created by God, and what's more, you were created for God. What if Hamlet were to try to change his lines, what then? He would cease to exist, at least he would cease to be all that he was intended to be. You were created by God to live for God, and if this day finds you no longer living for God, then hear this story.

April was a little orphan girl who had been placed in one home after another, and in each one she had been so abused she began to retreat into her own dream world. The so-called experts began to suspect retardation or autism. Actually, she was fine but had been terribly neglected. She finally ended up in an older couple's home with fifteen or so other kids. Turns out, the couple took her in just for the financial assistance the government programs provided. They were extremely hard on her, but they were cruel to all the kids.

April's fantasy world was one in which she found joy in her songs. She pretended to have a family and friends, and so she would write down the words to her songs and pretend to mail them. The lady caught her one day humming and writing and warned her to never write notes again. Someone might read them and take her away. The lady, of course, was worried only about the money. After she scolded the little girl, she went out into the hall and waited to see if she would disobey. April began to hum and write again, only this time she took the note she had scribbled and went down the stairs, out the door, and over to her favorite tree. She climbed up the tree and placed the piece of paper between two crossed branches.

The lady went and told her husband. He got a ladder out and climbed up to the note. He took it, and when he read it, he began to cry. He handed it down, saying, "You'd better read this." This is what it said: "Whoever finds this—I love you."

Two thousand years ago just outside a tiny city in the Middle East, between two crossed branches, God wrote this song: "Whoever finds this—I love you."

Here is what you have been waiting to hear: The God who

made you loves you. The One who knows you better than anyone loves you anyway. What a song! "Whoever finds this—I love you." You hear it now, don't you?

II. EXPOSITORY

8. Christ Incognito
Stephen Cherry

Luke 24:13–35

The story of the two disciples on the road to Emmaus must be one of a handful of classic Christian narratives. It ranks with the best of the resurrection appearances for both human and theological insight, and with the best of Luke's Gospel for sheer narrative power. It also prefigures the structure of the Communion service: there is a gathering, an opening of Scripture, and there is breaking of bread.

It is a story of the mysterious presence of God but at the same time of human misunderstanding and brashness. Christopher Evans maintains that there is a passion in the exchanges in the story that the translation does not bring out.[1] The exchange between the disciples is a *heated argument*. They are brought to a standstill with *glowering* faces. They ask a question that is *rude* ("Don't you know what's been going on," they say to one who has just said that he doesn't know what's going on), and they get a *rude* answer ("O foolish men, and slow of heart to believe . . ."). When Jesus pretends to go further he is *forcibly* restrained, and the inner sensation that marks the recognition of Christ is of their hearts *burning*.

The figure of the unrecognized Christ walking and talking with the two friends is inspiration in itself. I have known people who can hardly tear themselves away from the icon at Taizé in France that depicts this part of the story. Jesus was with two, but they did not know it. There is something beautiful about this kind of company. Understated and respectful, there is an openness about it that would not be possible if all had known each other equally well

Stephen Cherry is chaplain at King's College, Cambridge University, where he has pastoral and liturgical duties and conducts the Cambridge Liturgy and Theology Seminar. He has published articles in *Christian, Theology,* and *The Independent.*

or if there was a commitment for the three to live or work together. Many people will have had such conversations, perhaps while traveling; some of my best ones are from the time when I used to hitchhike a lot. Other people will know them from visits they have made. Visiting scholars and tourists know what it is to suddenly strike up a conversation that can be more meaningful because it is with strangers. I was in Prague recently, and a long conversation with a Swedish writer fell precisely into this category. We talked about our perceptions and preoccupations, our concerns, worries, and convictions in a way we never would have if a subsequent meeting had seemed likely or possible. It was a significant conversation with a stranger. I came away with a largely rethought appreciation of individualism, and whatever he came away with, he certainly heard what was for him a new and interesting statement of the importance of the idea of God as Trinity.

The first part of the story testifies to the gracious presence of Christ and witnesses to the value of speaking with strangers. I know this is an unfashionable point; stranger spells danger in our risk-sensitive minds. But for *adults,* meetings and conversations and encounters with strangers are fundamental to personal growth and holy and civil society.

We don't know much about the two people on the road. One was called Cleopas. The other? Who knows? Certainly we need not think of the other as just another youngish male. When a professor of biblical exegesis preached at the wedding of two friends of mine, he used this passage as his text. We don't know much about the two, he said. They could have been husband and wife, newly married. The two may well have been a couple. In any case Jesus, as stranger, certainly shared profound and significant intimacy with them.

But as they were walking along and talking, or at least while Jesus was talking, they had a sense that something special was happening. But they didn't acknowledge this to themselves or to each other until later. There's human truth in this. Religious sensibility is so closely related to memory that sometimes it seems to be a function of it. The paradigm is the Genesis story of Jacob, who having dreamed of the staircase between heaven and earth with angels passing both ways, subsequently realizes, "Surely the Lord is in this place, and I did not know it." But we have it here as well. Looking back, the disciples could confess that their hearts then burned within them. We can relate to this. Looking back, we can perceive realities about and presences within our experiences, our journeyings, our meetings, and our conversations.

Reading the passage in the Authorized Version, the words of restraint on Christ are "Abide with us, for it is toward evening." These words sprang to the forefront of the mind of the dying vicar of Brixham, H. F. Lyte, who on his deathbed composed the hymn "Abide with Me, Fast Falls the Eventide." English urban culture has not yet forgotten this vehicle of Christian conviction, and since the Hillsbrough tragedy, football culture has rediscovered this great hymn. Evening, death, darkness, meaninglessness is coming. Abide with us, with me, whoever you are, significant stranger. These are deep Christian and human sentiments. We learn something about ourselves when we appreciate that they were definitively expressed in the words of the two disciples on the road to Emmaus. We learn something about God when we realize that they were expressed to the incognito Christ.

The story bears interesting comparison with another Lukan narrative about an encounter with Christ on a journey, that of Paul on the road to Damascus (Acts 9:1–9). The two stories testify to two different, authentic, and foundational kinds of Christian experience. On the road to Damascus, Paul is still "breathing threats," he is hostile to Christianity, a danger to all. On the road to Emmaus, the disciples are in an emotional state but of sadness and disarray—if a danger at all, a danger to themselves. Paul encounters a vision his companions do not see, though they do hear the words, "Saul, Saul, why are you persecuting me"; Cleopas and partner see and hear Jesus and commune with him. Paul is immediately on the ground. Was he pushed, or is it a voluntary abasement? It is not clear from the text. The Emmaus road scene is not so apocalyptic, though it is not without its drama. When Paul rose from the ground, he could not see; he lost his sight for three days. At Emmaus, on the other hand, the experience was one of revelation. Everything was opened: the Scriptures, their hearts, and at last, their eyes. Then, when they saw, Jesus disappeared. After his encounter Paul could not eat; at Emmaus the *meal* was the place of vision. The Damascus road experience was the conversion of an individual; the Emmaus experience was social and communal.

My point is simple: We have two Lukan narratives of encounter and conversion, and although they are similar in this way, it remains the case that blinding light for the individual is not the same as breaking bread in community. Christians who warm to the Damascus road experience must learn to appreciate the Emmaus type—and vice versa.

But the breaking of bread is the crucial denouement at Emmaus. "And when he was at table with them, he took the bread and blessed and broke it and gave it to them. And their eyes were opened and they recognized him" (vv. 30 and 31). Those in the Judeo-Christian tradition can hardly pay enough attention to the significance of bread. Unleavened bread of Passover, manna in the wilderness, the bread of suffering and affliction, the daily bread, or bread for tomorrow, of the Lord's Prayer, the Bread of Life of John's Gospel, and of course the bread broken at the Last Supper, which is the Body of the Lord, and which is *for you.*

Bread is basic material, a nutritional and spiritual staple. But bread is at its most powerful, significant, available, and revelatory when it is broken. Western Christian liturgy has often lost sight of the power of breaking bread. Our spiritual ancestors saw the point and ritualized it, but in so doing they also removed it from real life. Bread broken in the sanctuary is significant, but the distance alienates as much as it communicates. We need to meditate on the tearing and crumbling of ordinary loaves, not the crisp, pious, crumbless divisions of sanctuary wafers.

Breaking bread is a way of divine revelation, and therefore and equally of human reconciliation. Sadly, the history of the Eucharist is one of blood and division; Communion seems to demand excommunication, just as church (as in fellowship) seems to imply schism. But the spiritual and historical truth is that either bread is broken and shared or the relationship is ruptured and broken. The embarrassing side of Christian history has not originated in the breaking of bread but in the *refusal* to break bread with certain others. The most awful twentieth-century example of this is that apartheid in South Africa had its origins in the breaking of table fellowship of Christians of different races.

But breaking bread with others *is* a powerful means of reconciliation. If you can't do this in practice, try it as a prayer for a relationship of yours that has lost its love or peace or well-being. Go to the person with a piece of bread. Break it with them and share it. The spiritual associations of bread are so deep in our understanding that simply to think this through is a prayer for reconciliation. To do it in practice would be a sacrament of love and vulnerability. It would be a risk. It would create something new and reveal something eternal. Jesus knew what he was doing when he broke bread with the disciples at Emmaus. He was terminating trouble as he was revealing himself; he was drawing the companions closer to each other as he was revealing where he was eternally present. When they saw the broken bread, they perceived it and him in a new and uncreated light. Jesus disappeared, the past came to life, and the broken bread remained.

NOTE

1. Christopher F. Evans, *Saint Luke* (London: SCM, 1990), 904.

9. A Diptych of Kindness
Peter Fribley

Mark 12:38–44; 1 Kings 17:8–16

Of the four lessons today, three refer to widows. To be a widow in the Bible is to be poor, unprotected, and without a voice. Indeed, it is the consensus that widows in some other ancient Near Eastern lands were better protected than were widows in Israel. The prophets do attack the harsh treatment of widows—thus telling us clearly how hard their lot was. Even the very word *widow* tells us worlds: it may be translated "mute" or "silent." "Without a voice." As a class widows were poor and on the margins of society, mute. Knowing that, one realizes just how out of character the cheeky widow who took on the unjust judge really was. Most widows would not have done that. They were poor, and society told them to keep quiet, and they mostly did. Some things don't change a whole lot, do they—Gray Panthers notwithstanding?

In Mark and in 1 Kings two stories, two widows: a diptych of kindness. I call them a diptych of kindness because, in art, a diptych is a painting, usually an altarpiece, consisting of two panels that complement each other. And these two widows do just that. Picture in your mind's eye these two stories as two panels, hinged together, as a diptych is. On the right, the widow in Mark's Gospel, perhaps just as she puts her two copper coins into the treasury.

Peter Fribley is pastor of First Presbyterian Church, Oskaloosa, Iowa. He was educated at Hanover College, Union Theological Seminary (New York), the University of Bonn (Germany), and Princeton Theological Seminary, where he received his Ph.D. He has taught at Princeton Theological Seminary, Pittsburgh Theological Seminary, and St. Cloud State University, and has served campus ministries and churches in British Columbia and Minnesota. He is a frequent contributor to periodicals and to *The Ministers Manual*. He and his wife, a special education teacher, have two sons and a daughter.

And on the left, the widow of Zaraphath, perhaps her cruse of oil and jar of meal in hand.

Consider first the panel to our right. Mark's widow. She is a model of piety and trust. Reinhold Niebuhr, in a sermon, has argued that we should translate *faith* as "trust," and I think he's right. For *faith* does not distinguish between what you believe "with the top of the head" and what you believe "from the bottom of the heart" (John Baillie). *Trust* does. Trust has an object. And she trusts God, and what is harder, she trusts that God will work through the formal religion of her day. She trusts that her money will be used well.

Why? After all, it is said in the previous passage that the scribes, the formally religious of her day, are hypocrites "who like to go about in long robes and to have salutations in the marketplaces ("good morning, Reverend") and the best seats in the synagogues and the places of honor at feasts but who devour widows' houses and for pretense make long prayers." They are, then, pretty far gone.

And presumably she knows all this. She may not keep up on church politics, and you may not get her to gossip or even to listen to gossip, but she isn't dumb. She knows. She knows all this. She can put two and two together.

One of my colleagues, a pastor, said that she is concerned about this widow's lack of anger. "Where is she loving herself?" she asked. After all, she's being taken advantage of. Ripped off. And she went on to say that in our society a lot of widows are barely making it, living in one room, and living a hand-to-mouth existence, and that even for ones who are doing well, when you're not a part of a couple, you can feel yourself a social outcast. Without a voice.

Perhaps Mark's widow trusts too much. Perhaps she sticks with the religious apparatus too easily. Perhaps my colleague is correct; perhaps she doesn't love herself enough. Yet our strength, our gift, is usually the flip side of our weakness, and that is surely the case here. The great kindness of Mark's widow is her trust. Her letting go. Her not worrying, even about needed reform that she perfectly well knows must come and will come. Her great gift, her kindness, is her sense that there will be enough. That God will supply her every need. Perhaps more assertiveness is called for, but perhaps a more assertive person couldn't teach us the lesson that it is this person's gift to teach us: the gift of trust in the course of history and of God working her or his purpose out.

The other story, in 1 Kings, raises a whole host of pictures and ponderings. The prophet Elijah is told to go to a widow in Zaraphath, who will feed and lodge him. "I have commanded a widow to feed you." It comes to that. High-minded seminary intentions, plans to change this or that, begin this or that, and it ends up with good people of limited means supporting you. Prophets and would-be prophets, evangelists and preachers, and all manner of reformers and improvers, from TV evangelists to the humblest storefront preacher to the pope to the great prophets—Isaiah, Jeremiah, Ezekiel, Moses, Jesus himself, and the disciples. Room and board provided by the likes of this lady.

There she is, gathering sticks. Women's work, then and now. In the third world, as wood becomes more scarce, it must be sought farther and farther away, and thus one must get up earlier and earlier—hours before the rest of the household—to go out and forage. Women must, that is. She gathers sticks. If you had told me the story is about someone who is gathering sticks and had asked whether the gatherer was a man or a woman, I would have said woman. It's a quite safe guess. Then and now.

At first, Elijah is Elijah. After all, God sent him. (Never mind that's what they all say.) He waltzes in through the gate of the city, spies her—his meal, that is—and calls to her, "Bring me a little water in a vessel that I may drink." I'm glad he didn't try that with my mother. She had a thing about people shouting wishes. You came into the room and expressed them, or wished you had. But no, she complies. But next he shouts, "Oh, and a morsel of bread."

On that count she draws the line. No. We've only a little, the boy and I, and we plan to eat it and die. Stop and realize what's going on here. This hotshot would-be prophet, reformer, out to rail at the rich on behalf of the poor, knows so little about his hostess and is so little interested that he asks her for her last meal. We all do it, clergy and laity alike. Impose on people in the name of God. Impose our agendas and our needs.

And her great gift is that she does love herself and her son enough to say no. At least until Elijah and implicitly God—for it is God who provides the jar of meal that is not spent and the cruse of oil that does not fail—until Elijah and God speak to her need and assure her. And that is why I see this story as a panel complementary to Mark's widow—why I see a diptych. Mark's widow knows, somehow, that the provisions of God will not fail. And that is Mark's widow's gift. But the widow in 1 Kings must ask, must challenge human agency (and as a person Elijah is that, prophet or no) to provide, to be a channel of, God's provisions. That is what we do when we open ourselves up to people from the third world and our own poor. For the mute are mute only because they have been ignored so long that they have ceased speaking. That is what we do when we listen to the voiceless—rape victims, incest victims, harassment victims, so-called uneducated. Widows, women.

By and large, I believe, the poor are silent and not angry. Not nearly as angry as one might expect them to be. In South Africa, some years ago, the whites in our Plowshares Institute trip were amazed at how gentle and lacking in anger toward us the blacks were. And the American blacks said to us whites, that's what we have been trying to tell you. There is indeed anger in us but not as much as you think. Because of the way you have treated us and your assumption that we should be boiling angry with you and should live out of that anger, you project your fears onto us. But by and large, no matter what group you are talking about that is "down," there is probably less anger than you think. And it has to do with trust. Trust in God working her purposes out through jaded religion and racist society and a callous society and much more. Trust in Jesus and how meaningful his presence is.

And the widow in 1 Kings, "Elijah's widow," in a way complements Mark's widow's gift of passivity with her gift of activity. She reminds one of the Syrophoenician woman who, when Jesus refused to heal her child because he was sent only to the lost sheep of the house of Israel, gave it right back to him *in his lap:* "Yes, Lord, but even the dogs eat the crumbs that fall from the table." Decked Jesus, and Jesus loved it. What's the Jewish saying? "God loves to be defeated by his children." I believe that.

Not that she fulminates or indulges in character assassination or behind-your-back, two-faced undercutting. She simply says no to his face and explains why. But her gift also contains this: She brings out the best in Elijah, for he turns to God to provide her need. To Elijah's credit, he doesn't split. He assures her that there will be more. Later, in the following scene, when her child is dying, she tells him he's bad luck: "*What* did I do to deserve *you* under my roof," she says, or, "What have you against me, O man of God? You have come to me to bring my sin to remembrance and to cause the death of my son!" She is animal-like in protecting the life of her son. Again, women's work. Today, on the dusty roads of refugees, 80 percent are women and children, and there are, I wager, *millions* of women similarly lionlike in "protecting their cubs" all they can.

Two panels. A widow putting in two copper coins, which together make a penny. And the other panel: a jar of meal and a cruse of oil. A mirroring (in turning into opposites also, as a mirror does, reversing), a mirroring, complementary *diptych of kindness.*

Mark's widow and the widow of Zaraphath: a diptych of kindness. Each needs the other. Truth does sometimes come in twos. Sometimes, of course, truth and kindness come in threes. But that would be a triptych, and that would be another story for another time.

10. Come Alive with 1 John— Stop Sinning!
Michael Quicke

1 John 2:1–6

I don't know whether anybody recently has called you "my dear children" and how you responded to it? It may be that you have an elderly relative who, in a rather quavering voice, really means it when they say "dear children." But most of us will not take that sort of language from others. Indeed, we find it patronizing and paternalistic. At the very least, it needs that somebody to be well known, older than us, and, of course, somebody who has a certain authority. And that's what hits you when you look at this first Letter of John. If you do find it difficult responding to somebody who calls you "dear children" you're going to have a tough time, especially in chapter 2—"my dear children" (v. 1); "dear friends" (v. 7); "dear children" (v. 12); "dear children" (v. 13); "dear children" (v. 18); "dear children" (v. 28)—and that's just the one chapter.

But you see, John *is* someone who is well known, he *is* an older person, and he *has* this extraordinary authority. There are lots of whys and wherefores as to whether the writer of the first, second, and third letters of John is the same as the writer of the Fourth Gospel and whether that same author can be identified with John, son of Zebedee, who left his nets and followed the Lord. By the end of the second century the general belief was that it was the same man, and that was the declared wisdom about the authority

Michael Quicke was born in London, England, and educated at Jesus College in Cambridge University and Regent's Park College in Oxford University. As a student he won both a university prize for Greek and the college preaching prize. Since 1980 he has been senior minister of the St. Andrews Street Baptist Church, Cambridge. He has preached at conventions and conducted Bible studies in Europe, Australia, Canada, and the United States.

behind these words *my dear children*. That John, son of Zebedee, the beloved disciple (John 21:20), was the longest-living disciple. He was the last of the links with the Lord, whom he had seen in flesh and blood, and that gave him the authority. Now, there are lots of aspects to balance concerning authorship. Linguistically, there are analyses that have taken place and also the examinations of context. What was going on when these letters were written? Could they be written by the same person? Indeed, you'll see as it began, in chapter 1, when it was in the plural (*we* have heard, *we* have seen) clearly there was a wider body of people involved. Yet I believe with *full* heart we have here someone speaking who knows these people so well he can declare "my dear children"; we have somebody who has an immense experience and is an elder in every sense, and we have somebody with that kind of authority. I believe there is a tremendous amount of evidence that this is the declared witness to us from John, the beloved disciple.

You know when people have got authority, of course. There's something about them. When Paul Negrut, pastor of the largest Baptist church in Romania, visited us just three Sundays ago, we noted, all of us, there was something about him. Just the way he was. Over lunch when he was staying with us with my family around the table, we got to know him a little better. It was extraordinary because, like I suppose all of us, we'd been riveted to the events in Romania, as the Ceaucescu regime fell in the events leading up to Christmas 1989. I'd read the story of Lazlo Tokes, the reform pastor whose church in Timosara was at the center of this revolution. And here was Paul Negrut, who was also in the heart of it. We asked him about it, and he began to describe what it was like to be involved in Romania in those days. I asked him about Lazlo Tokes, who he knows well. I asked him, "Was it not true, Paul, that at some point the people asked you to be part of the new government?" "Oh yes," he said, "that's true. In fact they came and asked me whether I would be foreign secretary." At this point the forks were suspended midway from the plates to our mouths. My boys couldn't believe it. Here was a man having lunch with us who'd been asked to become foreign secretary! "Oh," he said, "then a little later on they came and asked me to become prime minister of Romania." He paused. "It couldn't have been right. The kind of skills needed meant it would have been like driving a Rolls Royce car down a hill with nothing under the bonnet and no pedals to control it! . . . I knew it wasn't right," he said. As we heard him and looked at him, there was integrity that is the kind of integrity this author has for us today. Not just for the first readers but for *us* today, which is what we understand to be the inspiration of Scripture for all peoples in all places for all times.

When he says, "We've *heard* Jesus," you know what it is when you've *heard* somebody and it's in your experience forever. It may be years ago. I can remember as a small child certain things being said to me, certain good things being said, and I can capture even the nuance of the voice. I can see the face of the person who said it. And all through my life I can recall vividly the voices of those who've spoken to me and said things that mattered. And when we've *seen* and when we've *touched,* we're in a special place. And the writer here, John, has been there and speaks to us with an authority that means, I believe, we can come with full hearts and, when he says to you and me "my dear children," to respond in the best spirit.

Now he has several difficult things to say, and we begin unpacking these first six verses. I want to urge you to listen carefully to these verses for 1 John is rarely preached through because it's concentrated and it's tough and because you have an older man with authority saying painful things.

I.

The first thing that he says is *stop sinning*. Verse 1 of chapter 2: "My dear children, I write this to you so that you will not sin." Immediately there are at least two problems here. The first thing is that *most people misunderstand sin.* It's become so caught up with lapses of a sexual nature that we actually use words like "living in sin" entirely to do with a sexual relationship. When we talk about sinful acts, most people immediately think of something wickedly sexual. They're intrigued by it, and frankly, today as the mores move further and further away with people accusing us within the Church of great hypocrisy, the sense of sin has been lost in a vague feeling that it's something to do with sexual immorality and who cares anyway. You'll have heard before that there are different words for sin, and they're all significant, and they must be seen together. The particular word here comes from the stem *hamartia,* which means "missing the mark." We've heard that before, but it's so profound.

Because you see, sin is not just specifically wicked things that we can see, especially in others, and point them out. Sin is about us being made in the image of God—body, mind, and spirit, with the possibilities of living for him and then in body, mind, and spirit failing to be the best that our Lord calls us to be. That's what sin is. That's why Rom. 3:23 says that all of us are *in hamartia*—it's the same word. All of us have fallen short of the glory of God. None of us are the kind of people God intended us to be. And because none of us are, all the things that God first planned for us to be, belong together in, all the relationships—they're all spoiled and ruined. And worse than that, the whole *purpose* of us being alive has been lost in the offense that is *hamartia*.

Many people misunderstand that, and the second thing is *many people are comfortable with their sin*. There's a sense in which the shortcomings of our character are so well known to us that we've built them into our personality. We know that we're mean about certain things—well, that's the way we are. We know that we're envious and there's certain relationships that have been broken and we'll never get them right—well, that's the way it is. We know there's envy, and we know there's pride. Actually, we do! We know there's prejudice—but that's the way we are, people have to take us as we are. God has to take us as we are. And so we drift into this extraordinary state that we're actually comfortable the way we are. We hear challenges—we heard two weeks ago, "If you confess your sins" (1 John 1:9) and the need to be specific. But frankly, we're so comfortable we don't want to go through the process of beginning to recognize that there are parts of our personality that are so embedded within us they're taking us further from God. We're too comfortable, and we don't want to change, and so we don't. It's sometimes said in our house, "Huh, going to church hasn't made much difference to you, has it!" True! We can come to church, and we can listen to awesome truths about the promises of God for you and me, and we can go out exactly the same people, with the same mind-set and the same potential to fall short locked in because of the way in which we've organized our lives. And John confronts this. It will not do. If you are in any way serious about the message of God, then you need to understand that there must be a confessing. It must be specific. It must be directed to those areas of your lives where the shortcomings are so painful that they're even now causing such disaster in some of those things where the Lord calls you to be strong and good for him. And so John gently ("my dear children") but with great strength ("I write this to you that you will *not* sin") says *stop it*. As a cross section of people, you're meant to be different from any other cross section of people because you should be walking in the light. Stop it!

There is a cutting edge of realism here that we should be taking so seriously. And sadly, the more the preacher talks about sin, often the more generalist we become and the more we place it at a distance. Oh, we do feel slightly uncomfortable, but we make certain there is no action in our lives. You know about that impoverished young man in tatters who went to ask his bank manager for a loan for a secondhand car, and the bank manager said, "Well, apart from your job, have you got any security?" There was a long pause, and as the young man pondered, he said, "Well, have you got any property, any possessions?" There was another long pause. The bank manager said, "Do you own a car?" "Yes," said the young man, "a Porsche." "Oh, do you own any shares?" "Yes, yes," he said, "hundreds of them." "And you own a house?" "Yes," he said, "yeah, worth a quarter of a million pounds in the latest valuation. Five bedrooms." Said the bank manager looking over his spectacles, "You must be joking." "Well," said the young man, "you started it!"

When the Lord deals with you and me, he's not joking. He knows the truth. He's not interested in exaggerating, and he's certainly not interested in taking us down avenues where we move further and further from reality. Because today—and it may be a tiny step relative to some of the issues—today he needs us wherever you and I may go out and continue being the people we have been, he wants you to hear *Stop! Do not continue!* All this talk about walking in the light and about living for the Lord, he wants it to be real. So the first words of the elder with authority to us are *stop sinning*.

II.

And the second words are very important, too. *Face the cross*. Now, for John there is obviously this extraordinary experience of encountering the Risen Lord. He knows that wherever you are in need now there is this amazing Lord whom he can offer without reservation as the answer to our needs in trouble and in sin. You have this awesome ending of verse 1 and into verse 2 where he says, when there is sin "we have one who speaks to the Father in our defence, Jesus Christ the righteous one." Oh, we could spend so much time just unpacking this. There's a wonderful word here that you will know quite well, translated in the NIV "in our defence." It's the word *Paraclete,* translated of course in the Fourth Gospel sometimes as "Comforter," describing the Holy Spirit, but often left as it is, a Greek word, because it says so much. *Para,* "alongside," *clete,* "called"—one who comes alongside. As one commentator says, "lends his presence to his friends." Someone who stands alongside with awesome authority and, when we're in need, speaks for us and holds us that truth might be done but also mercy and love.

I think that's why within many of us this interest in advocacy and those who defend us is there. We're taken up, many of us, with John Mortimer's rascally Rumpole of the Bailey. I have Judge Gerald Sparrow's book *The Great Defenders,* and I love it. When I first read it, I gobbled up those chapters about Marshall Hall and Norman Birkett and Thomas Erskine—these greats who spoke in defense. In his preface to the book, Judge Gerald Sparrow says, "The real gift of the great defenders has been their insight into the hearts and hence into the motives of men and women. There's always been the impact of a forceful personality and undoubtedly they must have great compassion . . . but it follows that a mean, cantankerous, vindictive little man could hardly be a great defender." There never has been a less mean, a less cantankerous, a less vindictive, a less little man than Jesus. He's the righteous one, he's the biggest and the greatest, the most generous and the most understanding, sympathizing with us in all our weaknesses. And he comes alongside, not in some general sense, not to give us a vague feeling, not just emotionally to unlock a sense of "oh, it could be all right after all," but specifically to show in one place and in one place only, verse 2, "he is the atoning sacrifice for our sins and not for ours only but also for the sins of the world."

You need to know, though preachers can often conceal such things, that there's a very difficult word here. In NIV it's translated "atoning sacrifice." But if you have the Authorized Version, there's the word *propitiation* for our sins. *Propitiation* is a heavy, controversial word. It has a kind of background where people offer things to appease an angry god. So propitiate means that something is offered in order to make sure that the god changes his mind. And the feeling is that that could have no place in the Christian understanding of God, because whatever else is happening we're not talking about a barrier *within* God, we're talking about a barrier *within* us. So a word like *propitiate* is no good at all. It speaks about an uncomfortable dynamic, and we won't have it. And so RSV translates "expiate," and that has a better tone to it. That means rather than something happening within the nature of God, it's something happening where we ourselves are being changed—the responsibility is within us. The difficult thing is that the word here is actually *propitiate!* There is a sense where the holy, wonderful Lord of lights has a controlled antipathy and hatred of all that is dark, and there has to be a confrontation between light and dark, between justice and love. And should it be that the God who is offended by sin takes the initiative to propitiate himself through his Son, we're into such a uniqueness of language and of understanding that it blows the mind, because any such thing like this—that the very justice that repudiates sin should be overwhelmed by a love that meets that sin through the Son—well, we're taken out of our depth. And that's why we have a verse like 1 John 4:10. "This is love, not that we loved God but he loves us and sent his Son to propitiate for our sins"—that's Authorized Version language. Friends, there is upon the cross an extraordinary event, and no matter how many words we try to use and how we try to bring together the teaching of the New Testament, the dazzling truth is that the just God deals justly and yet he suffers within that justice because of the quality of his love. And this Lord who will not close his eyes to sin, offensive though it is, it is as though on the cross his eyes are wide open to the consequences of sin, to the shortcomings that have ruined this world and blotted out our possibilities, through the very sacrifice and suffering of Jesus.

Why are we so blind about the cross? Why do we have so little theology? Why is it that we're not concerned about whether we use the words *atoning, propitiation,* or *expiation?* I tell you why. It's because it's hard. It's hard work. It takes us to one place where in awesome truth men and women find themselves shredded of rationality because the Lord begins where he chooses to begin: upon a cross. And in this offense, which is a stumbling block, which Jews and Greeks and people in present day Cambridge would rather wish hadn't happened, the Lord begins. And he speaks about amazing justice and love meeting. The consequences of sin, which he cannot bear, being borne and of the outcome of mankind falling short in the wickedness of lives, which have perverted and twisted and rebelled against God's purposes being put right with him who comes to our defense upon a cross. John will not let us slacken in our understanding of the cross. Those with minds, he says, you're using them in all sorts of other ways, will you use them to ponder the miracle of the cross? Face the cross.

III.

Stop, face, and then the last thing is, of course, *obey.* There is for John one experience—he's met Jesus and he wants other people to know him. And their initial reaction might be, "Well, *you* saw him, *you* heard him, *you* touched him, *you* were right close. How can *we* know Jesus?" And John says something amazingly profound. He says you can know Jesus by obeying his commands. The more you obey him, then the more you'll know him. Now this is a question primarily of ethics, of so growing close to him that you find you're taken up into his way and you live his kind of life. Yesterday, in the romance of the day, I recollected how it was that my assistant Simon and Clare first met each other here within the life of this church. And one recognizes the only way that we can grow close to people we'd like to get to know is to spend more time and to be willing, understanding that they will have different experiences and different ways of looking at life, to try and understand them, to get inside what they're thinking and they're feeling. And that's the way it happens, and so romance overwashed many of us yesterday.

I was reflecting on my relationship with Carol, in fact reflecting with her about it, how in former lives she was very keen on somebody who was a keen tennis player, who in fact played for his country. And she found her desire to come close to him involved a great deal of tennis—watching tennis; having her own techniques of tennis perfected; all sorts of ways, but tennis was the thing. And then a little while after that there was somebody who was very keen on opera, and as Carol wanted to know this particular person, she found herself going to a tremendous amount of opera—a vast amount! And week after week her horizons were opened to the miracles and marvels of the whole new world up to that point entirely closed to her. And then, as she pointed out, she met *me* who was into the *church*. She found herself being drawn more and more into the church, and it probably didn't have quite the same ring—but I assured her and continue to do, that that's the most glorious dimension to go into to!

But when Jesus touches our lives, as he has done for so many of us here, he calls us to grow so close that we actually live for him and grow like him. That Christianity is not some set of principles worked out, it's the way of our lives. And that we find ourselves so caught up that we *are* being changed, and we're changed because we listen to his words and we grow in the relationship. And this morning before we came here, yes, we said our prayers to him, and we began the day with him, because he's real and he's vital. Obeying him, we find ourselves knowing him.

I met somebody just this week who said, "It's extraordinary, you know, when I made my Christian commitment, it's worked because somehow as I sought to live a Christian life, to read the Bible, and to do the things I'm told to do, Jesus has become more and more real." Yes! As we obey him, we know him. If you say, "Oh, I know him," but in your life there's a major area of disobedience, then you can't. In fact John says very bluntly, "The man who says I know him but does not do what he commands is a liar" (v. 4). I always feel that people like John must have gone through traumas, because in that group of close disciples there was a Judas who actually said, "I know Jesus so well that I'm going to kiss him, and then you can go for him and arrest him and take him away and kill him—and where's my money?" You can know him. You can know him well enough to kiss him and identify him. You can know him well enough to sing and to speak about him, to argue about him, actually to come to worship and feel a certain sense of comfort with the worship and the singing and even the preaching of hard words. But the Word of God to us is, if you're not obeying, if within your life there isn't that stopping of sin, which if it continues bedevils the relationship, if there isn't a facing of him in the awesome work of the cross, then you can't know him and you won't walk as Jesus did.

Stop, face, obey—these are the words of the elder with authority to us, dear children, and they're words to be applied. For if you and I know right now those tiny steps to be taken, he wants you to do it in his strength, to walk with him, obeying him in them. And he wants you to see again that upon that cross is the place where heaven's love and heaven's justice meet. Where your life and mine are changed for evermore. Where it all begins and where for evermore we look and see, we have a friend, we have an Advocate, we have the Righteous One who enables us to be right with God forever in his love.

11. Defeating Fortune and Misfortune

J. Alfred Smith

At this Job got up and tore his robe, and shaved his head. Then he fell to the ground in worship and said: Naked I came from my mother's womb and naked I will depart. The Lord gave and the Lord has taken away, may the name of the Lord be praised.

—Job 1:20–21 NIV

Introduction

Oscar Wilde once wrote, "In this world there are only two tragedies. One is not getting what one wants and the other is getting it."[1] Wilde was really describing Job's life. For Job knew the tragedies of getting all that he wanted and the loss of all that was precious.

I. The Prologue

He lived in the land of Uz. The place of Uz is uncertain. The Bible speaks of Uz only twice. In Jer. 25:20 Uz is a land of kings and in Lam. 4:21 Uz is a neighbor to Edom. Scholarship places Uz east of Edom in northern Arabia. This view is supported by the fact that

J. Alfred Smith is the senior pastor of Allen Temple Baptist Church, Oakland, California, and professor of Christian ministry at the American Baptist Seminary of the West and the Graduate Theological Union of Berkeley. He was educated at Western Baptist College (B.S.), Missouri School of Religion (B.D. and Th.M.), American Baptist Seminary of the West (Th.M. in American church history), and Golden Gate Baptist Theological Seminary (D.Min.). He has served as visiting professor at several seminaries and as adjunct professor. He has published more than a dozen books, including *Preach On!*, *New Treasures from the Old*, and *The Overflowing Heart.*

Job lived near the desert. Chapter 1, verse 9, speaks of a mighty wind that blows in from the desert. The land of Job was fertile for agriculture and livestock raising like the land of northern Arabia. Chapter 1, verses 3 and 14, speak of Job's livestock. He owned seven thousand sheep, three thousand camels, five hundred yoke of oxen, and five hundred donkeys. He was prosperous in *Qedem,* the word translated to mean "the East." He was the largest stockholder on Wall Street. No one could buy him out. He had the highest credit rating at the bank. He was a shrewd business man who participated in international trade. He had business associates from neighboring countries. There were three partners: Eliphaz from Teman, Bildad from Shuah, and Zophar from Naamah, a Judean town mentioned in Josh. 15:41. As a prosperous business man Mr. Job had a monopoly on the transportation industry. He had bought out smaller transportation firms and now controlled the travel routes with three thousand camels. He had a franchise of enviable proportions in the rug and fur coat business because he owned seven thousand sheep, and with five hundred yoke of oxen to do the plowing, Mr. Job did not have to take a back seat to any farmer. Because the pay was good, the benefits generous, and the kind spirit of Job treated the employees with a dignity that Caesar Chavez and the unions never won through negotiations, verse 3 tells us that Mr. Job never had trouble with servants. Everyone wanted to work for Mr. Job. Little did Mr. Job know that in a few days his fortune would turn to misfortune. He would learn by personal experience Jesus' words, "A man's life consisteth not in the abundance of the things which he possesseth" (Luke 12:15, kjv).

Mr. Job was not only prosperous, but also he was a parent. Chapter 1, verse 2, tells us that he had seven sons and three daughters. These ten children were young adults with homes of their own. They spent their time fellowshiping with each other. They were a very closely knit family. With seven strong sons to carry on the family name, the Job family would be a strong family for generations to come. Job continued to worry about his children. He provided for their physical, mental, and social well-being, but now he was more concerned about their souls. Would to God that more fathers cared about the souls of their children! Did Job have a premonition of their death? We don't know. But we do know that when Job's children were through feasting and partying, he would send to have them purified. Early in the morning he would bring his children to the altar with prayer and sacrifice. Thank God for the prayers our parents and grandparents prayed for us.

Job was prosperous, prayerful as a parent, and also pious in his personal and public life. Chapter 1, verse 1, tells us, "This man was blameless and upright; he feared God and shunned evil" (NIV).

Blameless (tam) implies genuine sincerity and complete integrity.

Upright (yā s hār) implies complete fairness and pure honesty.

Fearing God (ye rē elohīm) indicates that Job hated above all else the violation of the known will of God.

Turning from evil (sār mērā) means that he was not attracted by any form of vice or wickedness.

II. The Scene Changes from Earth to the Scene of God in Counsel

But *there is an enemy* who dislikes the prosperity of the pious and the success of the saints. His name means *Adversary. Satan,* the one who disobeys God and discredits God's servants. *Satan,* the hindering personality of God's program. *Satan,* the reckless foe of redemption. *The Satan* who in Zech. 3:1 accused Joshua, the high priest of Israel, before the angel of the Lord, seeking to have him condemned for his and the errant nation's transgressions. *This Satan* is always for retributive justice because he is a warrior against forgiveness, an enemy of grace, and an opponent of mercy. *This Satan,* whom Isaiah in chapter 14, verses 12 to 15, chided with these chilling words:

> How have you fallen from heaven, O morning
> star, son of the dawn! You have been cast down to
> the earth, you who once laid low the nations! You
> said in your heart, I will ascend to heaven, I will
> raise my throne above the stars of God; I will sit
> enthroned on the mount of the assembly on the
> utmost heights of the sacred mountain. I will
> ascend above the tops of the clouds; I will make
> myself like the Most High, *But you* are brought
> down to the grave, to the depths of the pit. (NIV)

Luke 10:18 tells us that Jesus saw this Satan falling as lightning from heaven, from the blessed level of fortune to the cursed level of misfortune. This fallen and falling Satan had his eyes on Job for the express purpose of pulling him down from integrity and uprightness to the depths of disgrace and death.

Hear God say to him, "Have you considered my servant Job? There is no one on earth like him; he is blameless and upright, a man who fears God ["me"] and shuns evil" (Job 1:8, NIV). God knows Satan, and he wants us to know that Satan is like a hungry hunter, a devouring lion, or a deadly cobra. He spoils the pure, makes fools of the wise, and makes midgets of giants. Trust God and watch Satan.

Respected theologian A. C. Knudson in his book *The Doctrine of Redemption* states the following:

> Satan occupies no logical place in the Christian
> system of belief. His existence does not explain the
> origin of sin nor does it make temptation any
> more intelligible. In so far as it implies a
> nonhuman source of human sin, it is a relic of
> dualism and cancels the concept of sin.[2]

Those of us who are pastors must disagree with this famous theologian. We see young lives with rich potential that are ruined by Satan. We see seasoned saints and war-weary Christian soldiers tainted by the poison of Satan's arrows. We who preach believe that the cleverest wile of the devil is to convince us that he does not exist.

Satan exists, but he is limited by God's almighty power. With God's permissive will he inflicts Job with four crushing disasters. First of all, the Sabeans kill Job's servants and steal his oxen and donkeys. Second, an electrical storm used forked lightning to kill the sheep and all servants, save one spared to bring Job the bad news. Third, three platoons of experienced Chaldean raiders with careful strategy cut off every possible exit and steal three thousand of Job's fleet-footed camels. This destructive desert Mafia kills Job's servants, save one, with sharp swords. For the Mafia believes that dead men tell no tales. The government looks the other way. Now, the Mafia controls the transportation systems, and importing drugs into the city from the Far East is no longer a problem. Choice young minorities and queenly minority women whose charms enraptured Moses and Solomon are now turned to work the streets for animalistic pimps controlled by the Mafia.

Fourth, a catastrophic hurricane destroys the million-dollar mansion in which Job's children are having a banquet. At one fell swoop the children are dead. Overnight, without a hint of warning, Job's work of a lifetime and Job's children, whom he deeply loves, flee into nonbeing like a flashing meteor.

Look at Job now.

He tears up the clothes he is wearing. *Clothes* aren't that important now. He shaved his hair from his head. *Pride* is not that important now. He doesn't mourn for long. This prominent, prosperous, prayerful, pious parent is now in the pits of poverty and pain. He is knocked down but not out. He is beaten but not defeated. He is hurt but not killed. He has nothing, yet he possesses everything.

He decides that the way up is by the posture of prayer. Chapter 1, verse 20, reads, "Then he fell to the ground in worship" (NIV). When you don't know what to do, when you have done all that you can do, fall down on your knees. No one is ever so tall as when one is on one's knees in prayer. Fall down on your knees. Talk to God. Fall down on your knees and tell Jesus. Fall down on your knees and wait for deliverance.

Pray with Job: "Naked I came from my mother's womb, and naked I will depart."

Stand up and praise the Lord.

Stand up and praise God with your lips.

Stand up and praise God with realism: "The Lord gave and the Lord has taken away; may the name of the Lord be praised. Blessed, blessed, blessed, be the name of the Lord."

Blessed be the name of the Lord in summer and winter. Blessed be the name of the Lord in sickness and health. Blessed be the name of the Lord in sorrow and joy. Blessed be the name of the Lord in tragedy and triumph. Blessed be the name of the Lord in life and death. Blessed be the name of the Lord in fortune and misfortune.

NOTES

1. Quoted in Harold Kushner, *When All You've Ever Wanted Isn't Enough* (New York: Summit Books, 1986), 3.

2. A. C. Knudson, *The Doctrine of Redemption* (New York: Abingdon-Cokesbury Press, 1933), 251.

12. Memorable Munificence
Thomas J. Gibbs, Jr.

John 11:45–12:8

Introduction

At first thought, there is not very much about Bethany that is memorable. The very meaning of the word would almost involuntarily cause one to relegate it amid the mind's gladly forgotten places and events. It means the house of the poor or afflicted one, a house of poverty, or a house or place of unripe figs. And there is surely nothing there to stir or prod the mind to memory.

But, of course, you do remember Bethany. It was the home of Lazarus, of Martha and Mary. There also lived Simon the Leper, a friend of Jesus' and one healed and redeemed by him. And we remember it was at Bethany that Jesus was last seen and from there that he ascended. But it is true that none of these things in themselves cause us to remember Bethany.

And yet there was an incident at Bethany that has and always will redeem and reclaim it from the list of unconscious memories. It was an incident I like to call "Memorable Munificence," or remembered liberality.

Let me tell you the story.

It took place in the evening in the house of Simon the Leper. It was supper time. Around the sumptuous table of Simon reclined Jesus and his disciples and, of course, the host, Simon. Jesus and

---

Thomas J. Gibbs, Jr., is Long-term Senior Interim Minister for South Gate First Christian Church in South Gate, California. A Disciple of Christ, Gibbs received his Bachelor of Divinity from Phillips Seminary. In addition to preaching, Reverend Gibbs is a licensed Marriage, Family, and Child Counselor.

the Twelve were on their way to Jerusalem, and for him it was his last trip. For he had, as the Gospels indicate, "determinedly set his face to go to Jerusalem," and he knew full well what awaited him there. And while they were eating, a woman, named by John as Mary, quietly slipped in from the street and, going directly to Jesus, knelt at his feet. And pulling from the folds of her garment an alabaster vase of ointment called spikenard—among the costliest of perfumes—she anointed his feet. This was unusual enough, but it was not all. With a quick gesture, she pulled the ribbon that bound up her long and beautiful hair. Then, kneeling again, she wiped the feet of Jesus with her hair. The onlookers, whose attention was riveted to the scene being enacted before them, were stunned when Mary deliberately broke the cruse containing the ointment. But now when Mary unbinds her hair and wipes his feet they can hardly believe it. Unbound hair was the badge of the harlot; the use of expensive ointment and the breaking of the flask was a Roman custom.

There is the old story, perhaps apocryphal, that long before Jesus had found Mary, the sister of Martha and Lazarus, living a dissolute life of harlotry in northern Magdala, a long distance from home, and that he had restored her to womanhood, to better things, and to her family. At any rate, it makes the story understandable and more plausible. This beautiful act—the meaning of which was known only to Jesus—was carried out without regard to her own feelings of embarrassment or humiliation and signified to him that Mary had not forgotten all that he had done for her.

But it did not signify this to Judas. His retort is instantaneous, "Why was this ointment thus wasted? It might have been sold for three hundred denarii and given to the poor." And the disciples reproached her. But Jesus said, "Let her alone; why do you trouble her? She has done a beautiful thing for me. For you always have the poor with you, and whenever you will, you can do good to them; but you will not always have me. She has done what she could; she has anointed my body beforehand for burying. And truly, I say to you, where the gospel is preached in the whole world, what she has done will be told in memory of her."

Mary's memorable munificence, her beautiful extravagance, her remembered lavish, liberal, bountiful generosity! No, I cannot forget Bethany, can you? I cannot forget it, for it unforgettably reveals the four attitudes or minds taken toward life, its acts and its expressions.

I.

The first is the *miserly mind*. Listen to Judas: "Why was this ointment wasted?" Here is the miserly mind speaking, and its echo is found in many hearts. The miserly mind is seldom if ever moved to generosity; rather it is cold, calculating, even uncomfortable in the presence of liberality. Its chief joy is in keeping, saving, storing up, even hoarding—and it doesn't matter whether it is words, actions, or faith that it is dispensing. Always and ever it measures out its affections in scant, precise, exact quotas. A little here, a little there, not too much; now mind you, can't afford to lose your head, you know.

It is sadly true that our miserliness puts the greatest blight on our lives. Or to put it even more clearly, the miserly mind is always miserable, wretched, unhappy, disconsolate, forlorn. Now, of course, most of us think of the miser in terms of that person whose attic or garage is stored with all sorts of scarce or choice items or who has a safe-deposit box stocked with all kinds of valuables. But I doubt if there are many in this category. On the other hand, how many people are miserly when it comes to the things money can't buy, which are not necessarily tangible, can't be passed over the counter or stored up?

Think of the things we possess in abundance that we often deny one another—affection, understanding, a cheerful smile, a listening ear, a pat on the back, expressions of appreciation, acts of gratitude—things that, for the most part, cost nothing but are worth worlds when given in sincerity! Many hearts within reach of each of us, often known to us intimately, are at this hour growing cold and lonely because of withheld sympathy, because of miserliness that forbids a kind word and stops cold an action of gratitude before it begins. Surely, it was a keen awareness of the ability of each one of us to give the things money can't buy that prompted Emily Dickinson to write,

> If I can stop one heart from breaking,
> I shall not live in vain;
> If I can ease one life the aching,

Or cool one pain,
Or help one fainting robin
Unto his nest again
I shall not live in vain.

The strange lamentable fact about miserliness is that in the end, it is its own worst enemy. Ever intent on saving, hoarding, it goes one day to its supposed storehouse, and instead of resources aplenty, it finds the larder depleted. The things it sought to keep could only have been kept if they had been given, bestowed, used. So Judas the miserly went one day when the time had finally come to use his sympathy, his understanding, his affection, but alas, he came back empty-handed. All this is perceptible in his quick and caustic comment about Mary's deed. "Why all this waste?" Even so is he who lays up treasure for himself and is not rich toward God (Luke 12:21).

II.

Then there is the *market mind*. And it is ever so closely akin to the miserly mind. In the further words of Judas, it goes on quickly and always says, "For this ointment might have been sold for more than three hundred denarii and given to the poor." Life measured in the marketplace, weighed on the scales, and carefully computed as to its worth in dollars and cents!

And the market mind has taken most of us in. George Bernard Shaw had a word of insight on the market mind when he once said, "It is true that the world is governed to a considerable extent by the considerations that occur to stockbrokers in the first five minutes of the day." The president's heart flutters, and the stock market goes down $2.5 billion. Look, for instance, at the host of important things in front of which we put the dollar sign.

A college education is mainly thought of as costing so many thousands of dollars and taking so many years, not as equipping one to live and serve adequately.

A home is measured by its cost and its market value, not by how much happiness and comfort it brings.

A new church or school is first weighed by the number and amount of pledges it will take to build or by the increase in taxes necessitated rather than the growing in grace and knowledge it brings.

A car is judged by its resale value or trade-in value, not by the places it enables one to go or the service its owner may thus render.

We often think of children with the market mind—sadly shaking our heads and decrying the expense of bring up children today— never stopping to think how poor and blighted our lives would be without them.

It might have been sold—it is the market mind and the possibility of profit that scandalized Judas and the others, for remember, they all joined in. As Mark says, "They reproached her."

> Ointment might have become a factor in the real
> world, the good, solid, substantial world of copper,
> silver, and gold, instead of being wasted in a vain
> gesture of devotion, an unsubstantial waste which
> paid no dividends. They were the sort that would
> have answered the poet: "Getting and spending we
> lay waste our powers? Nonsense! What is not
> getting and spending is the real waste!"[1]

So life becomes, for many, a matter of barter. We sell ourselves to the highest bidder, never mind the consequences or the terms, for that matter, so long as the end figure totals up to expectations. Making good has become god. Financial or numerical success, whatever brings the reward, regardless of principles or scruples, family considerations or religious convictions. It is the end that matters, not the means.

> On this basis you would have to say that Francis of
> Assisi wasted his life—he might have been a lord
> of the manor instead of an impecunious beggar.
> Father Damien's life on the scales was a waste. So
> was John Wesley's—what a major general or
> parliamentary whip he would have made with all
> that executive capacity! And so of course with the
> life of Jesus. The King of the Jews, a power to
> have made Rome tremble—instead an itinerant
> teacher dying the death of a criminal![2]

This ointment might have been sold—ah, Judas, you are still with us—the market mind has more devotees today than ever.

III.

Contrast, if you will, the miserly mind and the market mind with the *munificent mind*—the mind of Mary, of beautiful extravagance, of remembered generosity.

Hers was unmeasured generosity. It was, as has been said, a glorious maximum of sacrifice that never stopped to calculate what might have been a passable minimum—the kind of mathematical computation that so easily besets us. This was no ordinary gift—it was a treasure. Its value has been estimated to have been $240, at least, and perhaps as high as $500. Here, indeed, was giving in "good measure, pressed down, shaken together, and running over." She did not pour out a few drops and say, "Well, I guess that ought to be enough for this occasion." She was lifted clear out of herself in a great devotion. This spontaneity of love was not smothered with caution and prudence. She was lifted clear out of arithmetic into love—one of the greatest leaps a life can ever take.

It is no wonder that Jesus came to Mary's defense. "Let her alone," he said. "She has done a beautiful thing." How he loved open-hearted, generous liberality, and how he paid tribute to it wherever he found it. There was the widow who cast her all in the temple treasury; there was Zachaeus, who restored four times as much as he had embezzled; there was the man whose son Jesus healed, even though he was many miles away, because the father manifested this same abundant, generous, munificent faith; and there was Mary, who poured out her devotion in large unmeasured quantity and of whom Jesus said, "Wherever the gospel is preached in the whole world, what she has done will be told in memory of her."

Memorable munificence—Jesus does not require it of us, but how he loves to find it in us!

Now, whether we will admit it or not, life is not only made livable, but such beauty as it does possess comes from just such munificence. Love's little excesses are too few and far between in most lives. And yet how gloomy the world would be without them.

> Consider the young man about to buy an
> engagement ring for his betrothed. His father, a
> hard-headed fellow, wants to give him some
> practical advice. "Son," he says, "it's silly to spend
> several thousand dollars on a diamond ring. If

your young lady expects that kind of extravagance, you'd better think twice about this marriage. It would be unfair to her. Later on there will be something she really needs, like a washing machine or a vacuum cleaner. And then you won't have the money. Let me give you some advice; get her a zircon. It will only cost a few dollars and no one will ever know the difference."[3]

Sound advice, but what does the young man do? He buys the diamond anyway. And however practical the girl may be, you can be sure of one thing, she wears that ring. She may wish many times she had the money it cost, but she will see herself reduced to the depths of poverty before she parts with it. For the extravagance of the gift is the seal of her husband's love. The gift has bound giver and receiver together, and there is something here that puts to shame all dutiful philanthropy. There is a treasure laid up in memory that far outlives the gift itself.[4]

You may remember O. Henry's Christmas story entitled "The Gift of the Magi." It tells of a poor young couple who lived in a wretched flat. They had little, but of two of their possessions they were very proud. One was Jim's gold watch, a family heirloom. The other was Della's long, brown hair. Christmas was at hand and neither Jim nor Della had the means to buy the other a present worthy of their devotion. So Della went out and sold her beautiful hair. With the money she bought a platinum fob chain for Jim's watch. That evening Jim came home to dinner. He, too, brought a present—it was a set of jeweled combs for Della's hair. To pay for the combs, Jim had sold his watch. That story will abide in American literature when many a more polished tale has long been forgotten. Why? Because it tells so beautifully the power of sacrifice to outlive the giving and receiving of mere things.

Such was the gift of Mary to Jesus—a gift of memorable munificence.

IV.

The miserly mind and the market mind—two of a kind. And so also the munificent mind and the *Master's mind*. For surely this was the kind of extravagance our Lord manifested again and again. "For their sakes I sanctify myself," he said to the Father. "No man takes my life from me, but I lay it down of my own accord. For you know the grace of our Lord Jesus Christ that, though he was rich, yet for our sakes he became poor."

We can well imagine that Satan might have whispered in the ear of Jesus that night in Gethsemane, "This is foolishness. The human race is not worth it. Let them stew in their own juice. Let them be brought before the judgment bar and destroyed. Your life is more precious than all the sinners in creation."

That, too, was sound advice. But Jesus, thank God, did not heed it. He gave, he gave extravagantly, and we remember. We remember because in that giving was a power that redeems. By the account book of prudence we are not worth it, but by the grace of God we are saved.

And here was Mary, by all our standards, foolish Mary. But not by his. "She has done a beautiful thing, and truly I say to you, wherever the gospel is preached in the whole world, what she has done will be told in memory of her."

We remember, Mary. We remember Bethany, and we remember you. Would that our hands might so anoint that brow with beauty. For, by our sins, we have encircled it with a crown of thorns!

Be pleased, O Lord, to have received our moods, thoughts, silences, and meditations this day. And enable us to daily live lives of abundant generosity. Amen.

NOTES

1. *Interpreter's Bible,* vol. 7 (New York: Abington-Cokesbury Press, 1951), 869.
2. Ibid., 870.
3. *The Pulpit,* August 1957, 16
4. Ibid.

13. How, Then, Shall We Live?

Cheryl B. Rhodes

Luke 4:1–13

"It is becoming clearer every day that the most urgent problem besetting our church is this: How can we live the Christian life in the modern world?" This is a concern that most of us have felt very deeply. How can we live as Christians in the world that is around us, a world of hunger and poverty and oppression, a world filled with people who are prisoners to sin, a world filled with those who are blinded to the truth that was in Jesus Christ, a world that seems as if it is trying to constantly test us? But the question I began with is not from our immediate time. It was asked in 1937 by Dietrich Bonhoeffer during a time of war and religious upheaval in Germany. Bonhoeffer was concerned because he felt that people looked at life without the benefit of religious interpretation. He felt that his world, and his Church, had become secularized, and he was bothered. It may be that he foresaw that his question would continue to be the question for those who seek to live a life that is pleasing to God. Indeed, it does remain the question of God's people. But the question is timeless, and it is universal—it has always been asked by those called to be God's people in the world. In fact, if we were to summarize the temptations of Jesus—that time when he was tried and tested—we could say that Jesus was struggling with this same question: How, then, shall I live? It is in the asking

Cheryl B. Rhodes is pastor of Grace United Methodist Church in Hartwood, Virginia. A graduate of the University of South Carolina, Rhodes went on to receive her Master of Divinity from Wesley Theological Seminary. She has served various pastorates in the U.S. and Germany.

of the question and in the struggling for the answer that the decision is made whether to place faith and trust completely in God or in something or someone else. It is a question that is only asked by those who have faith; others simply do not care. It is a question that is timeless and universal and found throughout the Bible.

When the Lord called Israel into a covenantal relationship as the people of God, Israel's history became the story of a nation trying to learn what it meant to be involved in such a relationship, trying to learn *how* to live now that they were the people of God. After Moses had given the Israelites a review of how God had shown mercy to them, even in their stubbornness, he asked, "What then, O Israel, does the Lord your God ask of you?" The answer was to "fear the Lord your God, to conform to all his ways, to love him, and to serve him with all your heart and soul" (Deut. 10:12), and this was to be accomplished by keeping the commandments.

Micah asked, "What does the Lord require of thee?" (Mic. 6:8), and the answer, "to seek justice, to love mercy, and to walk humbly with thy God," was but a summary of "Amos's demand for justice, Hosea's appeal for the steadfast love that binds people in covenant with God and with one another, and Isaiah's plea for the quiet faith of the 'humble walk' with God."[1]

The New Testament records examples of people who continued to ask the same question. John the Baptist was asked, "What then shall we do?" (Luke 3:10) by those he baptized and in the anticipation of the salvation of God for all humankind. His answer stipulated that the expression of love for God be shown through the expression of love to neighbor.

After the coming of Jesus, we find Luke writing of a member of the ruling class (Luke 18:18) and Matthew of a Pharisee (Matt. 22:35)—each coming to ask the same question of Jesus. And we find that Jesus' reply combined the Old Testament answer from the Law with the answer from the Prophets: "Love the Lord your God with all your heart, with all your soul, with all your mind . . . love your neighbor as yourself" (Mark 12:29).

After Jesus' death, resurrection, and ascension, the question continued to be asked. Peter in Acts 2:37, St. Paul on the Damascus road. Then the church at Corinth approached St. Paul concerning how they should live now that the new age had dawned and the return of Christ was soon expected (1 Cor. 7:1). Paul's answer reiterated that of Jesus, and to Corinth and other congregations, remained unchanged as he continued addressing the same issue (Gal. 5:6). The concern continued throughout New Testament times, as Christians were faced with the delay of Christ's return, the beginning of persecution, the closing of the age of the apostles, and the realization that the Church was to be the agent of God in the time between Jesus' in-breaking of the Kingdom and his return (1 Pet. 4:12; Rev. 22:7).

As the church grew and aged, its members reformulated the same question, and the answer remained unchanged. Ambrose, St. Francis of Assisi, St. Augustine, Martin Luther, John Calvin, John Wesley, Dietrich Bonhoeffer, and millions of anonymous Christians throughout the centuries continued to ask, "How, then, shall we live?" And today those who are God's people in the world still ask the same question. And we still unite in agreeing that the answer lies in love of God and love of neighbor. Yet, believers disagree, as they have in the past, as did Peter and Paul, as to exactly how that love is to be expressed. I would suggest to you this morning that only those who have been in the wilderness are in a position to offer an answer, for it is in the wilderness that the struggle takes place.

Let us return to our text and to the one who knew what it means to be in the wilderness and to struggle with the question of the ages, "How, then, shall I live?"

Jesus has been baptized and the confirmation has come: "Thou art my beloved Son; in thee I am well pleased" (Luke 3:22). He must have pondered, struggled: How, then, Lord, shall I live? What's next? Where do I go from here? Exactly how was he to fulfill God's plan? He is to be the Messiah, the Savior of the world. How is this to be done?

Is he to be the glorious, conquering, kingly figure sitting on a throne of judgment—the Son of man figure in Daniel 7? Or is he to achieve God's plan for the world by becoming the silent, suffering servant of Isaiah 53? Is he to achieve God's purpose by becoming a ruler or by becoming a servant? The way of a crown? Or the way of a cross? Where is the answer to be found?

And Jesus, filled with the Holy Spirit, is led into the wilderness—into solitude, thought, testing, struggle. Just like Jacob and Moses and David and Elijah—forty days in the wilderness. And it is there that he is tempted, tested by the devil—not to break specific laws (Barth) but to disregard the total plan of God for the salvation of the world and the part that he was to play in that plan.

The first temptation was the temptation of bread. If you are the Son of God, command these stones to become bread. Now, while I don't want to belittle the fact that Jesus was hungry and was being tempted to use his divine power to satisfy his physical needs, he did know that he only had to leave the desert to get food. But like Esau, who sold his birthright—God's plan for his life—for a piece of bread, and Adam, who sold his for the bite of an apple, the message here, too, runs much deeper than hunger. The devil is trying to get Jesus to use bread as a means of being the Messiah, trying to show him that with this one thing he could make the world his own; he could be the Savior of the world if he'd just give the people all the bread they wanted!

It is hard for us to understand the force behind this temptation because most of us have never really known hunger. But if we can take the place of someone who is starving for just a moment, perhaps we can better understand. What we are dealing with is the kind of hunger that has no hope, no possibility of being satisfied. The type of hunger that was experienced by a group of Christians whose plane crashed on a mountain, and they knew it would take months before they could be rescued because of their location and the weather. They also knew that they would die, and so in desperation and in what they considered to be a religious act, they began eating the flesh of those who died. We are dealing with the type of hunger that Israel experienced in the desert, where they had no means of getting anything to eat and so they began to doubt God and wished again for slavery. The hunger that causes people to steal and to kill. The hunger that causes people to flee from their homes seeking other lands in hope of food. The hunger that is a cause of sin and destruction in the world. The hunger that is so great that it tempts people to forget about God and follow anything or anyone that will feed them. Feed them, the devil is saying, and they will be yours! How right the devil was!

If you can control the source of someone's bread, you can control the person. Our clichés are oftentimes based on truth: "The way to a man's heart is through his stomach" or "If you be a good girl/boy, I'll give you a piece of candy." Control through food, and it works! It was reported that when Castro first took power, he sent his army into the schools and had the children put their heads on their desks and pray to God for candy. When they lifted their heads there was none. They then were told to put their heads down and ask Castro for candy, and when they lifted their heads, there was candy on their desks.

The devil is trying to persuade Jesus that if he can give them bread, the basic substance of life, he can control the people, they will do what he wants. But for how long? Like the Israelites who received manna, like people who have been temporarily fed, like those who again feel hunger after a totalitarian takeover, the momentary devotion will not last. When hunger comes again, the people will turn to whoever offers bread! And when hunger is alleviated through an increase in abundance? Then, too, the people will forget who first fed them. Isn't that what we're experiencing in America and in other prosperous nations? So many of those who now have everything they want are no longer turning to God to supply their needs. Religion—no, God—gets pushed aside in a self-satisfied, self-sufficient world. And so Jesus replied, "Man shall not live by bread alone." The remainder of that sentence from Deuteronomy says, "But by every word that proceedeth from the mouth of God." Jesus is not rejecting bread. Jesus is rejecting the idea that only bread is the source of life and that bread alone is a means to win people's allegiance. Jesus does not want us to follow him only because we are seeking to fill our physical needs. God has provided through creation for those, and if there are people who suffer from the lack of daily bread, it is not to heaven but to earth we should look to place blame. You cannot buy souls with bread. A starving person will do anything for food, say anything, but it just won't be lasting. Jesus will not succumb to the temptation to turn stones into bread as a means of achieving salvation for the world.

What's next? What's the devil got up his other sleeve? Ah, worldly kingdoms, with all their wealth and power! It's just what the rulers of the past had tried. Alexander the Great believed that he could truly bring peace and harmony if only he could conquer the world. He then could control everything and everyone in it. One united world—one harmonious ant heap, as Dostoyevski described it. Everyone believing and doing the same thing, and someone in power telling them what to do, how to do it, when to do it. If Jesus could be the ruler to lead Israel into dominance of the world—wow! The Kingdom of God *forced* upon every living creature—controlling their lives by controlling all of the wealth and power in the world. Utopia! Or hell?

To have the power of earthly kingdoms is to have dominance over the lives of other human beings—to control people's lives—and Jesus will have no part of this. Allegiance to Christ and his kingdom is to be based completely upon freedom. It comes from within a person, it is not forced from without. God gave us free wills, and Jesus guaranteed that we continue to have that freedom—we are free to worship God or not, we are not forced to worship God because of the control of a worldly kingdom. It didn't work when Constantine made Christianity the religion of the empire; it didn't work when the church tried it during the Spanish Inquisition; it has never worked for Israel. It will never work.

When the Kingdom of God comes in its fullness, the kingdoms of this world will pass away. But the devil gives it his best shot, and all he wants in exchange is for Jesus to worship him! That's all Caesar wanted, too. Worship me and you can even keep your other God. The early Christians were fed to the lions, not for worshiping God, but for refusal to worship Caesar as well. Forget God and worship those who would give you earthly kingdoms with their wealth and power, and life will be good. Jesus says no! "You shall worship the Lord thy God, and him only shall thou serve" (Deut. 6:13).

The devil knew well how earthly wealth and power dazzles people, controls them, and leads them straight into idolatry! Jesus says no! No! The earth does not belong to Satan. The earth is the Lord's and the fullness therein, and God will reclaim what belongs to God through Jesus and his death upon the cross. The ends—God's plan for the salvation of the world, the reconciliation of the world to the divine nature—cannot be justified by any means: The cross cannot be avoided.

Well, Jesus certainly knows the Scriptures, but so does the devil. He uses the Word of God to test Jesus with the next temptation, to test Jesus to use the miraculous: "If you are the Son of God . . . jump down from the pinnacle of the Temple. The Scriptures say that the angels will protect you, nothing will harm you." God promised! Now call upon God to keep his holy Word. Again we find the devil speaking truth. He's got it right again. What better way to prove to the people that God keeps promises and that you are the Son of God than by putting God to the test—go ahead and make

God prove the validity of Holy Scriptures. The people will love it; you'll have them following after you like flies. Give them a spectacular show, give them miracles, and they'll do what you want, just as if you gave them bread or controlled them through worldly kingdoms. Jesus refused: "You shall not tempt the Lord thy God."

To demand that God prove the reliability of Scriptures is to make God our servant. It is casting trust and faith aside and asking God to play by our rules, for our ends rather than for God's end. Jesus says no, that's not the way God wants it done.

Jesus is saying to the devil, "Get off my back! Just let me be. You cannot break my trust in God. You cannot keep me down, not with your bread, not with your offer of worldly kingdoms and power, not with miracles for my safety." And the devil departed from him until an opportune time.

Have you noticed that the only words Luke records Jesus using are quotes from the Old Testament? All of his struggling, all his dealing with temptation was based first and foremost upon Scripture. His answers to his testing were from Scripture. And yet, even in Scripture there were different aspects of what the Messiah would be. So Jesus used his brain, letting the Holy Spirit guide him into truth and understanding. He struggled in that wilderness.

And temptation continued to be part of his ministry. He will call Peter Satan when Peter tries to shield him from suffering and death. He will refuse the request for a sign, showing that he will not adapt to a scheme of some of the Jewish expectations of messiahship (Matt. 16:1). He will constantly be tried, tempted, put to the test by the Pharisees and scribes (Mark 8:11; 10:2; 12:15; Matt. 22:35; Luke 10:25; 11:16). Some will try to make him king, but he will refuse. He will be challenged to prove his identity as the expected Messiah. And he will refuse. He will pray in the Garden of Gethsemane, "Not my will, but thy will be done." And the cross— where the shout comes, "*If* you are the son of God . . . save yourself" (Mark 15:21)—is seen by some to be the final temptation in his life. His final temptation to reject God's plan of salvation for the world.

When he was twelve, he knew he must be about his Father's business. He was baptized, confirmed as God's, and led into the wilderness to struggle. When he came out from that wilderness, he went into the synagogue knowing what the Messiah was to be and do, and he read from the scroll of the prophet Isaiah: The spirit of the Lord is upon me, because he hath appointed me to preach the gospel to the poor; he hath sent me to heal the brokenhearted, to preach deliverance to the captives and recovering of sight to the blind, to set at liberty them that are bruised, to preach the acceptable year of the Lord. And Jesus tells them that this day this text is fulfilled.

Jesus had no doubts as to how he was to live. Redemption was to come through a message, not through bread or worldly kingdoms or miracles, but through a message, through the Word of God and the people of God. Salvation comes through Jesus Christ and his death upon the cross. Jesus did not succumb to temptation to save humanity by any other means than by the path that had the cross as its goal and the text from Isaiah as the way to get there. Today our response to temptation depends upon whether the world will remain separated from God or be reconciled to God. This first Sunday of Lent calls us into a time of repentance and a time to look again at this man called Jesus, to go into the wilderness and ask, "How, then, shall I live, knowing what I know about God and what Jesus the Christ has done for me?"

Ultimately, the question of the ages becomes the question of every believer. How is one to live after the realization of what God has done, freely offering salvation through grace alone. How shall we live so that the world may be reconciled to God? How do we respond to temptation?

Sometimes we ask, but like Jonah we don't really want to know because we don't want to go to Nineveh. To really want to know means spending a lot of time studying the Bible and time studying the world. Sometimes we come humbly before God, like Moses, as a last resort, and we pray, "God, how shall we live?" And sometimes we come boldly, with the force of an Isaiah, the stamina of an Ezekiel, and the self-assurance of an Amos, and we lift our voices to God, and we cry out, "Lord God, how shall we live?"

And sometimes we go into the wilderness because we know the awesomeness of our responsibility as the Body of Christ in the world, and we tremble and struggle and pray, "Help me, Lord, for I know how I shall live, but I cannot without your help!" And like the psalmist long ago, our help, too, cometh from the Lord! The answer is always the same: Love the Lord your God with all your heart, with all your strength, with all your mind, and love your neighbor as you love yourself. This is not possible without the Holy

Spirit, without the knowledge that Christ died for us while we were yet sinners, that God's grace has been given to us, and that faith itself is a gift from God.

Go into the wilderness, struggle with the question of the ages, but don't stay too long. God has work for you to do in the world! Amen.

NOTE

1. Bernard Anderson, *Understanding the Old Testament* (Englewood Cliffs, N.J.: Prentice Hall, 1957).

14. Casting the First Stone
Bruce Hedman

John 8:2–11

Jesus offended the religious people of his day by the company he kept. One might have expected him to have preferred the company of religious people. In that day the most scrupulous of such were the Pharisees, who attended synagogue regularly, contributed generously, prayed often, and read their Bibles. Yet, Jesus associated with thieves and prostitutes rather than with them. The Pharisees berated Jesus as a "friend of sinners" and chided his disciples that their Master even ate and relaxed with such dregs of society. But to these religious people Jesus replied, "Truly, I say to you, the tax collectors and the harlots go into the Kingdom of God before you."

Jesus sought to make a fundamental change in human attitudes that religious people, of his day and of ours, strongly resist. Religious people use God's Law as a yardstick against which to measure others. Jesus wants us to use God's Law as a mirror in which to examine ourselves. The Ten Commandments, morality, and conscience were given to us so that we might know right from wrong. With this knowledge we are to look at our own lives and see how far short we have fallen. This sense of our own failings makes us

Bruce A. Hedman is a full-time faculty member of the University of Connecticut as well as pastor of the Abington Congregational Church, which boasts the oldest meetinghouse in Connecticut (1751). A member of the United Church of Christ, Hedman received a Ph.D. in mathematics from Princeton University in 1979 and an M.Div. from Princeton Theological Seminary in 1980. His special interest is the relation between science and Christian faith.

seek God's mercy. By convicting us of sin, the Law leads us to the gospel, by which we are forgiven.

But religious people prefer to use God's Law to judge the visible and public sins of others, rather than the inward and private sins of their own hearts. Frankly, Jesus preferred the company of those whose sins were more public, as they could not hide their failings behind a hypocritical veneer of piety. As their sin was more visible, they were more ready to seek the forgiveness Jesus brought. Jesus commanded the religious people to look inside themselves to see the blackness of their own hearts, lest their self-righteousness miss the Kingdom of God. Jesus' basic insight into human nature has become a well-known idiom in our English language: "Let he who is without sin cast the first stone."

The Pharisees thought that Jesus was compromising God's Law just to attract a following. The Pharisees believed that they made themselves right before God by following the Law, by living a disciplined religious life. They abhorred Jesus' suggestion that they could not really keep the Law. They believed a person could come to God only by the Law, only by following the self-disciplined life of the Pharisees. Thus, the common people were lost unless they embraced this discipline. The Pharisees were angry that Jesus dared to forgive sins, especially of those who were unworthy. These religious people thought Jesus blunted the demands of God's Law.

The Pharisees had a trick question by which they hoped to trap Jesus by his own words in front of his followers. Jesus was sitting in the Temple, teaching a large crowd gathered there. The Pharisees roughly pushed into this crowd a woman whom they had caught red-handed committing adultery. They asked Jesus, "Now, in the Law, Moses commanded us to stone such. What do you say about her?" They thought they had Jesus. If he were lenient and forgave her sin, then they proved to everyone that Jesus contradicted God's Law, and they had a legal basis on which to accuse him in court. If Jesus upheld Moses' command to stone adulterers, he would contradict his compassionate image and would disillusion his followers.

The Pharisees utterly misunderstood Jesus. He did not blunt the demands of the Law. He did not relax any commandment. He did not wink at adultery or any other sin. Jesus said, "Think not that I have come to abolish the Law and the Prophets . . . till heaven and earth pass away, not an iota, not a dot, will pass from the Law until all is accomplished." Jesus did not come to change the Law; he came to change people. The purpose of the Law is not to tell us how bad other people are; it is to tell us how bad we are, so that we will come to Jesus for forgiveness. To the Pharisees and to all religious people, Jesus gave this warning. "Judge not, that you be not judged. For with the judgment you pronounce, you will be judged."

Jesus wanted people to apply God's Law to themselves, not others. But the Pharisees were particularly judgmental toward this woman. They were using her just to build a case against Jesus, which made them unusually vindictive. The three greatest sins under the Law were idolatry, murder, and adultery. Yet in the first century adultery was rather common and was settled by divorce, not capital punishment. The Pharisees could have posed their question to Jesus without dragging the woman into the central courtyard and humiliating her publicly. But to exact the death penalty, they had to stir up mob violence, because the Roman governor would never have allowed a legal execution. The Old Testament required the witnesses of a crime to do the stoning of the guilty. These Pharisees were ready to become "judge, jury, and executioner" in order to use this woman against Jesus.

Judgmental self-righteousness had worked itself into a fevered pitch. But Jesus met their violent accusations by graciously turning the tables. He summoned these Pharisees to judge themselves, not the woman. "Jesus bent down and wrote with his finger on the ground. And as they continued to ask him, he stood up and said to them, 'Let he who is without sin among you be the first to throw a stone at her.'"

The Pharisees could not accuse Jesus of contradicting the Law of Moses, because he did not forbid the stoning by those who were fit. He would have the Pharisees apply the strictures of the Law to themselves, not the woman. We do not really know what Jesus "wrote with his finger on the ground." This word for "wrote" means "to write down a record against someone." A later Greek tradition says that Jesus wrote in the sand the sins of which the Pharisees themselves were guilty.

Jesus "himself knew what was in a man" and so knew the sins lurking in the hearts of these Pharisees: pride, greed, lust, envy, anger. Jesus was not trying to expose these Pharisees publicly to humiliate them, as they were this woman. He wanted them honestly to come to themselves in the privacy of their own hearts that they might see their own guilt and repent. At first he quietly wrote their sins in the sand, saying nothing. As they pressed him, Jesus arose and challenged these accusers to examine themselves. "'Let he who is without sin among you be the first to throw a stone at her.' And once more he bent down and wrote with his finger on the ground." Slowly the force of Jesus' words struck home, as they recognized the secrets of their hearts written on the ground at their feet. "They went away, one by one, beginning with the oldest."

Jesus did not come to change God's Law; he came to change people. He wanted people to use morality not as a yardstick against which to judge others but as a mirror in which to examine themselves. He wanted people to look at themselves in sober self-honesty, so that they might regret their selfishness and come to him for forgiveness. We need to recognize our need before we will seek God's supply. Contrition and repentance must come before forgiveness. Our fear to own up to our sins is the stumbling block, not God's willingness to forgive. God stands right ready to forgive all who will but ask.

Jesus came into this world to bring the forgiveness of God. He convicted people of their sin, only that they might come to him for forgiveness. But these Pharisees, though convicted of their sin, refused Christ's invitation. He had shown them to themselves, and they left, fearing he would show them to the world. How many indeed are lost because they care more to save their reputations than to save their souls.

Jesus would have all of us examine ourselves as closely as we examine our neighbors, that we may be driven by the sight of our own sin back upon the mercy of God. Notice that the woman left standing alone before Jesus had not herself come to Jesus. She had been dragged there, used, and humiliated. She had not come willingly out of a sense of her own need, nor did she seek forgiveness. So Jesus did not pronounce her forgiven. Instead, he said, "Neither do I condemn you; go and do not sin again."

Jesus had aimed to bring her accusers to repentance by showing them their sin. Now he aimed to bring the accused to repentance by showing her his mercy. Jesus deferred judgment to give her another chance. He showed her the mercy of God and called her to live a righteous life in the hope that someday she would come herself to him. Jesus did not come to condemn the world; it was already condemned by its own sin. Jesus came to free the world from this condemnation, if it would simply receive by faith the forgiveness the gospel offers in the blood of Christ's cross. Jesus said, "I did not come to judge the world but to save the world."

This account of Jesus and the woman taken in adultery will forever witness to us of our hypocrisy in judging others. But if we only suspend our judgments of others, we still will have fallen short of the kingdom of heaven. The Pharisee and the woman herself may have been convicted of their sin, but neither turned for mercy to the Savior. May we approach our Savior, not like this woman taken in adultery, but like that prostitute in Simon's house who wet Jesus' feet with her tears of remorse. For then we will hear him say to us, as he did to her, "Your sins are forgiven. Your faith has saved you; go in peace."

III. DOCTRINAL/ THEOLOGICAL

15. What Is Man?

Jan M. Lochman
(Translated by James W. Cox)

What is man that thou art mindful of him, and the son of man that thou dost care for him?

—Psalm 8:4 RSV

What are human beings that you are mindful of them, mortals that you care for them?

—Psalm 8:4 NRSV

I.

"What is man?" That is the question of all questions, the essential, decisive question with which human beings have had to deal again and again since the beginning of their history. We meet it in the leading thinkers. When Immanuel Kant undertook the difficult task of reducing the great themes of philosophy to one essential common denominator, he chose our sentence: What is man? Not only with professional philosophers, but also among us all, as thinking people, this question sooner or later comes to our attention.

It can be stated in several distinct ways. The question can arise in entirely different, indeed actually contrasting, experiences and feelings. In modern times, it appears mostly as an expression of admiration coming from exultant joy in being human. "Glory be to

---

Jan M. Lochman, a native of Czechoslovakia, is a member of the Swiss Reformed Church. Dr. Lochman has been professor of systematic theology at the University of Basel since 1969 and is the author of a number of books, most recently *Christ or Prometheus: A Quest for Theological Identity.* This sermon was translated from the German by James W. Cox.

man in the highest, for man is the lord of all things." With these words the English poet Alexander Pope sang the credo of the Enlightenment. And in our century as well, a Russian poet, Maxim Gorky, coined the sentence "Man—that sounds magnificent," a sentence repeated again and again in Communist eastern Europe and unfortunately also misused. Such pathetic sentences are painful to us today. Of course, we should not judge too quickly. They address important matters. Hasn't man, especially and precisely modern man, accomplished astonishing things? Isn't the history of modern times a history of mighty conquests and achievements? Were there not unlocked in them astonishing possibilities in nature, culture, and society for us? Indeed, man is a rich, creative, and an incomparable being. Whoever, as a human being, could not perceive any astonishment, admiration, and joy behind our question? Such a person would be indeed rather shortsighted, dense, or simply unthankful.

But one can also express the question "What is man?" in a quite different way—now not as praise, in pride and exaltation, but more as a cry from the depths, an expression of doubt, even of despair, because of all that man produces in terms of what is destructive, malicious, and insidious down to the last detail! It is true, we have brought about magnificent discoveries and achievements. But we have not placed them solely in the service of the good and of the public welfare; we have instead even employed them in a sinister complex of persecution and destruction. It is true, we have brought the powers of nature into dramatic movement and in that way enhanced our chances of survival. But we have at the same time also vastly polluted our natural environment. Though we were once called the hope of creation, we have become the problem, the risk factor, the *enfant terrible* of the universe. A shady character—that is man! "What is man?" An enigmatic, ambiguous question!

II.

How is such a question taken up by the psalmist: "What is man, *that thou art mindful of him?*" This is an amazing expression. It is a question about man, and yet another is questioned; a *thou,* that before was called the "Lord, our God," is addressed. How are we to understand this approach of the psalmist? Does he simply bypass our question, as we have just put it? Should it be piously diverted from our creaturely experiences? I believe not. They are—in *both* aspects of them—obviously well known to the psalmist. Unmistakably, there bursts immediately from our psalm the *praise* of the human condition.

> Yet thou hast made him little less than God,
> and dost crown him with glory and honor.
> Thou hast given him dominion over the works of
> thy hands;
> Thou hast put all things under his feet,
> all sheep and oxen,
> and also the beasts of the field,
> the birds of the air, and the fish of the sea,
> whatever passes along the paths of the sea.
> (Ps. 8:5–8, RSV)

No humanist could speak of man with greater reverence. The exaltation of the awe-struck poet is in no way alien to our psalmist.

And he knows also that *other* dark, contrapunctal side, the abyss of the failing, sinful human being. In Psalm 8 we are dealing, of course, with the psalm of David. And David was the biblical man who experienced in an especially clear and bitter fashion the sinful, tragic entanglement of the human heart in the presence of God and his fellow human beings. One has only to read the Fifty-first psalm, this outcry of yearning for the forgiveness of sin and for a new heart, in view of his abysmal failure:

> Create in me a clean heart, O God,
> and put a new and right spirit within me.
> Cast me not away from thy presence,
> and take not thy holy Spirit from me.
> (Ps. 51:10–11, RSV)

David entertains no illusions about himself—and none about his fellow human beings. Recall that scene at the end of the second book of Samuel: The elderly David is allowed to choose his judge —a court of justice at the hand of God or at the hand of human beings. His decision is clear-cut: "Let us fall into the hand of the Lord, for his mercy is great; but let me not fall into the hand of man" (24:14b, RSV). So David chose pestilence (24:15ff). A shocking choice! Yet we understand right off that such a choice was made on the basis of the experience of a lifetime: Whatever you do, do not become a victim to unmerciful humans and their systems!

So it is clear: The psalmist and the Bible in no way avoid the human experiences behind the question "What is man?" Our common human experiences, the good and the bad, amount to a great deal in the presence of God; we should, we dare bring them before God. However, where the question is raised about the ultimate *ground* of our humanity, precisely there our experience of life is certainly not pushed aside but rather broken open, placed into the new decisive relationship *to God*. Therefore, the psalmist does not ask proudly, "What is man, who by such achievements is powerful?" Nor does he ask despairingly, "What is man, who is capable of such atrocities?" Rather, he asks, "What are human beings that you are mindful of them, / mortals that you care for them?" (NRSV).

This expression belongs in the center of the biblical message; it *is* the good news of the Old and New Testaments. What is the fundamental theme of biblical history, of the history of the covenant of God with us human beings? That God faithfully remembers us humans and that we mortals are not products of blind cosmic processes and that we are more than aimless nomads at the edge of the universe, that we are the allies of God, the "citizens" protected by his covenant, given our names—his adopted children. Such is the heart of biblical faith. We may and we should live our story, the story of humanity or even our own little life story from this point of view: *sub specie aeternitatis* (as the noted Czech thinker T. G. Masaryk was wont to express it), "under the viewpoint of eternity." We may, indeed we should, lead a well-founded and purposeful life. That is the dignity of humankind: "What are human beings that you are mindful of them, / mortals that you care for them?"

III.

My dear friends, what does this view of humanity mean for us today? What *can* it still mean for people in our time? Is it not hopelessly outdated and, of course, not merely in some details of the psalm, but precisely in its basic orientation, in its quest of the secret and dignity of humanity *beyond* this world? Is it not proven in this very setting as testament of the times in which man was still immature, still unable to take his destiny into his own hands, and therefore, in the state of underdevelopment, that man sought to understand himself from a heavenly source? Will not, then, our present-day seeking, the longing for self-fulfillment and self-development in history, be left actually in the lurch by the psalmist? I believe not. To be sure, we can find in history and in the present time many an example of pious prattle about God, which has a debilitating effect. However, I am most profoundly convinced that our psalm points in a different direction, that its reference to the mindfulness of God and to our condition as God's adopted children has something valid and liberating to say today (and precisely today!) to our quest for the true identity of man's being, if it is related to contemporary needs and perils of our human existence.

The Comfort

With the word of the faithful mindfulness of God, the psalmist relates himself to an especially bitter need of man: man if forgotten, ignored, overlooked, not accepted. He experiences himself as a forsaken, abandoned being; he looks like a lost sheep. That always signifies pain and shock, bitter danger to our quest for the meaning of human life. It is no coincidence that in the Bible the lot of "widows and orphans" (and of prisoners!) is especially made a matter of deep concern for the people of God, because they are precisely the ones who, as the "abandoned" and isolated, were especially affected by the distress of loneliness.

There are other kinds of loneliness. The psychologists show us convincingly how the experience of "being forgotten," the denied acceptance, the lack of interested attention, obstructs and strains the development of children—a constant problem for parents, teachers, the entire adult world. And how bitter it is for old people to have to experience the fact that they are no longer needed, that they are even half or entirely forgotten by their neighbors. About that, every seemingly comfortable old people's home could tell many heart-wrenching stories. And doesn't this human distress also spread silently and broadly in the midst of active life? Don't many people of our time in the modern workday world appear to be largely superfluous, replaceable at any time, economically expendable, and precisely, therefore, in their personal lives as humans, destined to be overlooked, not taken seriously, forgotten?

The psalmist's testimony now relates itself to this human distress. Therefore the answer comes: You are not forgotten. You are not a totally forsaken creature. You are not an abandoned, lost sheep. You are an adopted child. There is one who does not forget; one who seeks you. This one is the shepherd of Israel, the Good Shepherd Jesus Christ. It is precisely the psalms that attest to this motif most clearly and impressively: "The Lord is my shepherd, I shall not want" (Psalm 23). Moreover, "He who keeps you will not slumber. He who keeps Israel will neither slumber nor sleep" (Psalm 121). It is here a matter of memory, which remains true and lively even if our memory and that of others stumbles and betrays. In the sea of human forgetfulness we are before God and, for God, unforgotten and unforgettable people. Here we find the true identity of our endangered humanity. That is the comfort of our being Christians, just now, it seems to me, right in the midst of the alienating conditions of our time. Our reforming fathers were correct when, just at the beginning of the Heidelberg Catechism, they brought to expression loud and clear this very word of comfort: "My only comfort in life and in death is that I am in body and soul not my own, but my faithful Savior Jesus Christ's own." This is the comfort of our psalm: "What are human beings that you are mindful of them?"

IV.

This psalm at the same time deals with the question of the *right of man*. In what is the right of our humanity grounded? We speak often today about human rights. Quite properly! For we live in the time of a many-sided denial of these very human rights—downright alarmingly in the third world and depressingly so in the second world. But even in our world we are challenged in the same way; perhaps not so sharply and directly, but indeed in relation to the fundamental question: In what is the right of man based, the right of every human being? From the atmosphere of our time and, it seems to me, from the propagandized mentality, the following answer in most cases is suggested: Earnings and achievement set the standard for what is our right to life. Productivity, outstanding success, brilliance—these are the things that count. So we have a hard time with the young and the old, the "unproductive."

Today we often speak of the *meritocracy.* I would not like to make a sweeping statement. There is a genuine human merit. Where would our society be if there were not among us able people, workers, craftsmen, scientists? Everyone knows how important it is in an emergency to come across a good doctor or a conscientious official or simply a neighbor ready to help. Nothing about that is to be disdained. Achievement surely has its meaning. But where it has to do with the final inalienable rights of man, where it is a question of the final measure of humanity, there the psalmist in concert with the entire Bible points in an entirely different direction: "What is man that thou art mindful of him, and the son of man that thou dost care for him?"

Man's right to life does not depend, therefore, on human achievements and advancements, on accumulations of great works. Man is more than he produces, more than the sum of his accomplishments, and more, also, than his slip-ups. Our right to life is based beyond that which is successful or unsuccessful: it is precisely in God's faithful memory, in God's acceptance. It is *unconditionally* so.

One picture in the New Testament impresses me again and again: "Our citizenship is in heaven" (Phil. 3:20). Almost everyone knows to treasure his *earthly* citizenship. It is painful to be denied it. But it is more important to know this: There is a citizenship that no one can be denied—the dignity established in the presence of God, sealed in Jesus Christ, therefore the inalienable dignity of being human. Not that we have achieved it, not that any sort of institution has bestowed it on us. So then neither can it be taken away from us. "Our citizenship is in heaven."

This gives freedom from all human hands. But this gives us at the same time the task of proving ourselves as witnesses of this unconditional right to life. In our human relationships we do not consider people as neighbors by what they can do for us; we do not deal with them as mere pawns in our private chess game. Rather, we respect the rights in them that are protected by God. Also, as Christians living in a society oriented to achievement and profit, we are advocates of people not so interesting as measured by the prevailing standards and who for that reason alone are undervalued, overlooked, forgotten. The faithful mindfulness of God also sharpens our memory, our understanding of people on the shadow side of everyday life in church and society. When we ask ourselves with the psalmist for comfort, "What is man that thou art mindful of him, and the son of man that thou dost care for him?" we are asking at the same time about the forgotten and abandoned, about their right to life.

V.

Dear friends, with this train of thought we have taken up that line that was stressed emphatically in the history of the church by the *Reformation* of the sixteenth century. *Justification* not by works but by faith, *by faith alone*—this was the program of that Reformation, on which today, Reformation Day, we especially think. Thus it opposed all self-righteousness—therefore, every human attempt to justify oneself before God, before neighbor, and before one's own self—and to assess the value of the neighbors by their achievements. In opposition to the old religious (but also to the new worldly) works-righteousness, it advocated the *right of grace*. Today many of the battles of the Reformation can appear to us as faded and strange. Their central message is burningly contemporary. By playing fast and loose with both law and grace, man is destroyed—in personal and social life. About that, bitter proofs are daily supplied far and near. More than ever, all of us have need of the active recollection of the right of grace grounded in the faithful memory of God. We should, we may, keep it under a watchful eye in our churches: for us and our children, for our neighbors in this perilous time. At stake is our true humanity. "What is man, that thou art mindful of him, and the son of man that thou dost care for him?" Amen.

16. Christianity and the Survival of Creation

Wendell Berry

I.

I confess that I have not invariably been comfortable in front of a pulpit; I have never been comfortable behind one. To be behind a pulpit is always a forcible reminder to me that I am an essayist and in many ways a dissenter. An essayist is, literally, a writer who attempts to tell the truth. Preachers must resign themselves to being either right or wrong; an essayist, when proved wrong, may claim to have been "just practicing." An essayist is privileged to speak without institutional authorization. A dissenter, of course, must speak without privilege.

I want to begin with a problem: namely, that the culpability of Christianity in the destruction of the natural world and the uselessness of Christianity to any effort to correct that destruction are now established clichés of the conservation movement. This is a problem for two reasons.

First, the indictment of Christianity by the anti-Christian conservationists is, in many respects, just. For instance, the complicity of Christian priests, preachers, and missionaries in the cultural destruction and the economic exploitation of the primary peoples of the Western Hemisphere, as of traditional cultures around the

---

Wendell Berry, a native Kentuckian, has spent the last thirty and more years farming seventy-five acres in Henry County, Kentucky, and writing fiction, poetry, and essays. Prior to that, he lived and taught in New York and California. Some of his numerous books are *Collected Poems, The Gift of the Good Land* (essays), and *Remembering* (a novel).

world, is notorious. Throughout the five hundred years since Columbus's first landfall in the Bahamas, the evangelist has walked beside the conqueror and the merchant, too often blandly assuming that his cause was the same as theirs. Christian organizations, to this day, remain largely indifferent to the rape and plunder of the world and of its traditional cultures. It is hardly too much to say that most Christian organizations are as happily indifferent to the ecological, cultural, and religious implications of industrial economics as are most industrial organizations. The certified Christian seems just as likely as anyone else to join the military-industrial conspiracy to murder creation.

The conservationist indictment of Christianity is a problem, secondly, because, however just it may be, it does not come from an adequate understanding of the Bible and the cultural traditions that descend from the Bible. The anti-Christian conservationists characteristically deal with the Bible by waving it off. And this dismissal conceals, as such dismissals are apt to do, an ignorance that invalidates it. The Bible is an inspired book written by human hands; as such, it is certainly subject to criticism. But the anti-Christian environmentalists have not mastered the first rule of the criticism of books: You have to read them before you criticize them. Our predicament now, I believe, requires us to learn to read and understand the Bible in the light of the present fact of creation. This would seem to be a requirement both for Christians and for everyone concerned, but it entails a long work of true criticism—that is, careful and judicious study, not dismissal. It entails, furthermore, the making of very precise distinctions between biblical instruction and the behavior of those peoples supposed to have been biblically instructed.

I cannot pretend, obviously, to have made so meticulous a study; if I were capable of it, I would not live long enough to do it. But I have attempted to read the Bible with some of these issues in mind, and I see some virtually catastrophic discrepancies between biblical instruction and Christian behavior. I don't mean disreputable Christian behavior, either. The discrepancies I see are between biblical instruction and allegedly respectable Christian behavior.

If, because of these discrepancies, Christianity were dismissable, there would, of course, be no problem. We could simply dismiss it, along with the twenty centuries of unsatisfactory history attached to it, and start setting things to rights. The problem emerges only when we ask, Where then would we turn for instruction? We might, let us suppose, turn to another religion—a recourse that is sometimes suggested by the anti-Christian environmentalists. Buddhism, for example, is certainly a religion that could guide us toward a right respect for the natural world, our fellow humans, and our fellow creatures. I have a considerable debt myself to Buddhism and Buddhists. But there is an enormous number of people, and I am one of them, whose native religion, for better or worse, is Christianity. We can turn away from it or against it, but that will only bind us tightly to a reduced version of it. A better possibility is that this, our native religion, should survive and renew itself, so that it may become as largely and truly instructive as we need it to be. On such a survival and renewal of the Christian religion may depend the survival of that creation which is its subject.

II.

If we read the Bible, keeping in mind the desirability of those two survivals—of Christianity and the creation—we are apt to discover several things that modern Christian organizations have kept remarkably quiet about, or have paid little attention to.

We will discover that we humans do not own the world or any part of it: "The earth is the Lord's, and the fullness thereof: the world and they that dwell therein" (Ps. 24:1). There is in our human law, undeniably, the concept and right of land ownership. But this, I think, is merely an expedient to safeguard the mutuality of belonging without which there can be no lasting and conserving settlement of human communities. This right of human ownership is limited by mortality and by natural constraints upon human attention and responsibility; it quickly becomes abusive when used to justify large accumulations of "real estate," and perhaps for that reason such large accumulations are forbidden in the twenty-fifth chapter of Leviticus. In biblical terms, the "landowner" is the guest and steward of God: "the land is mine; for ye are strangers and sojourners with me" (Lev. 25:23).

We will discover that God made not only the parts of creation that we humans understand and approve but all of it: "All things were made by him; and without him was not anything made that was made" (John 1:3). And so we must credit God with the making of biting and stinging insects, poisonous serpents, weeds, poisonous weeds, dangerous beasts, and disease-causing microorganisms. That we may disapprove of these things does not mean that God is in error or that he ceded some of the work of creation to Satan; it means that we are deficient in wholeness, harmony, and understanding—that is, we are "fallen."

We will discover that God found the world, as he made it, to be good; that he made it for his pleasure; and that he continues to love it and to find it worthy, despite its reduction and corruption by us. People who quote John 3:16 as an easy formula for getting to heaven neglect to see the great difficulty implied in the statement that the advent of Christ was made possible by God's love for the world—not God's love for heaven or for the world as it might be, but for the world as it was and is. Belief in Christ is thus made dependent upon prior belief in the inherent goodness—the lovability—of the world.

We will discover that the creation is not in any sense independent of the Creator, the result of a primal creative act long over and done with, but is the continuous, constant participation of all creatures in the being of God. Elihu said to Job that if God "gather unto himself his spirit and his breath; All flesh shall perish together . . ." (Job 34:14–15). And Psalm 104 says, "Thou sendest forth thy spirit, they are created. . . ." Creation is God's presence in creatures. The Greek Orthodox theologian Philip Sherrard has written that "Creation is nothing less than the manifestation of God's hidden Being."[1] Thus we and all other creatures live by a sanctity that is inexpressibly intimate. To every creature the gift of life is a portion of the breath and Spirit of God. As the poet George Herbert put it,

> Thou art in small things great, not small in any . . .
> For thou art infinite in one and all.[2]

We will discover that, for these reasons, our destruction of nature is not just bad stewardship or stupid economics or a betrayal of family responsibility; it is the most horrid blasphemy. It is flinging God's gifts into his face, as of no worth beyond that assigned to them by our destruction of them. To Dante, "despising Nature and her gifts" was a violence against God.[3] We have no entitlement from the Bible to exterminate or permanently destroy or hold in contempt anything on the earth or in the heavens above it or in the waters beneath it. We have the right to use the gifts of nature but not to ruin or waste them. We have the right to use what we need but no more, which is why the Bible forbids usury and great accumulations of property. The usurer, Dante said, "contemns Nature . . . for he puts his hope elsewhere."[4]

William Blake was biblically correct, then, when he said that "everything that lives is holy."[5] And Blake's great commentator, Kathleen Raine, was correct both biblically and historically when she said that "the sense of the holiness of life is the human norm. . . ."[6]

The Bible leaves no doubt at all about the sanctity of the act of world-making or of the world that was made or of creaturely or bodily life in this world. We are holy creatures living among other holy creatures in a world that is holy. Some people know this, and some do not. Nobody, of course, knows it all the time. But what keeps it from being far better known than it is? Why is it apparently unknown to millions of professed students of the Bible? How can modern Christianity have so solemnly folded its hands while so much of the work of God was and is being destroyed?

III.

Obviously, "the sense of the holiness of life" is not compatible with an exploitive economy. You cannot know that life is holy if you are content to live from economic practices that daily destroy life and diminish its possibility. And many if not most Christian organizations now appear to be perfectly at peace with the military-industrial economy and its "scientific" destruction of life. Surely, if we are to remain free and if we are to remain true to our religious inheritance, we must maintain a separation between church and state. But if we are to maintain any sense or coherence or meaning in our lives, we cannot tolerate the present utter disconnection between religion and economy. By *economy* I do not mean *economics,* which is the study of money-making, but rather the ways of human housekeeping, the ways by which the human household is situated and maintained within the household of nature. To be uninterested in economy is to be uninterested in the practice of religion; it is to be uninterested in culture and in character. Probably the most urgent question now faced by people who would adhere to the Bible is this: What sort of economy would be responsible to the holiness of life? What, for Christians, would be the economy, the practices and the restraints, of "right livelihood"? I do not believe that organized Christianity now has any idea. I think its idea of a Christian economy is no more or less than the industrial economy—which is an economy firmly founded upon the seven deadly sins and the breaking of all ten of the Ten Commandments. Obviously, if Christianity is going to survive as more than a respecter and comforter of profitable iniquities, then Christians, regardless of their organizations, are going to have to interest themselves in economy—which is to say, in nature and in work. They are going to have to give workable answers to those who say we cannot live without this economy that is destroying us and our world, who see the murder of creation as the only way of life.

A second reason why the holiness of life is so obscured to modern Christians is the idea that the only holy place is the built church. This idea may be more taken for granted than taught; nevertheless, Christians are encouraged from childhood to think of the church building as "God's house," and most of them could think of their houses or farms or shops or factories as holy places only with great effort and embarrassment. It is understandably difficult for modern Americans to think of their dwellings and workplaces as holy, because most of these are, in fact, places of desecration, deeply involved in the ruin of creation.

The idea of the exclusive holiness of church buildings is, of course, wildly incompatible with the idea, which the churches also teach, that God is present in all places to hear prayers. It is incompatible with Scripture. The idea that a human artifact could contain or confine God was explicitly repudiated by Solomon in his prayer at the dedication of the Temple: "Behold, the heaven and the heaven of heavens cannot contain thee: how much less this house that I have builded?" (1 Kings 8:27). And these words of Solomon were remembered a thousand years later by St. Paul, preaching at Athens:

> God that made the world and all things therein,
> seeing that he is lord of heaven and earth,
> dwelleth not in temples made with hands. . . .

For in him we live, and move, and have our being;
as certain also of your own poets have said. . . .
(Acts 17:24, 28)

Idolatry always reduces to the worship of something "made with hands," something confined within the terms of human work and human comprehension. Thus Solomon and St. Paul both insisted upon the largeness and the at-largeness of God, setting him free, so to speak, from ideas about him. He is not to be fenced in, under human control, like some domestic creature; he is the wildest being in existence. The presence of his Spirit in us is our wildness, our oneness with the wilderness of creation. That is why subduing the things of nature to human purposes is so dangerous and why it so often results in evil, in separation and desecration. It is why the poets of our tradition so often have given nature the role, not only of mother or grandmother, but of the highest earthly teacher and judge, a figure of mystery and great power. Jesus' own specifications for his Church have nothing at all to do with masonry and carpentry but only with people; his church is "where two or three are gathered together in my name" (Matt. 18:20).

I don't think it is enough appreciated how much an outdoor book the Bible is. It is a hypaethral book, such as Thoreau talked about—a book open to the sky. It is best read and understood outdoors, and the farther outdoors the better. Or that has been my experience of it. Passages that within walls seem improbable or incredible, outdoors seem merely natural. That is because outdoors we are confronted everywhere with wonders; we see that the miraculous is not extraordinary but the common mode of existence. It is our daily bread. Whoever really has considered the lilies of the field or the birds of the air and pondered the improbability of their existence in this warm world within the cold and empty stellar distances will hardly balk at the turning of water into wine—which was, after all, a very small miracle. We forget the greater and still continuing miracle by which water (with soil and sunlight) is turned into grapes.

It is clearly impossible to assign holiness exclusively to the built church without denying holiness to the rest of creation, which is then said to be "secular." The world, that God looked at and found entirely good, we find none too good to pollute entirely and destroy piecemeal. The church, then, becomes a kind of preserve of "holiness" from which certified lovers of God dash out to assault and plunder the "secular" earth.

Not only does this repudiate God's approval of his work; it refuses also to honor the Bible's explicit instruction to regard the works of the creation as God's revelation of himself. The assignation of holiness exclusively to the built church is therefore logically accompanied by the assignation of revelation exclusively to the Bible. But Psalm 19 begins, "The heavens declare the glory of God; and the firmament sheweth his handiwork." The Word of God has been revealed in facts from the moment of the third verse of the first chapter of Genesis: "Let there be light: and there was light." And St. Paul states the rule: "The invisible things of him from the creation of the world are clearly seen, being understood by the things that are made, even his eternal power and godhead." (Rom. 1:20). And from this free, generous, and sensible view of things, we come to the idolatry of the book: the idea that nothing is true that cannot be (and has not been already) written. The misuse of the Bible thus logically accompanies the abuse of nature: If you are going to destroy creatures without respect, you will want to reduce them to "materiality"; you will want to deny that there is spirit or truth in them, just as you will want to believe that the only holy or ensouled creatures are humans, or only Christian humans.

By denying spirit and truth to the nonhuman creation, latter-day proponents of religion have legitimized a form of blasphemy without which the nature-and culture-destroying machinery of the industrial economy could not have been built—that is, they have legitimized bad work. Good human work honors God's work. Good work uses no thing without respect, both for what it is in itself and for its origin. It uses neither tool nor material that it does not respect and that it does not love. It honors nature as a great mystery and power, as an indispensable teacher, and as the inescapable judge of all work of human hands. It does not dissociate life and work or pleasure and work or love and work or usefulness and beauty. To work without pleasure or affection, to make a product that is not both useful and beautiful, is to dishonor God, nature, the thing that is made, and whomever it is made for. This is blasphemy: to make shoddy work of the work of God. And such blasphemy is not possible so long as the entire creation is understood as holy and so long as the works of God are understood as embodying and so revealing his Spirit.

IV.

I have been talking, of course, about a dualism that manifests itself in several ways; it is a cleavage, a radical discontinuity, between Creator and creature, spirit and matter, religion and nature, religion and economy, worship and work, etc. This dualism, I think, is the most destructive disease that afflicts us. In its best known, its most dangerous, and perhaps its fundamental version, it is the dualism of body and soul. This is an issue as difficult as it is important, and so to deal with it we should start at the beginning.

The crucial test is probably Genesis 2:7, which gives the process by which Adam was created: "The Lord God formed man of the dust of the ground, and breathed into his nostrils the breath of life: and man became a living soul." My mind, like most people's, has been deeply influenced by dualism, and I can see how dualistic minds deal with this verse. They conclude that the formula for man-making is: man = body + soul. But that conclusion cannot be derived, except by violence, from Genesis 2:7, which is not dualistic. The formula given in Genesis 2:7 is not man = body + soul; the formula there is soul = dust + breath. According to this verse, God did not make a body and put a soul into it, like a letter into an envelope. He formed man of dust; by breathing his breath into it, he made the dust live. Insofar as it lived, it was a soul. The dust, formed as man and made to live, did not *embody* a soul; it *became* a soul. *Soul* here refers to the whole creature. Humanity is thus presented to us, in Adam, not as a creature of two discrete parts temporarily glued together, but as a single mystery.

We can see how easy it is to fall into the dualism of body and soul when talking about the inescapable worldly dualities of good and evil or time and eternity. And we can see how easy it is when Jesus asks, "For what is a man profited, if he shall gain the whole world, and lose his own soul?" (Matt. 16:26) to assume that he is condemning the world and appreciating the disembodied soul. But if we give to *soul* here the sense that it has in Genesis 2:7, we see that he is doing no such thing. He is warning that, in pursuit of so-called material possessions, we can lose our understanding of ourselves as "living souls"—that is, as creatures of God, members of the holy community of creation. We can lose the possibility of the atonement of that membership. For we are free, if we choose, to make a duality of our one living soul by disowning the breath of God that is our fundamental bond with one another and with other creatures.

But we can make the same duality by disowning the dust. The breath of God is only one of the divine gifts that make us living souls; the other is the dust. Most of our modern troubles come from our misunderstanding and misvaluation of this dust. Forgetting that the dust, too, is a creature of the Creator, made by the sending forth of his Spirit, we have presumed to decide that the dust is "low." We have presumed to say that we are made of two parts: a body and a soul, the body being "low" because made of dust and the soul "high." By thus valuing these two supposed-to-be "parts," we inevitably throw them into competition with each other, like two corporations. The "spiritual" view, of course, has been that the body, in Yeats's phrase, must be "bruised to pleasure soul." And the "secular" version of the same dualism has been that the body, along with the rest of the "material" world, must give way before the advance of the human mind. The dominant religious view, for a long time, has been that the body is a kind of scrip issued by the Great Company Store in the Sky, which can be cashed in to redeem the soul but is otherwise worthless. And the predictable result has been a human creature able to appreciate or tolerate only the "spiritual" (or mental) part of creation and full of a semiconscious hatred of the "physical" or "natural" part, which it is ready and willing to destroy for "salvation," for profit, for "victory," or for fun. This madness constitutes the normality of modern humanity and of modern Christianity.

But to despise the body or mistreat it for the sake of the "soul" is not just to burn one's house for the insurance, nor is it just self-hatred of the most deep and dangerous sort. It is yet another blasphemy. It is to make nothing, and worse than nothing, of the great Something in which we live and move and have our being.

V.

If we credit the Bible's description of the relationship between Creator and creation, then we cannot deny the spiritual importance of our economic life. Then we see how religious issues lead to issues of economy and how issues of economy lead to issues of art, of how to make things. If we understand that no artist—no maker—can work except by reworking the works of creation, then we see that by our work, by the way we practice our arts, we reveal what we think of the works of God. How we take our lives from this world, how we work, what work we do, how well we use the materials we use and what we do with them after we have used them—all these are questions of the highest and gravest religious significance. These questions cannot be answered by thinking but only by doing. In answering them, we practice, or do not practice, our religion.

NOTES

1. Philip Sherrard, unpublished manuscript.
2. George Herbert, "Providence," lines 41 and 44.
3. Dante, *Inferno*, Singleton translation (Princeton: Princeton Univ. Press, 1970), 11. 46–48.
4. Ibid., 11. 109–11.
5. William Blake, *The Marriage of Heaven and Hell*, the final line.
6. Kathleen Raine, *Golgonooza: City of Imagination* (Ipswich: Golgonooza Press, 1991), 28.

17. God in Three Persons
Dana Martin

Romans 8:9–11; Ephesians 2:15–18

Alister McGrath, theologian at Oxford University, recalls an incident from childhood that happened one Sunday at church. On this particular Sunday the congregation had come to that portion of the service where they recited the Athanasian Creed. They had just solemnly intoned the words "The Father incomprehensible, the Son incomprehensible, and the Holy Spirit incomprehensible" when the man sitting next to him muttered, much too loudly, "The whole damn thing incomprehensible!"[1]

Professor McGrath's seatmate might be faulted for his irreverence but not his accuracy. The Christian language of Trinity *is* incomprehensible. We can break that language down into manageable units, but the reality the language tries to express is ultimately incomprehensible. There is no use pretending otherwise. Yet, as I tried to illustrate from the Scripture I read this morning, the language of Trinity has marked Christian-speaking from the very beginning. Only by the language of Trinity can we speak of God who is utterly unlike us but infinitely committed to our well-being.

Still, there remains the fact of it being incomprehensible language. Why can't theologians and scholars find an easier way for those in the pews to speak of God? Why complicate matters with language of Trinity, which is so difficult for the specialist and more so for the ordinary believer? The answer, I'm afraid, is that the

---

Dana Martin is interim pastor of the United Church (Baptist and Presbyterian) of Marion, New York. An American Baptist, Martin was pastor of the First Baptist Church, Iowa City, Iowa, from 1985 to 1992. He is a graduate of Princeton Theological Seminary, the University of Chicago Divinity School, and Yale Divinity School.

difficulty is built-in. If we would talk about God who raised Jesus from the dead, if we would talk about God whose Spirit calls us and gathers us, then we necessarily speak about God whose reality challenges and breaks our language.

Imagine that somehow you could step into a cartoon strip, be it "Peanuts," "Doonesbury," "Garfield," "B.C.," or whatever. Imagine that you, a three-dimensional person, could somehow step into a cartoon strip of only two dimensions. If you could, something about you would be limited and distorted by virtue of being bound to that two-dimensional world. You could never fully explain yourself to cartoon characters who have length and width but not thickness. You would soon realize that three-dimensional language would be incomprehensible in a two-dimensional world.

In a comparable way, our language can never fully explain the fullness and the glory of God's absolute being. Unlike us creatures of time and space, God's being transcends those categories. God dwells beyond the limitations of time and space. Yet the language of Trinity makes it possible for us to speak of God in ways that somehow cut through our time and our space. Through the language of Father, Son, Spirit, we can begin to speak, though imperfectly, about the eternal God who has come to be intimately involved *in* our time and space, the infinite God who has chosen to be intimately connected with us.

Let me take a detour for just a moment. In the last twenty years or so a growing number of women and some men have complained that the language of Father, Son, Spirit has created a male bias. In their opinion, calling God Father and Son deifies maleness. In their opinion, calling God Father and Son has rationalized a male dominance within the church.

For myself, I find that I cannot simply jettison the church's ancient language of Father, Son, Spirit. But their complaints are not without merit. Christians have indeed misused trinitarian language. God transcends the biology of male and female. Even if God is called Father, God is not made of male genitalia and hormones. Even if God is called Father, males are not more like God than females. God's fatherhood is not a matter of sexual differentiation. God's fatherhood is a matter of God being the Progenitor, the Source of all life—male and female. The trinitarian language of Father, Son, Spirit does not justify a male dominance or male bias. Where we choose to use that ancient language of Father,

Son, Spirit, we must carefully and explicitly acknowledge that God's fatherhood ought not create the least sort of privilege for males.

So why then keep on speaking this language of Trinity? It is always difficult. It is sometimes misused grievously. Why should we be bound to this ancient language that God is Father, Son, Spirit—three persons in one?

If we wish to speak to God only in vague, ill-defined ways, we do not need the language of Trinity. If we wish to mean by *God* only a warm fuzzy with no discernible power to move in our lives, much less the power to call and to command our lives, we do not need the language of Trinity. If we wish to mean by *God* only a variable that can refer to any generally religious thought we want to put in, we don't need the language of Trinity. But if we ever wish to speak of God as a supreme reality who at God's choosing can enter our lives, change our lives, command our lives, if we ever wish to speak of God who was revealed in Jesus of Nazareth, proclaimed by Peter, James, and John, by Paul, Priscilla, and Lydia, that specificity requires the language of Trinity. Only as we speak of God as Father, Son, Spirit, only then, can we describe God as Christians have actually experienced God.

We Christians confess one God and one God only; still, God's reality requires that we speak of God as Father. Remember, God's fatherhood does *not* deify males, nor does God's fatherhood justify a male bias. By the language of Father, we speak of the Transcendent One. We speak of the One who is Source and Creator. We speak of the One who is the Given for all that is holy and good. If we do not speak of Father, then we do not speak of the divine at all but only ourselves. With the language of Father we speak of God who is before us, to whom we are accountable, for whom we are brought into life.

My father served as a pilot during the Second World War. He flew for the navy's transport service, shuttling supplies across the Pacific. His was a critical but generally not dangerous assignment. Once, though, he and his crew were flying alone across the Pacific late one night when he happened to spot an unidentified plane on the horizon. When he related the incident, I asked him if the plane was an enemy aircraft. He said he didn't wait around to find out; instead, he immediately took evasive action. Then he said—and I've never forgotten his phrase—"If I hadn't, you might not be around." He was reminding me, correctly, that my life has flowed from his life. In that sense, my life has depended on his life and is grounded in his life.

God's fatherhood names that dependence of all humanity upon God as the Source and Progenitor of life. God's fatherhood describes God's creative and procreative dimension. Without that fatherhood, we simply would not be. But *Father* says something even more than that.

The twentieth-century theologian Paul Tillich was fond of referring to God as the Ground of Being. Who could disagree? God is the ultimate being, which makes possible every other being. But God's fatherhood says more than just that.

Tillich would have done well to have read Gregory of Nyssa, a theologian of the Christian church in the fourth century after Christ. Gregory wrote that calling God Father recognizes God as the Being who is the source and cause of all other beings (which sounds very much like what Tillich tried to say). But Gregory went on to say that calling God Father also recognizes that God has a relationship with us as persons.[2]

God is called Father not only because God is the procreative power by which we exist; God is called Father also because this same God continues to live in relationship with us. If we cannot comprehend the whole of God's being, then we need to comprehend this: God stands as the procreative power for us, but God is not an abstract distant power. God is still the one in infinitely close relationship.

We Christians confess one God and one God only; still, God's reality requires that we also speak of God as Son. As Son, God puts on a human face. As Son, God's being resides in human flesh and form.

Again, what is significant about the Son is his humanity, not his maleness. The great prologue of John's Gospel does not say, "And the Word became male." No, it says, "And the word became *flesh* and lived among *us*." Through this flesh, male and female alike beheld the glory of God. Through the Son, God knows us from the inside, and we behold God as One with us.

For the second time in a decade, a member of India's powerful Gandhi family has been assassinated. I watched the satellite news as his son, in accordance with Hindu custom, lighted the funeral pyre to cremate the body of Rajiv Gandhi. Hundreds, thousands gathered to witness the ceremony, including leaders from all over the world.

Vice President Quayle and his wife were among those in the crowd, sent as the personal representatives of our president. We make jokes about vice presidents attending a lot of funerals, but in truth his presence there was very important. Sending a letter of condolence or merely making a courtesy telephone call would not have been enough for our president. It was appropriate that our president sent a person to embody the sorrow and concerns of our nation.

Remember how moving a sight it was when the leaders of the world walked behind the casket of John Kennedy? I can still see how French President Charles DeGaulle towered over everyone else and how his height was emphasized all the more by that peculiar military cap he wore. He and other leaders did not merely send consoling words; they bore their sorrow in the flesh.

God who transcends our time and our space does not merely wish us well from afar. God puts on a human face. God bears human sorrow and suffering. God feels human thirst and hunger. In so doing, God draws us into the deepest fellowship possible. God embodies a form with which we can commune. God creates in human terms a saving relationship for us, both men and women. If we cannot comprehend the whole of God's being, we can comprehend what God has made evident through the Son who, for us, put on a human face.

We Christians confess one God and one God only; still, God's reality requires that we speak of God as Spirit. Robert Jenson put that in a fairly academic way: "[T]he 'Spirit' is God as the power of the future to overturn what already is, and just so fulfill it. The Spirit is indeed a present reality."[3] What he is saying is that, as Spirit, God is still present; God is still active; and God's presence and activity are so powerful that they will shape the future in conformity to God's will.

This is what the Deists of an earlier age could not bring themselves to believe. To them, God was the Creator who had initiated the world, and God was the Provider who had set the physical laws to regulate the universe and the moral laws to provide for the well-being of people. However, they could not fathom God as Spirit who continued to be present and active in the world. They could not fathom God as Spirit whose power is such that ultimately it bends even the future to God's will. The Deists, along with their predecessors and successors, have an insufficient understanding of God as they have pursued their self-styled rationality. As theologian Geoffrey Wainwright wrote, "Try as I may, I cannot find anything positive for Christianity to learn from the deist position."[4]

Where we do not know and acknowledge God as Spirit, we do not know and acknowledge God as present and active among us. Because God is Spirit no less than Father and Son, Jesus could promise a Comforter for his followers. Because God is Spirit no less than Father and Son, the Apostle Paul was not daunted by his imprisonment but held fast to the hope of victory in Christ Jesus. Because God is Spirit no less than Father and Son, the Church was gathered, nurtured, and preserved.

But I tell you that that presence, that activity, that power of God who is Spirit is not just for the ancient people of the Bible. It is for us now as well. Because God is Spirit no less than Father and Son, the church in China endured the decades-long hostility of its government. Because God is Spirit no less than Father and Son, seminaries are opening, Bibles are being distributed, restrictions are being lifted in Eastern Europe. Because God is Spirit no less than Father and Son, lives around us are being touched and changed. Addictions are being broken. Forgiveness is being born, and reconciliation is being nurtured. Despair is turned to hope. Failure is softened by signs of promise.

God is Spirit—present among us, active in our world and in our affairs, powerful enough to create a triumphant future freed from our own weaknesses and sin.

This is God whom we worship in the name of Jesus: Father, Son, Spirit; one God in three persons. And yes, we could imagine simpler theologies, but only the language of Father, Son, Spirit links together what Professor McGrath calls "the non-negotiables of the Christian understanding of God."[5] Only the language of Trinity presents to us God as God revealed God's own self. In this strange but wonderful language of Trinity, we meet God the Source of life who yet relates to us, God who puts on a human face for our sake, God who is still active in the world and who is bringing triumphant power to bear on the future. This is the God who stands before us and who calls us into blessed fellowship.

NOTES

1. Alister McGrath, "Making Sense of the Trinity," *Princeton Seminary Bulletin* 12(1991):1.

2. As cited by Deborah Malacky Belonick, "Revelation and Metaphors," *Union Seminary Quarterly Review* 40(1985):31.

3. Robert Jenson, *The Triune Identity* (Philadelphia: Fortress Press, 1982), 23.

4. Geoffrey Wainwright, "The Doctrine of the Trinity," *Interpretation* 45(April 1991):125.

5. McGrath, "Making Sense of the Trinity," 6.

18. Who Art in Heaven
Paul F. Rack

Matthew 6:9b

Some of you may have heard the story about one of the first Soviet cosmonauts. The Russians were the first to go into space, you may recall. And as this cosmonaut sailed through the sky in his capsule, he is said to have radioed down to earth triumphantly that he was looking around and there was no sign of God anywhere.

There was nothing up there but empty space: no air, no clouds, no pieces of solid matter, not even much light. It was just an empty vacuum of nothingness. Having had our first glimpse of heaven, this is what it was.

The Greek word used in the Bible for heaven means "sky." Ancient people had all kinds of theories and myths about the sky and what it was made of. It has always symbolized something beyond human experience.

But with air and space travel the sky ceases to be as much of a mystery. Now people can go up there and see it firsthand. Through observation we now know that heaven, the sky, is virtually empty space. Beyond the dome of the earth's atmosphere, there is a vast and nearly infinite expanse of nothingness, where distances are unimaginably great, where even stars and planets are scattered specks of matter.

The ancient mind may have thought that God literally dwelled in the sky. The modern mind knows that God is apparently nowhere to be found up there. Heaven is vacant.

Paul F. Rack is Pastor of Christ Presbyterian Church in Martinsville, New Jersey. He is a graduate of Princeton Theological Seminary and is religion columnist for the Bridgewater, New Jersey, *Courier-News*. He has also been manager of the Thomas More Bookshop in Cambridge, Mass.

In theology, the idea of heaven has traditionally been used to talk about God's transcendence. God is distant, remote, unknowable, and high above us in every way. Heaven is the way theologians have talked about God's otherness and unreachability.

This understanding of God as transcendent and beyond the world and human experience is absolutely basic to the theology of the Bible. This why God's people are not permitted to make any images or statues of God. God is beyond anything that can be represented in a recognizable form.

In the Bible the greatest sin is idolatry. Idolatry is even seen as the root of all other sins. We cannot attempt to make God something in our own experience, something we can grasp and deal with as we please.

Even the place where God was said really to dwell, the Holy of Holies in the Temple in Jerusalem, was basically an empty space. Except for a few furnishings, God lived there invisibly and intangibly and at God's own good pleasure.

This was a totally foreign idea to every other nation. The consensus view was that an invisible god was no god at all. So when the Babylonians came to destroy the Temple, the swaggering and brutal soldiers broke into the Holy of Holies and triumphantly declared it to be empty. In other words, they had the same reaction as the cosmonaut. By exposing the apparent absence of God, they thought they were exposing the whole religion as a fraud.

What the modern cosmonaut and the ancient soldiers failed to understand was that the emptiness and vacancy of these places was precisely the point. A visible, tangible, knowable, and available god could not be the transcendent God who created the universe.

Heaven, or the sky, was the last place we could put God and preserve our tendency to idolatry, which thinks of God as literally living somewhere, like any other object in our world. By pointing out heaven's emptiness, the cosmonaut is actually doing us a favor.

After all this, what does Jesus mean when he has us pray to God "who art in heaven"? Does he mean that God literally dwells in the sky somewhere? Does he mean to use the word *heaven* as a metaphor for God's transcendence, a way to say that God is not here, that God is distant and remote from our experience on earth? Or is his intention something else?

The scientific understanding is that we on the earth sail through empty space. But scientists tell us things about our world that appear to be even more bizarre than this. Not only is heaven an empty void, but matter as well is mostly empty space.

At the bottom of the Pacific Ocean, scientists are building a giant apparatus designed to catch and measure some tiny subatomic particles that are zooming through the galaxy. These particles can only be perceived after they pass through the earth. So this giant device is supposed to collect particles from space that have come through the planet.

My point is that these particles are so tiny, and the earth is so porous, that they pass this solid mass of rock as if it wasn't there. On that level of reality the atoms and molecules that make up the earth are as sparse and distant from each other as planes in the air over Nebraska. Particles can pass through the whole planet without bumping into anything.

This is because what we consider to be solid matter, like rock or wood or metal, is really mostly empty space. Between the atoms and molecules and particles and waves that make up our physical, substantial world, there is a vast expanse of nothing. Tangible reality is mostly space. In this respect a piece of stone is very similar to heaven. Both are mostly made of nothing, as are we and everything else.

There is this sense then that space is not just "out there." It is also all around and within us. The sky does not begin where the atmosphere leaves off, it permeates everything. Space, heaven, is something that is very close to us, even if it is also very far away.

Christian theology has always understood this. The resurrection and ascension of Jesus never meant that he abandoned us to go and live somewhere in the sky, far away. Believers have always known that precisely because of his ascension into heaven, Jesus is also always with us. We are in him, and he is in us. Christ gives to the Church his Spirit by which he is always present.

Certainly, heaven still means God's radical otherness and transcendence. Yet at the same time there is a sense in which heaven is in our hearts. So that when we say Christ ascended into heaven, we are also saying that now Jesus is closer to us than we are to ourselves.

Maybe it is not too much to say as well that the God of heaven, while infinitely far from us, is also so intimate with us as to inhabit the empty space between our cells, molecules, and atoms, and even the empty space between our thoughts and feelings.

When Jesus has us address God with the words "our Father who art in heaven," he is making us aware at once of God's otherness and of God's self-emptying love in being present with and within us. God is at the same time "in heaven" and also "our Father." God is at the same time the transcendent Creator and also one who can be addressed when we gather together or even in the secrecy of our own hearts.

The good news is that in Jesus Christ God's closeness to us is revealed. In him we realize that we can seek and find God's presence within us and among us. This new Reality is near and at hand, as Jesus himself proclaimed in his ministry.

Jesus Christ brings heaven down to earth. He brings the hopelessly remote right down next to us. He makes that from which we were alienated in sinfulness to be our new and true home. In Christ the dwelling place of the transcendent God is with us, among us, full of grace and truth.

When the soldiers discovered that the Temple was empty, and when the cosmonaut discovered that the sky was empty, it is really not all that different from the experience of a group of women who go to a cemetery very early on a particular Sunday morning. The tomb they are visiting is also found to be empty.

The emptiness of this tomb is good news because its meaning is that Jesus has risen. And by his resurrection and ascension Jesus reveals to us that heaven, the saving presence of God, is located precisely where we see nothing, where we do not identify or recognize God. Heaven reaches into the space between and within us and is closer to us than we are to the cells of our bodies. God's grace in Christ permeates every part of our being. Truly in him heaven has come to us.

In Christ God lightens our darkness and fills our emptiness with his presence. God's transcendent love is revealed to be so close to us that we can feel the heartbeat and hear the breathing.

To pray to a God "who art in heaven" is to know the powerful energy of the infinite in the empty and lost places in your heart. It is to recognize that the emptiness all around us—in our souls and in our culture—could be places where God's invisible power is already at work.

In this prayer we turn our attention outside of ourselves and away from our visible, tangible circumstances. Instead, we look to the person of Jesus Christ. He is the one who brings heaven to us. He makes what is remote from us to be immediate. He is the condensation in our flesh of God's living Word, which is to us otherwise inaudible and invisible.

In him we listen for what we cannot hear. In him we look for what we cannot see. For in him the infinite, transcendent God enters our lives and saves us by dwelling in the space within and between us and making it, and us, an extension of the space "above" where God dwells.

19. I Would Kiss the Cardinal's Hands
SERMON FOR GOOD FRIDAY

Richard Mazziotta

During Nazi occupation of Poland in World War II, Karol Wojtyla supported himself working by day in a quarry and later in a chemical factory near Kraków. By night, the young man turned actor, poet, and playwright, performing in a clandestine stage company called the Rhapsodic Theater. After the war, he did not become a poet-actor as he had expected; instead, Wojtyla became a priest. His poetry continued and was published after ordination under a pseudonym. It was not until the quarry worker and actor of the underground resistance was elected pope in 1978 that the real identity of Andrezej Jawien, his pen name, became known. One poem is entitled "The Quarry." In this poem, Wojtyla writes,

Hands are the heart's landscape. They split sometimes like ravines into which an undefined force rolls.

When I distribute Communion during the Eucharist, I often find myself looking at your hands. Though Jesus tells us in the Gospel that the eyes are the window of the soul, at Communion time, I'm inclined to agree instead with the pope: "Hands are the landscape of the heart. . . ."

Many of your hands, toughened by work and daily toil, tell the story of the years. The deep, expressive lines across your palms reveal the strain of daily life, of marriage, parenthood, sickness, and fatigue and its distress. During the days before you brought

---

Richard Mazziotta, C.S.C., is Assistant Professor of Religious Studies at Stonehill College in North Easton, Massachussetts. A graduate of Boston University and the University of Notre Dame, Mazziotta is the author of *Jesus in the Gospels* and *We Pray to the Lord*.

those hands here to receive Christ, maybe they carried a sick child to the hospital or nursed an aged parent or changed a thousand diapers or paid a hundred bills or mopped an acre of floors or held a phone during an argument or steered a car on a difficult journey or failed a math test or turned the pages of a depressing report or opened a letter filled with sad news. They are hands that have reached perhaps for the one-too-many drink or for the cigarette, pill, or drug that diminishes life rather than restores it.

When some of you come to Communion, you are carrying infants in your arms, and toddlers are trailing at your side. It takes a second for you to rearrange your family so that you can free a hand to receive Christ. As parents of the very young, you have your hands full all the time, and it seems right to me that at the moment of Communion you bring your responsibilities with you, too.

Some of your hands, I know, are unemployed or underemployed. You come here to reach for Christ with them, hoping that the Savior, in turn, will fill them with meaningful work and satisfying labor.

Some of you are nurses and physicians, and your hands give life and hope all week long. You come here on Sunday so that they can receive the gift of life again.

Teenagers, you have special hands. Maybe they passed the basketball through the net in the championship game for Sharon High last Monday night. Maybe they were held for the first time by your boyfriend this week. When you open them wide to receive Christ, your hands show your youth and excitement, your joy in life, your perfect health, perfectly undaunted by the coming years.

Children, we love your hands especially. Yes, they are smaller than those of your parents or older sisters and brothers, but they are just as large as we see them. At the altar, when you open your hands, I see in your upturned palms your own openness to God and to the Catholic faith. Your hands are so essential, so important, to the spiritual life of our parish. I do not think that I have ever seen hands more open than the hands of little children. The lines that travel across your palms are perfect trust untouched by fear.

The hands we open to receive Christ are, of course, hands that have sinned as well. They have sinned in what they have reached for, perhaps, in what they have struck in violence, in what they have grasped or only merely touched. These are hands that have closed the door on reconciliation. Ours are the hands that have brushed away homeless on the street or hands that have not been raised to make a point of mercy in defense of others. If your hands have sinned, you must remember what great feast this is, and you should not be afraid. Have trust today. When your hands reach for the Communion cup, remember that our Lord's cup of the new covenant is the Blood of Christ, which is poured out—as Jesus said that very night on which hands and kiss betrayed him—so that sins, yours and mine, might be forgiven.

On Good Friday I always recall a poem by Wilfred Owen, a young British soldier of World War I. Though not a Catholic, Owen attended liturgy in a Catholic church on one Good Friday. He watched worshipers file down the aisle and approach a server, who stood holding a crucifix. Owen watched as each worshiper knelt in turn and kissed the figure on the cross, as you and I soon will do. Moved by what he saw, soldier Owen took a place in line and advanced with the rest. When his turn arrived, however, his own action was unpredictable, even to himself, as the final words of the poem reveal:

> Then I, too, knelt before that acolyte.
> Above the crucifix I bent my head:
> The Christ was thin, and cold, and very dead.
> And yet I bowed, yea, kissed—my lips did cling.
> (I kissed the warm live hand that held the thing.)

Wilfred Owen died in battle seven days before the armistic that brought an end to that terrible modern war. I have thought of Wilfred Owen, soldier-poet, a great deal these months. I thought of him especially after the ground phase of the Gulf War ended. I saw the scenes of Iraqi war diaries discovered near bunkers. Their pages were blowing lost and uncollected across the desert sands. Occasionally, a journalist found a page and had it translated from Arabic for his English-speaking audience. Unlike Owen's vivid war poetry, which was saved, these are poems that only God has collected for the saddest book in heaven's library, the book of war poetry. Am I wrong to think that it is this book, much-expanded in 1991, that God reads on this Good Friday, in what has been, in fact, a long, Good Friday winter of devastation and war, nation against nation, West against East, East against West, color against color, creed against creed, and now, brother against brother.

Hands are the landscape of the heart. "They split sometimes / like ravines into which an undefined force rolls."

I wish, my friends, that on this Good Friday I could kiss your hands, young hands, old hands, hands of boys and girls, of teenagers and grandparents, of the addicted and the healthy, hands full and hands unemployed, hands of police and restaurant workers, hands that run the government, hands of laborers and secretaries, of artists and mechanics, hands that run bulldozers, those that manage businesses, hands that play pipe organs, hands of the saint, hands of the sinner.

And kiss them all I would—believe me, I would—if it were not for one thing. I am sure that someone, well-intentioned though they be, would be offended and call the cardinal to complain that on Good Friday they came here for Communion and instead had their hands kissed. Then I would get called on the carpet, on a cardinal-red carpet, and asked to explain such giddy behavior for such a sober day, Good Friday.

Even that, though, would be all right. You see, I would tell the cardinal about the poem the pope wrote long ago about the hands of a quarry worker. I would tell him of the poem's apocalyptic words, now being fulfilled across Eastern Europe, words that saw the day when workers hands would split like ravines and into them an undefined force would roll. I would explain how in the poem the pope keeps calling hands the landscape of the heart. And if all my words were not enough, then I would kiss the cardinal's hands as well.

IV. ETHICAL

20. Covenant with Creation
Al Gore

Genesis 9:8–17

When God made his covenant with Noah and gave the rainbow as a symbol of his promise, he went on to make another covenant, expressed in the very next verse, a covenant with all living things and the entire earth.

What is *our* relationship to all living things and to the entire earth? The purpose of life, I was taught in Sunday School many years ago, is to glorify God. If we destroy that part of creation within our grasp—if we heap contempt upon it—what does that say about our relationship with or our attitude toward the Creator?

Our relationship to the earth is, therefore, critical in expressing our relationship to God.

In three of the Gospels, those of Matthew, Mark, and Luke, there is the parable of the unfaithful servant, wherein the master, upon leaving for a journey, instructs his servant that he must take care of the house. The master gives one very simple rule: If, while I'm gone, he says, vandals come and ransack this house or thieves come to steal my belongings, it will not be a good enough excuse if you say you were asleep.

We are now witnessing in our lifetimes environmental vandalism in God's home on a global scale:

> Forests are being destroyed at the rate of one-and-a-half acres per second and with them thousands of species that can never be replaced;

Albert F. Gore, Jr., is vice president of the United States, following sixteen years as a U.S. congressman and then senator from Tennessee. He is a graduate of Harvard University and attended Vanderbilt University's divinity and law schools. During his service in public office, Vice President Gore has demonstrated a particular interest in environmental issues. He is the author of the 1992 book *Earth in the Balance.*

Each day almost forty thousand children under the age of five die from hunger and malnutrition caused in significant part by ecological devastation;

We continue to generate waste in the United States every day at a rate exceeding twice the average body weight of every American;

Dead dolphins are being washed up along the Mediterranean coast, their immune systems weakened by too much pollution; thousands of seals wash up along the shores of the North Sea; our own children dodge hypodermic needles washing in with the waves.

It will not be good enough for us to say we were asleep. It is an insufficient excuse for us to claim we were unaware of what is going on in God's home right now. As humans, we have been given dominion over the earth, dominion that is meant to be keeping as well as tilling. In other words, we are required by God to be good stewards of the earth.

To redefine our relationship with the earth, we must reawaken ourselves to a truer understanding of our relationship with other living things. We are not separate and isolated from the world around us. Instead, we are part of the whole—a powerful force like the winds and the tides.

I asked a group of elementary school students recently the questions "Where is God?" and "Where is heaven?" You know, of course, where they pointed. They pointed straight up. We have, all of us, absorbed the notion that God is way out there somewhere, perhaps an old man with a white beard, living far from the earth. Where is hell? We've been taught to point straight down to the center of the earth.

But Jesus told us that the Kingdom of God is within. Is God in us? Why are so many uncomfortable with that notion, and if God is within us, is God not also within other living things? Is God not also in the rest of creation?

Early in the history of Christianity, the message of Christ was wrapped tightly in the language and metaphors of Greek philosophy, a rich tradition from which we selected some things and left out others. In the process, we understood and kept some of Christ's message. Other parts were set aside.

The Church faced an existing body of religious beliefs in much of the world where the gospel was preached. Paganism and animism derived a revelation from the physical world. Some believed that in each separate, individual animal and plant and rock there was a separate motivating spirit.

In the desire to overcome this superstitious way of relating to the world, our tradition placed heavy emphasis on a disembodied spirit that we worshiped intellectually.

We still worship God intellectually. But we can also feel his presence, understand God emotionally and physically and receive a revelation from all of the world.

We are not separate from the earth. God is not separate from the earth.

All the new technologies we use have convinced us that we can employ our intellect to completely understand the world, to master it, to manipulate it, to do with it as we wish. We have acquired new technologies and new powers, and the scale of humankind's existence on the earth is out of all proportion to what it has been throughout all of human history up until now.

I talked with some scientists about a new technology called holograms. Because of the unique laws of optics, every tiny part of the hologram screen has the entire three-dimensional image very faintly represented. When the full screen is brought into view, then a large image becomes visible.

It seems to me that God's relationship to creation, as we perceive it, is not unlike that phenomenon. We have an obligation to act, first of all, in our own lives and then in our own communities, in our nation, and in our world. We have an obligation to see the whole picture, the entire image.

We have an obligation to those who are less fortunate, to social justice. We have a responsibility to protect this earth against the rapacious destruction now underway.

Is there hope that we can succeed in this task? Those of us who are believers believe in a God of hope, a God of miracles, a God who promises us that we can have a future completely outside the boundaries of our own imagination, that what comes in the future need not be what has come in the past, and that we have a responsibility to cocreate that future.

In Revelation, John says we will praise the lamb triumphant with all creatures, and we are told the earth is the Lord's and the fullness thereof.

Let us take that feeling of joy and join with it a commitment to pray, to act, to change, and to protect God's creation.

21. Not by Might, Nor by Power, But by My Spirit
Margaret Moers Wenig

Zechariah 4:1–14

In an age long before television,[1] God often communicated through images, not on a screen, of course, but out in the desert or in a dream: a bush burning unconsumed, a gold lamp stand with seven lamps thereon and olive trees beside it. Sometimes those images spoke for themselves. Sometimes they required commentary. Zechariah was humble enough to admit that he needed help with this one. So he consulted a reliable secondary source: "What do these things mean, my lord?," Zechariah asked the angel. The angel explained, "This is the word of the Lord to Zerubbabel: 'Not by might, nor by power, but by my Spirit' says the Lord of hosts."

Now, Zechariah was not a military leader. He was among those who returned from exile, entrusted with rebuilding the Temple (which had been destroyed by the Babylonians). Zerubbabel certainly understood that his people had not survived exile nor won their return to Jerusalem through military power. So we can safely assume that when Zerubbabel heard God's message, "Not by might, nor by power, . . ." he heard it not as a challenge but as a confirmation.

But when the rabbis chose this text as the prophetic lesson for the Sabbath in Chanukah (which today happens to be) they did not mean it as a confirmation. They meant it as a challenge.

Margaret Moers Wenig is rabbi at Beth Am, the People's Temple in New York City. She is also a lecturer on homiletics at Hebrew Union College. A graduate of Brown University, Wenig was a contributor to *Womanspirit Rising,* edited by Carol Christ and Judith Plaskow, and *The Mishnah: A New Translation* by Jacob Neusner. She was a first place winner in the competition in *Best Sermons 5.*

I know that you are not observing Chanukah with me. I know that you do not tell and retell its story among your sacred stories. None the less, I have a sense that this particular year, this particular date, you, too, may be able to hear a Word of God in this story:

Antiochus IV of Syria, as the very partisan account goes, overran Judah and Jerusalem as part of his conquest of Egypt. Insecure about dissident groups, he apparently used force to Hellenize the country. As 1 Maccabees reports (1:41), "The king then issued a decree throughout his empire: His subjects were all to become one people and to abandon their own law and religion." Jews were prohibited from observing the Sabbath, maintaining dietary laws, circumcising their sons, reading the Law and offering daily sacrifices in their Temple. In fact, to drive his point home, Antiochus apparently erected idols in that Temple and offered unclean animals on its altar.

As in many such situations, some of the oppressed people observed Antiochus's decrees, others flaunted them and were put to death, but a third group, led by Judah the Maccabee, launched a military initiative to liberate Jerusalem and the Temple from Syrian hands. Surprisingly, they succeeded. Something of a miracle, I'd say. Three years, to the day, after the promulgation of Antiochus's decrees, three years after the defiling of the Temple's sacred altar, Judah and his band recaptured the Temple, cleaned it out, fashioned new holy vessels, and a new lamp stand. They destroyed the altar defiled by swine and dedicated a new one. And they proclaimed that day to be a festival for all time to celebrate their military victory and the dedication of the altar. Thus Chanukah (which means "dedication").

Worth celebrating, right?

Not if you are the rabbis (in the first few centuries of this era). Not if you know what happened to the Maccabees after the dedication ceremony. For it turned out that power rather than religious freedom was Judah's goal: No sooner had he secured religious freedom than he turned around and forcibly circumcised uncircumcised Jewish boys. Call that freedom? Hardly! Moreover Judah and his band didn't lay down their arms. After the victory celebration they continued fighting. Judah was eventually killed in battle. His fellow warrior and brother, Jonathan, became high priest, and thus began the Hasmonean dynasty, which moved of its own accord from high priesthood to kingship (with no legitimacy) and sank slowly in its own corruption for two hundred years until Rome finally sacked Jerusalem, destroyed the Temple once and for all, and sent the Jews into exile.[2]

For the rabbis, that was nothing to celebrate, especially in their time, especially in light of the constant talk of revolt against Rome that they had to rebut. Can you believe it, revolt against Rome? For some, I guess, history teaches no lessons. No, the rabbis were not in favor of celebrating the military victory of the Maccabees. So they excluded 1 and 2 Maccabees from their sacred canon, they proclaimed that the miracle of Chanukah was not military victory but that a little cruse of oil (the only one found in the Temple) lasted not for one but for all eight days of the festival of dedication, and they prescribed as the prophetic reading for the Sabbath in Chanukah: Not by might, nor by power . . . is life secured for a people under siege. To any would-be heirs of the Maccabees, that was a challenging word.

Had Zechariah said to Roosevelt in 1941, "Not by might, nor by power, . . ." that surely would have been a challenging word.

Fifty years later, however, on this the fiftieth anniversary of the Japanese attack on Pearl Harbor, after fifty million deaths, after Hiroshima and Nagasaki, after Korea, Vietnam, and Iraq, the message that life ultimately prevails not by might, nor by power, but by God's Spirit is hardly a challenging word. Especially not for us. For we are, after all, the ones who preach of the life-giving power of the Spirit of God, a Spirit not content to hover over the face of the waters; a Spirit restless and yearning to be made manifest; a Spirit that gives strength to a new shoot growing from the stump of an old, felled tree; a Spirit that plants seeds in virgin soil and from barren terrain brings forth life; a Spirit that splits the sea to let slaves go free and enables ordinary people to prophesy; a Spirit that breathes life into life-less bodies and inspires men and women to holy words and holy deeds. No, we are not likely to feel challenged by the message "not by might, nor by power, but by my Spirit"—unless, of course, we hear the whispered warning.

The Spirit, by taking the form of flesh and blood, by finding expression in the words and deeds of real people, the Spirit has allowed itself to be vulnerable—vulnerable, for instance, to an insecure government seeking to diminish dissidence by imposing the will of the majority on the minority. The earthly manifestations of the Spirit are vulnerable to those in power, who from time to time would have them silenced or shackled. My tradition portrays the Shechinah (the indwelling presence of God) bound in chains, forced into exile with her people. Your tradition, too, knows that an earthly manifestation of God's Spirit can be bound and hung to die on a cross. People inspired by the Spirit may be bound, and deeds that people inspired by the Spirit believe they must do may also be circumscribed. A warning: Not by might, nor by power, but by God's Spirit will life prevail—as long as we don't allow the vulnerable human manifestations of God's Spirit to be proscribed. For we must prepare a way for God. For some mysterious reason God has chosen to need us. Judah the Maccabee, all his ambitions for personal power aside, understood this.

And the rabbis—though they objected to the original meaning of Chanukah—did not eliminate its observance; they merely transformed it. For as much as they wanted to play down Judah's military victory, the rabbis must have understood how much this people needed to hear a story of a minority who refused to allow the Spirit of God, as it lived and breathed through them, to be held captive by the majority. A warning: Not by might, nor by power, but by God's Spirit shall you have life. So you dare not placidly allow a government to hamper your ability to live as the Spirit says you should live.

It was a warning to generations past, and it is a warning to us. For in our own time an Antiochus reigns again. This time disguised in the black robes of a Supreme Court judge. Antiochus of Syria outlawed Sabbath and dietary observance, circumcision, study of the Law, and daily sacrifices. This Antiochus has already threatened the wearing of religious garb on the job, refusals of autopsies and blood transfusions, and more. This Antiochus went much further than he even needed to go to secure his government's interest. In the now infamous Smith case, Supreme Court judge Antonin Scalia could have ruled that it was or was not in the compelling interest of the State of Oregon to prohibit the use of peyote for sacramental purposes. Instead, Scalia eliminated altogether the compelling state interest test for infringement of the free exercise of religion, calling it "a luxury we can no longer afford."

In one year fifteen cases have already been affected by the Smith decision.[3] Lest you think that the decision threatens only Native Americans, Jehovah's Witnesses, Muslims, and Jews, know that you, too, may lose the protections you have enjoyed to express the Spirit as you see fit. In one case Boston Jesuits were almost prohibited from relocating their church altar because even the interior of the church had been designated a landmark. In New York City, St. Bartholemew's Episcopal church did lose its free exercise claim against landmarking restrictions. If these issues don't concern you, perhaps this one will: After Smith, state courts may now be permitted to decide the role of lesbian and gay people in your church. In a case pending in liberal Minnesota a church may be prohibited from discriminating against a gay rights group wishing to lease church space that is regularly shared with community groups.[4] While that may please some of you, know that the Smith case can also have the opposite effect in a conservative state such as Georgia where the attorney general gets away with firing a woman on his legal staff for having a religious service of commitment with another woman at which a member of the clergy presided.[5] I don't want someone to lose a job for participating in a religious ceremony that my denomination permits me to perform. Do you?

This week, of all weeks, the warning rings loudly in my ears. For it was on December 15, 1791, that the State of Virginia ratified the Bill of Rights. On December 15, 1941, eight days after Pearl Harbor, President Roosevelt declared a Bill of Rights Day. (Ironically, in an act reminiscent of Judah the Maccabee, Roosevelt then turned around and deprived 120,000 Japanese Americans of the very rights he declared we should celebrate.) This week, on the two hundredth anniversary of the Bill of Rights, I hear the warning: Yes, by God's Spirit does life prevail—but remember, the Spirit speaks in many tongues. Some have a large number of voices; some, only a few. I hear the warning: Fight government's attempt to silence any one of those voices without demonstrating compelling interest.

"But how, my lord, shall we fight, we who are only preachers and teachers of preachers?" I ask the angel. And he responds, "Not by might, nor by power, but by my Spirit." And this time, he can mean only one thing: By God's Spirit, namely, through preaching; preaching to keep free the human manifestations of the very Spirit that enables us to preach. Preach not only in the pulpit but also in the press, not only in the halls of seminaries but especially these days in the halls of Congress. Preach to our representatives to pass legislation that would restore the compelling state interest test to protect our free exercise of religion.

This is an auspicious time, the anniversaries of Pearl Harbor and the Bill of Rights, the season of Chanukah and Advent. It feels as though God is waiting, waiting for us to ensure that the spirit may be free so that life may ultimately prevail.

NOTES

1. A theme of the 1991 meeting of the Academy of Homiletics (where this sermon was delivered) was "Culture, Symbol, and Media," and a few papers dealt with the visual medium of television.

2. This sentence is borrowed from a sermon by Rabbi Margaret Holub.

3. See "Religious Freedom Under Fire," *The Lutheran* (July 17, 1991).

4. "First a California church dismissed an organist based on his gay lifestyle. The court found for the church. 'In a post-*Smith* situation, it is highly unlikely the case could have been decided that way,' [constitutional lawyer Douglas Laycock] said. Second, a local civil rights commission told a Minnesota church, known for sharing its facilities with community groups, that it could not exclude a gay-rights group. The case is still in the courts, and legal experts anticipate more suits against churches involving gay rights issues." *The Lutheran* (July 17, 1991), 12.

5. This summer, Attorney General Bowers rescinded an offer of a job to Emory Law School graduate Robin Shahar after she celebrated her commitment to her lover of five years in a religious ceremony of Kiddushin under the supervision of Rabbi Sharon Kleinbaum. The leadership of the Reconstructionist movement (which ordained Rabbi Kleinbaum) and the president of the Union of American Hebrew Congregations (the Reform movement, for which Rabbi Kleinbaum now works) support Rabbi Kleinbaum and the ACLU's suit against Attorney General Bowers.

22. Plowshares and Swords
Allan M. Parrent

Joel 3:1–2, 9–17; 1 Peter 1:1–12

From the Old Testament lesson: "Beat your plowshares into swords and your pruning hooks into spears." And from the Epistle: "By his great mercy he has given us a new birth into a living hope through the Resurrection of Jesus Christ from the dead and into an inheritance that is imperishable—for a salvation ready to be revealed in the last time."

It was a bright but chilly Sunday morning, and I had been to church, as usual, with my parents and siblings. My mother was organist and my father was head usher that day. I was ten years old. After church we went to my aunt's house for a big Sunday dinner, as we then called the midday Sunday meal. After dinner I turned on the radio, that wonderful new technological achievement that allows one to listen to a program without having to watch it—great for the imagination. I always listened to "Father Flanagan's Boys' Town" at 2:30 on Sunday afternoon. My life in those years was not unlike the idyllic, small-town American existence that today's more sophisticated society tends to pass off as an Ozzie-and-Harriet myth that never really existed. Well, it did to some degree, at least in the bluegrass region of Kentucky in the late 30s

Allan M. Parrent was educated at Georgetown College (Kentucky), Vanderbilt, Duke, and Durham (England) universities. He served as foreign service officer, U.S. Department of State, and was a member of the U.S. delegation to the Eighteen-Nation Disarmament Conference, Geneva, in 1964. He was director of program in Washington, department of international affairs, for the National Council of Churches, 1967–72. He currently serves as professor of Christian ethics, associate dean for academic affairs, and vice president at the Episcopal Theological Seminary in Virginia. Dr. Parrent contributes frequently to scholarly journals and speaks widely on ethical issues.

and early 40s or at least until that Sunday fifty years ago: December 7, 1941.

I, of course, didn't fully realize at the time what was happening. In fact I got a little irritated because some announcer kept interrupting "Boys' Town." But in retrospect it seems clear that that day marked symbolically the end of an older America and the beginning of a new era that has had, and continues to this day to have, a profound effect on all of us and on millions more around the world. The possible ending of the third world war, the Cold War, which we may now be witnessing, is linked directly to those events of fifty years ago.

World War II was in many ways, of course, merely a continuation of World War I, just as Woodrow Wilson had predicted after the Versailles treaty. It cast an isolationist and reluctant America onto the world scene in a way it did not seek and in a role for which it was not prepared. In the two decades between the wars many nations, reacting to the horrors of World War I, had either naively or cynically signed an agreement outlawing war, as if that would settle the matter once and for all. The same mentality led the democracies to disarm, beating swords into plowshares as fast as they could.

Those in the churches and elsewhere who wished so strongly for peace after Passchendaele, the Somme, and the Marne, joined with the isolationists to insure that spears would be turned into pruning hooks and that this nation would study war no more. Just a year before Pearl Harbor, a bill to extend the draft and beef up our skeletal military forces passed the Congress by one vote, in spite of the conquest of most of continental Europe. FDR had to stretch the powers of the president considerably, given U.S. neutrality, just to send a few old ships to the equally unprepared British who were at that moment standing alone, fighting the Battle of Britain.

All of that fifty-year-old history, which probably no more than a few of us here remember firsthand, came flooding back as I read those words from Joel in today's lesson that so jar our Isaiah-formed ears: "Beat your plowshares into swords and your pruning hooks into spears." Is that a misprint, some might ask? Did Joel unintentionally misquote Isaiah? Perhaps this could be explained in psychological terms—a result of Joel's sexual repression or perhaps a dysfunctional family.

No, Joel's admonition to beat plowshares into swords, when contrasted with Isaiah's vision of the latter days when nations will beat swords into plowshares, illustrates and exemplifies the paradox of human existence itself. It is a paradox that is fundamental to living the Christian life in a world not yet fully reconciled to God in Christ. It illustrates the fact that we live the Christian life between Joel's valley of decision and Isaiah's mountain of the Lord and his universal reign, between the already and the not yet, under both Law and gospel, as both justified and sinners. When, in our Eucharistic Prayer B, we say, "We remember his death, we proclaim his resurrection, we await his coming in glory," we are acknowledging that we live right where that second comma occurs, between resurrection and glory, in the valley of decision.

We know and affirm the vision of an Isaiah, in which the nations are invited to go up to the mountain of the Lord. Here they will be taught his ways and walk in his paths. Here swords will be beaten into plowshares. Here the lion will lie down with the lamb. But we also know and must acknowledge the sense of injustice in the world perceived by a Joel, in his case concerning the treatment of Israel, though it is a perennial phenomenon of human history in a world not reconciled to God. It is in such a world that he calls the nations to beat plowshares into swords and to come, not to the mountain of the Lord, but to the valley of Jehoshaphat, the valley of decision. Here God will judge the nations and vindicate his moral order, which has been violated by injustice and oppression. But for the present, Joel sees the world as a world in which Israel's oppressors, like oppressors in every age between resurrection and glory, show contempt for God the Creator by showing contempt for those he created. It is a world where, in Woody Allen's words, the lion may lie down with the lamb, but the lamb won't get much sleep.

This is the world Dietrich Bonhoeffer knew when he wrote, in July 1939, to his professor at Union Seminary who only a few weeks before had been instrumental in getting Bonhoeffer out of Germany. That professor was Reinhold Niebuhr, and this is what the young Bonhoeffer wrote:

> I have come to the conclusion that I have made a
> mistake in coming to America. I must live through
> this difficult period of our national history with

the Christian people of Germany. . . . Christians in
Germany will face the terrible alternative of either
willing the defeat of their nation in order that
Christian civilization may survive, or willing the
victory of their nation and thereby destroying our
civilization. I know which of these alternatives I
must choose, but I cannot make that choice in
security.

The valley of decision.

This is the world Winston Churchill knew when, amidst
charges of warmongering, he mobilized the English language and
sent it into battle, along with an inadequate set of spears and
swords in the form of a few Spitfires and Hurricanes. The valley
of decision. This is also the world the United States woke up to
suddenly in December 1941. It was fortunate to have the time and
the protection of two oceans to allow this sleeping giant, with little
sense of the tragic dimensions of history, to turn plowshares into
swords in an effort to prevent what Bonhoeffer himself had re-
ferred to as the destruction of our civilization. The valley of decision.

As we near the fiftieth anniversary of one of those awful days
of history, at least for this nation, when people can tell you where
they were at the time, we might ask once again how our formation
and self-understanding as Christians might shape our response to
such darker moments of history. One part of a possible two-part
answer is found in a statement by the Archbishop of Canterbury,
Robert Runcie, made at the time of the Gulf War:

The Christian has a built-in resistance to the use of
force. We are to be peacemakers. But the Bible
insists that we live in a world in rebellion, a world
which has rejected the order given to it by its
creator. Christianity does not lack realism about
the intransigence of conflict. The scriptures speak
of our responsibility for seeking justice and the
well-being of creation in the world as it exists. The
hard fact is that the use of force is caused as much
by human virtues—our sense of justice, our belief
in the difference between right and wrong, our
readiness for self-sacrifice on behalf of others—as
it is by any of our failures.

In other words, Christian conscience *may* prompt a challenge to unjust power in the world, and this *may* prompt, reluctantly, the beating of plowshares into swords. But conscience must at the same time acknowledge that whatever new level of justice may emerge from a conflict, it will be less than the vision of perfect justice that inspired the challenge. It will not bring in the kingdom. It could even contribute to new forms of injustice. Such possibilities, however, should not lead to inaction. Without martyrs like Bonhoeffer, we might live under the illusion that a kingdom of this world is the Kingdom of God in embryo and forget that there is a fundamental contradiction between the two. Without prophets like Joel and Isaiah, we might forget that each moment of history is always open to better and higher possibilties. Without statesmen like Churchill and FDR and other always flawed and fallible men and women we entrust with the authority of government, willing to risk turning plowshares into swords when required, we might allow the vision of the Kingdom of God to become a luxury of those who can afford to accept present injustice because they do not suffer from it.

That is one part of a possible answer to the question of what the Christian faith offers in the darker moments of history. Another, however, is even more fundamental. It is found in today's second lesson, from 1 Peter. "By his great mercy he has given us a new birth into a living hope through the Resurrection of Jesus Christ from the dead and into an inheritance that is imperishable — for a salvation ready to be revealed in the last time."

This is a picture of the Christian drama of salvation, a *new birth* into a *living hope* and into an *imperishable inheritance*. It speaks not of any progressive human triumph of good over evil but of God's great *mercy* in the midst of the perennial struggle of good and evil. It speaks not of the gradual eradication of tragedy in human history but of the *living hope* in the midst of tragedy, given to us by the Resurrection. It speaks not of the solution to the contradictions of human existence but of those contradictions being swallowed up in the life of God himself, the God who has redeemed us and who has prepared for us an *imperishable inheritance,* ready to be revealed in the last time. In the words of the old prayer book, "as we joyfully receive him for our Redeemer, so we may with sure confidence behold him when he shall come to be our judge."

The intermingling of good and evil, order and chaos, love and hate in the world may indicate at one moment in history the wisdom of plowshares and pruning hooks, at another the wisdom of swords and spears. Usually it is a mix, and one function of politics is to find the right mix for the occasion. Today we rejoice at the velvet revolution in central and eastern Europe. But at the same time we watch with trepidation the revival of ethnic rivalries, blatant anti-Semitism, and civil war in the same area. Today we rejoice at the seeming demise of totalitarianism in the old USSR and the growth there of political freedom and a free economy. But at the same time we watch with trepidation the disintegration of the Soviet empire into ethnic and religious enclaves that are not economically viable and that could result in major nuclear proliferation. Today we rejoice in the unilateral U.S. proposal for the elimination of at least some forms of nuclear weapons, and the equally positive Soviet response, of real beating of swords into plowshares. But we watch with trepidation the increasing nuclear capabilities of Iraq and the growing violence or political regression in places like Yugoslavia, Myanmar, Liberia, Sudan, Zaire, China.

Clearly we do not live in God's perfect kingdom. Those latter days of which Isaiah spoke, when nation shall not lift up sword against nation nor learn war anymore, are not here in their fullness. The limited and unsatisfactory moral choices available in such a world may be unacceptable to those guided solely by the vision of a world without violence, without swords and spears.

In one of our prayers for peace, however, we pray, "Eternal God, in whose perfect kingdom no sword is drawn but the sword of righteousness, no strength known but the strength of love; so mightily spread abroad your Spirit, that all people may be gathered under the banner of the Prince of Peace, as children of one Father." *That* is the *living hope* into which we, in this less than perfect kingdom, have been reborn through the Resurrection of Jesus Christ. *That* is the *imperishable inheritance* that is ready to be revealed to us in the last time, the time of his coming in glory. In that we have sure confidence. The God revealed in Jesus Christ is *both* our help in ages past *and* our hope in years to come; he is *both* our guide while life, with all its ambiguities about swords and plowshares, shall last *and* our eternal home.

23. Commitment
AN ORDINATION SERMON
Donald Macleod

For their sakes I consecrate myself, that they also might be
consecrated by the truth.

—John 17:19

It is reported that during a visit to the campus of Harvard University several years ago, Billy Graham asked President Bok, "What in your opinion is the greatest lack in the mind-set of students today?" And Dr. Bok replied, "A sense of commitment."

Whenever we sing Frances Havergal's great hymn, "Take My Life and Let It Be, Consecrated, Lord, to Thee," I wonder how many of us pause to realize the risk we are assuming. Verse by verse we offer some one of our capacities or powers to God's exclusive use. We sing,

> Take my hands, and let them move
> At the impulse of thy love.
> Take my feet, and let them be
> Swift and beautiful for thee. . . .
>
> Take my voice, and let me sing,
> Always only for my King.

and so on, until in the final stanza, as a sort of summary, we add,

> Take my-self, and I will be
> Ever, only, all for thee.

Donald Macleod was born in Nova Scotia, Canada. Dr. Macleod was the founder and first president of the Academy of Homiletics and until 1983 was Francis L. Patton Professor of Preaching and Worship at Princeton Theological Seminary in Princeton, New Jersey. He is the author of ten books in the field of preaching and worship.

Can anyone sing such a hymn honestly and sincerely and ever presume to be the same again? For here is seemingly a yardstick by which we can measure the dimensions of our consecration; here is suggested how far we are ready to go with God; and here we sense the degree to which on occasion we are apt jealously and selfishly to hold back.

One day Philip de Neri, the sixteenth-century Italian mystic, was crossing the campus of a European university and he fell into conversation with a young man who was entering upon his studies in the field of law. "When you have completed your course," asked Philip, "what then do you plan to do?" "Why," the boy replied, "I shall seek to build up a wide reputation." "And then?" remarked Philip. "Well," the student replied, "I shall seek promotion to high office, earn money, and become rich." "And then?" continued Philip. "I hope to settle down," the boy replied, "and live in comfort, wealth, and dignity." "And then?" persisted Philip. "And then? And then?" the student stammered, "I suppose I shall die." And now Philip raised his voice and asked, "*And what then?*" The young man made no answer; he simply turned away.

Do not these instances suggest the tremendous responsibility God has placed into our human hands? Think, for a moment, of what is our right, our distinction, and privilege as members of God's human creation! Ours is the ability, yea the liberty, to rise to the heights of our own self-consciousness and from that vantage ground to examine ourself, evaluate our worth, and come to grips generally with the issues of our destiny. At the same time, however, this can constitute our biggest problem, for each of us can have herself or himself on our hands and the whole aim and business of our life can be summed up in one succinct question: Well, what am I to make of myself? Jesus said concerning his followers in his great soliloquy on the eve of Calvary, "For their sakes I consecrate myself, that they also might be consecrated by the truth." Now, each of us has the same two pronouns, *I* and *myself,* and the important question confronting us is, What word shall I place in between them? Too many will choose a word that focuses upon themselves alone, and hence the words *I* and *myself* are brought too closely together, which leads to either of two unfortunate results: either we worship ourselves or we retreat into and plaintively excuse ourselves. Some will take the word *glorify,* and the whole motto and slogan of their lives becomes "I glorify myself." While some others may take the word *excuse,* and hence the whole pattern of their living is colored by "I excuse myself." But Jesus said, "For their sakes I consecrate myself," and his inference is that this word takes us out of ourselves and points us to a reality above and beyond ourselves. This, therefore, is the kind of life he would have us all follow, appropriate, and support.

Let us look now more closely at our text and see what are its implications for this vocation we celebrate on this significant occasion.

I.

The first thing we note is that *the consecrated life is a concerned life.* Jesus said, "For their sakes I consecrate myself." His was always a serious concern for others, and a reading of the Gospels indicates how his very heart went out to the sick, the poor, and the underprivileged who had lost their way. In this he differed so radically from the other religious leaders and thinkers of his day, especially a group of philosophers called Stoics. These scholars believed in creating a desert in the human heart so that an attitude of "I don't care" colored any reaction they might have to cases of human need and helplessness. And one of the chief words in the Stoic vocabulary was the Greek term αεαθεια, from which comes our English word *apathy,* meaning a state of life in which the flame of sympathy had flickered out and was replaced by a grim sense of self-reliance and self-control. As William Barclay remarked, "The aim of the Stoic was to banish sympathy from life."

But Jesus said, "For their sakes." And here he indicated the greatest spiritual principle by which anyone of us can live. It is the principle by which we invest all we are, all we have, and all we can ever be into the spiritual well-being of others and into the realization through them of some high and sacred cause. And this principle cuts straight across the way of life of those twentieth-century Stoics we meet every day: those people in whose lives the springs of love, pity, and human concern have become dried up and a narrow individualism suppresses their sensitivity to the needs of others. Indeed no person can reach the highest fulfillment of God's will for his or her life until all the ambitions and ideals of their inner nature are baptized into the name of Christ and, under the aegis of his Spirit, are used in devotion to the needs of all humankind. Robert Southwell once said, "Not where I breathe, but where I love I live." And love is the partner of consecration, for when men and women love sincerely they truly care, and in God's service the outgoings of their lives are for somebody else's sake. The reality of our consecration is always tested by the quality of our loving concern. Jesus had this in mind when he said to his disciples, "Inasmuch as you have done it to one of the least of these my brothers, you have done it to me" (Matt. 25:40).

II.

A second thing we note is that *the consecrated life is a controlled life.* Originally, "to be consecrated" meant to be set apart for divine use. It implies, therefore, being set apart *to* something and *by* something. Here Jesus names *truth* as the all-embracing agent that should claim his followers once they were chosen. Now truth, it must be understood, is not an object. As John Baillie pointed out, "Truth is *the truth* with reference to something." And what Jesus came to do was to proclaim the truth about God and in his own life to show us the truth about human nature. Human God-likeness in its truest form is seen in Jesus, and when we turn away from him, we are apt to see humankind only at its poorest and worst. Seven evenings a week our TV stations bring us stories of shame and horror by which—as Robert Baker of the *New York Times* said—"we uglify the beautiful." The New Testament, however, shows us the truth about human nature as it came alive once and for all in a Person, and its very essence was love. This is the heart of the gospel, and Paul stated it well when he wrote, "God was in Christ reconciling the world to himself" (2 Cor. 5:19).

Moreover, Jesus' followers then and now must find the fulfillment of their lives in and through that gospel, and once they accept it, it will control their whole being and always for someone else's sake. This is not, however, some dry-as-dust biblical or theological theory; this is history. Look at it this way: One day a young Oxford don chose Christ, and eventually, through the consecration of John Wesley, the whole course and current of English history was changed. One day a young Boston shoe salesman chose Christ, and in time, through the consecration of Dwight L. Moody, this North American continent throbbed with the spirit of his evangelism. One day a young factory worker in Blantyre, Scotland, chose

Christ, and soon, through the consecration of David Livingstone, the heart of parts of central Africa became sensitive to the higher levels of moral living. And one day a young Roman Catholic girl in Albania chose Christ, and today, through the consecration of Mother Teresa, hundreds of houses of charity reach out to the starving, the destitute, and the lost throughout the world. We see, then, that theirs was a concerned life, but its secret was that they were claimed by the gospel; they were under its control. And their prayer could very well be that of Jeremy Taylor when he prayed, "Let my body be servant of my spirit and both my body and spirit a servant of Jesus Christ."

III.

A third thing we note is that *the consecrated life is a committed life*. When our life is fully consecrated, we have a new concern; we are under a new control; but the quality of it all depends upon the depth and vitality of our personal commitment to Christ.

Many years ago a young man went out from the town of Devon, England, to become a shipmate in the fleet of Sir Francis Drake. Once on a visit back home he met on the street an old schoolmate who had grown rich, fat, and lazy upon the land. He turned to the sailor and said, "Well, you haven't made much of all these years, have you?" "No," said the sailor, "I guess I haven't. I've been cold, hungry, shipwrecked, and often I've been dreadfully frightened. But don't you forget: I've been with the greatest captain who ever sailed the seas!"

Consecration! Yes, it can be a glorious adventure, but at the same time it can be also the costliest thing in all the world. Yet in every age it has been this decisive commitment to the person of Jesus Christ that has engaged the dauntless spirits of countless men and women and sent them out across the seas and into the jungles and over the mountains with banners emblazoned with these words: "For his sake and theirs."

Speaking of St. Paul and his personal commitment, the late James S. Stewart of Edinburgh put it this way:

> The great frowning mountain ranges of Asia were
> no barrier to this man, for beyond them people
> were dying without Christ. Down to the shores of

the Aegean Sea he came, and on the winds from
across the Western oceans he heard dimly the cry
of thousands without hope and without God.
Always as he turned his gaze toward Corinth or
Rome or Spain, the Christ in his heart was
yearning with a great compassion for the sheep
who were without a shepherd. Always within him
was a driving sense of an unseen compulsion:
Necessity is laid upon me. Woe is me if I preach
not the gospel. This was one man's commitment,
and although it carried him to stoning, shipwreck,
imprisonment, and death, yet he could say, "I
count all things but loss for the excellency of the
knowledge of Christ Jesus my Lord."
(Phil. 3:8, KJV).[1]

How small you and I can appear in the face of all this! How
trivial can be our life's story if we merely snatch at bits of things
wherewith to glorify ourselves or raise barriers behind which to
excuse and hide ourselves! But then someone among us commits
himself or herself 100 percent to Christ and the causes of humankind, and so each lives, toils, and prays until God's job is done, and
finally, with a shout of victory on life's last horizon they say, "We
may have lost everything in life's voyage, but we have been with the
greatest Captain who ever sailed the seas!"

NOTE

1. Paraphrasing *passim* from James S. Stewart, *A Man in Christ*
(London: Hodder & Stoughton, 1954).

24. A Sermon at the End of the Summer University Institut Kirch und Judentum Berlin
Sanford Ragins

I want to thank Dr. von der Osten-Sacken for the honor of being the speaker at our worship service today. It is a privilege for me to stand here at this hour, as we conclude our week of study together. And it is also, I believe, a symbol with powerful significance.

As you may know, the synagogue in Los Angeles that I serve is named after Rabbi Leo Baeck. When our congregation was established in 1948, just three years after the war, our founders sought a name that would assert something about the times in which we live, about our fears and our hopes and especially our visions. And

---

Sanford Ragins is Senior Rabbi of Leo Baeck Temple in Los Angeles, California. He is the author of *Jewish Responses to Anti-Semitism in Germany Before World War I*. Ragins received his Ph.D. from Brandeis University and M.A.H.L. from Hebrew Union College. He has been active in many religious and community affairs and is presently serving on the Racial Harmony and Ethnic Discourse Action Task Force of Rebuild Los Angeles.

This sermon was delivered at an interfaith service in Berlin, Germany. The congregation was made up largely of Lutheran seminarians who were completing a course of study at the Summer University of the Institut Kirche und Judentum of the Evangelical Church. The synagogue that Rabbi Ragins serves is named after the leading Reform rabbi of Germany during the Nazi period.

so, after much consideration, they settled on Rabbi Leo Baeck, the teacher of Theresienstadt, a leader of the German Jewish community in its darkest hour and, for many years, in a synagogue not far from where we gather today, a rabbi and teacher here in Berlin.

Hence for me to be here today as a rabbi from the synagogue named in his honor, to speak to a Christian community in his city, is very moving. There are ghosts here in the chapel with us at this hour. The spirits of our ancestors are with us now, listening to us and watching with "old eyes."

Old eyes. That is Leo Baeck's term. We are told that one Shabbat afternoon in the 1930s, after Hitler had come to power, Heinz Warschauer came by to visit Leo Baeck at his apartment overlooking a park in Berlin. This is how Leonard Baker recalls the meeting in *Days of Sorrow and Pain:*

> Warschauer had returned from Palestine where he
> had witnessed Arab-Jewish riots. The newspapers
> were filled with news of the civil war in Spain,
> representing another triumph of fascism. Outside
> in the streets the specter of Nazism hung over the
> city he had loved. In Baeck's study, after the
> sponge cake had been eaten and the tea sipped,
> Warschauer poured out his feelings, his concern
> for the future, to the sympathetic Leo Baeck.
> When he was done . . . Leo Baeck looked carefully
> at him and said: "Hitler and his like cannot turn
> back history. We Jews will suffer. Some of us may
> die. But we will survive. *'Wir Juden haben alte
> Augen.'* We Jews have old eyes."

That was half a century ago, and Baeck has been proven right about the suffering and the death, about Jewish survival, but also about our vision. "We Jews have old eyes." I think he meant that when we look out into the world and into the future, even in a time of darkness, what we see is always shaped by that which we have already seen. A people with "old eyes" has the gift of perspective and a special kind of vision so that everything we see, the shadows and the sunlight, has a unique luminescence that glows with comfort and at the same time forces us to humility.

Today one could say in the spirit of Baeck's insight, "We Jews— and also, we Christians—have old eyes. People of faith, even in these tumultuous days in the last decade of the twentieth century, have the gift and the burden of our ancient traditions. When we look out on the world around us, on the lives of the people we serve and into the hidden recesses of our own souls, we see what human beings have always seen, all the complex, highly ambiguous stuff of reality: love and hate, liberation and slavery, fulfillment and suffering, persecution and injustice, war and misery, and, sometimes at the same moment, human courage and dignity beyond belief.

In our era both the blessings and the curses of civilization have intensified, and the contradictions of existence are perhaps more evident than they have ever been. But the ancient words of the preacher Kohelet still echo: "There is nothing new under the sun" (Eccles. 1:9). For to be a serious Christian, a serious Jew today is to be imbued, to the core of our souls, with powerful memories that shape who we are, what we do, and especially what we see. Those memories are not always pleasant, nor are they, in a superficial or trivial sense, always comforting. But they haunt us inexorably, and when we are tempted to live in and for the moment, they reassert themselves, with stubborn insistence, to remind us whence we come, who we really are, and what is expected of us.

Take for example this midsummer season for us Jews. At the end of the Sabbath last week we joined our brothers and sisters around the world in the commemoration of Tisha B'Av, the ninth day of the month of Av, perhaps the saddest day in the Jewish calendar. According to tradition, on that day three of the most horrible catastrophes in the life of Israel took place. First, on that day in 587 B.C.E. the Babylonians destroyed the first temple, the Temple of Solomon, in Jerusalem. And on that same day, centuries later in the year 70 C.E. Titus's Roman legions stormed through the last defenders on the Temple Mount. They set fire to Herod's Temple, reduced it to ashes, and left only one retaining wall, which still stands, a mute testimony to the horrors that took place there. And finally, on that same day, the ninth of Av, in the year 1492 the Jews of Spain were expelled from the land that had been their haven and their home for centuries.

And now, right after Tisha B'Av, comes this Sabbath that will begin soon with the setting of the sun, a Sabbath with a special name: *Shabbat Nachamu,* the Sabbath of Consolation. It is called that because of the Haftarah, the special reading from the Prophets that is read on this Sabbath. Tomorrow morning we will listen to that magnificent passage from the beginning of Deutero-Isaiah: "*Nachamu, nachamu ami,* comfort ye, comfort ye, my people, saith your God. Bid Jerusalem take heart, and proclaim unto her, that her time of service is accomplished, that her guilt is paid off; that she had received of the Lord's hand double for all her sins" (Isa. 40:1–2).

At first glance, the pattern seems clear. Suffering is followed by consolation; punishment, by forgiveness. Those whom God has cast out are brought home once more. But the paradigm of tradition is more complex and more subtle. Consider this: On every *Shabbat Nachamu,* every Sabbath of Consolation, just before we read these comforting words of Isaiah, we are commanded to read a passage from the Torah, from the Book of Deuteronomy, some words from Moses that, unexpectedly, sound a highly discordant note. (The same passage was read last week on Tisha B'Av itself.)

Moses is near his death. He knows he will not accompany the children of Israel into the Promised Land, and as he pauses with them in the land of Moab, before they cross the Jordan without him, he says to them, "Should you, when you have begotten children and children's children and are long established in the land, act wickedly and make for yourselves a sculptured image in any likeness . . . I call heaven and earth this day to witness against you that you shall soon perish from the land which you are crossing the Jordan to occupy; you shall not long endure in it, but shall be utterly wiped out. The Lord will scatter you among the peoples" (Deut. 4:25–27).

How strange! Last week we relived the suffering of our people, and when we enter the synagogue this Sabbath seeking consolation, we must listen to these harsh words of reproach and warning. We want Isaiah, but first we must hear Deuteronomy. And such is the message of our tradition: reproach and consolation, destruction and repentance, are inextricably intertwined. They cannot be separated. Not in the synagogue. Not in life.

Perhaps that is what Leo Baeck meant when he said, We Jews— and I add, also you Christians—have old eyes. Those who have old eyes are never completely deceived by the appearance of things. Midst despair, they know how to discern hope. And when others are convinced there is nothing to be worried about, they can read the ominous signs of approaching destruction and bring a message of reproach.

To see with old eyes. Has that not always been our challenge? And those of us who are chosen to teach and to lead, do we not bear a special responsibility to serve our people by bringing them, so far as we are able, the penetrating vision of our ancestors.

Here we must be, I believe, extremely careful. If the traditions of our people have brought light to illumine the darkness in human life, they have also been responsible—this we know full well—for much human suffering. When traditions become too rigid and impermeable to new truths, they stultify the human spirit instead of ennobling it. When religious communities, the church or the mosque or the synagogue, allow their vision to become narrow and deny the humanity of those who faith is different, then the blessing of sacred zeal becomes a curse. And when religious leaders and the institutions they serve are more concerned about maintaining the status quo than they are about using the life-giving values of their faith to reshape reality and society, when they become circumspect or cautious or timid, then, as the history of this century shows, darkness of the spirit is destined to descend upon the earth.

Leo Baeck himself taught us this when he wrote his essay "Romantic Religion." The book in which it appeared was printed but never published. Almost the entire edition was destroyed by the Gestapo, but a few copies survived, and it was reprinted after the war. Why did the Gestapo suppress this work? The answer is evident, for at the end of a section entitled "Humanity," Baeck wrote, "And a spirit is characterized not only by what it does but, no less, by what it permits, what it forgives, and what it beholds in silence."

Haunting words, these. A reminder that the work we do in our communities as religious leaders and teachers will be judged not by what we think or feel or even believe in our hearts, but by what moral horrors we permit without making an objection, by what ethical monstrosities we are able to forgive, and by what injustice and human misery we will behold in silence.

Human beings at all times desperately need comfort and sensitive wisdom in the search for meaning, especially in an era of broken symbols and failed gods. There is so much suffering, so much injustice, so much loneliness that pervades modern life, so much yearning for guidance in the struggle to live with depth, and so few resources in our culture for achieving community and transcendence. And thus there is for all of us much work to do.

We are told that about two thousand years ago, in Roman times, two rabbis, Rabbi Ishmael and Rabbi Akiba, were walking by the way when they met a sick man. Nearby they saw a farmer plowing his field, and Rabbi Ishmael called out to the farmer and asked him to go quickly to the nearest town and summon a physician.

And the farmer said, "Oh, rabbi of little faith, it is God's will that this man has become ill. If God wants him to die, he will die. If God wants him to live, he will live."

The rabbi was angered, and he said to the farmer, "What do you have in your hand?"

"A plow, of course," answered the farmer.

And the rabbi said, "Why do you interfere with the earth that God has created, O farmer of little faith? If God wants your crops to grow, they will grow. If God does not want your crops to grow, they will not grow. But what do you do? You plow, and you sow, and you water, and you weed, and you work. You enter into partnership with God in the work of creation. And so it is," the rabbi concluded, "with the physician who is partner with God in the work of healing. Now go and summon a doctor."

And as it is for the farmer and for the physician, so it is for us. We, not God, bear ultimate responsibility for the kind of world in which we live. And if we realize that this world is sadly imperfect, we should also know that God is simply not going to take care of it for us or without us. We must know that our destiny is in our hands and that we human beings still have, as we have always had, the capacity to choose between war and peace, between hate and love, between creating a society built on destructiveness and a society devoted to nurturing and protecting life.

"We Jews have old eyes," Leo Baeck said half a century ago, before most of us were born. We Jews, and also you Christians, have old eyes, sad and wise with visions of the ages. And because we have seen so much, we know there is much work for us to do. We know we must use our lives to bring some tenderness and some warmth, some justice and some peace into the cold universe to make it, at long last, a fit habitation for the human spirit. And we also affirm with calm conviction, against all odds and all evidence, that when we live this way, we are in harmony with the deepest purposes of Existence. When we live this way, Something Mysterious, Unnamed and Unknowable, is working in and through us.

25. Reflections of a White Southern Male

David B. Freeman

Jonah 3:10–4:11; Acts 10:9–16

They are kind of like sunglasses. Except instead of filtering sunlight, these experiences filter—sometimes distort—the way we perceive life, reality. If you live through the Great Depression, that experience is a filter though which you view the use of money. You can be assured that someone who has lived through the Depression will view money usage differently than one of today's young urban professionals. The reason is not the difference in age, that one is old and one is young. The reason is their experiences, the filters through which they see life.

Divorce is another filter. It shapes how you view relationships. A near-death accident or illness is a filter that affects your attitude toward life. Those deployed in Saudi Arabia now have another filter through which they see life.

We are learning more and more about the filters of our childhood. Children who grew up in the home of an alcoholic parent see life through that filter. The adult children of alcoholic parent groups that have burst onto the scene in recent years testify to the power of that long-unrecognized filter.

We all have these filters, some good and some bad, that shape the way we experience reality. Since today is Race Relations Sunday, I want to share with you three of my filters. I am a white

---

David B. Freeman is Pastor of Indian Springs First Baptist Church, Indian Springs Village, Alabama. A graduate of Southern Baptist Theological Seminary with both the M.Div. and D.Min. degrees, Freeman is active in ministries to the disabled community, especially exceptional children.

Southern male. When you see me, it's obvious that I am a white male. And when you hear me speak, it is obvious that I am a Southerner. We have a tendency to slow things and add an extra syllable or two to words. White. Southern. And male. These are three powerful, powerful filters, especially as they relate to race relations.

I'll confess that I am quite proud of much of my Southern heritage. I have such fond memories of growing up in the heart of the Deep South. Those memories are kindled when I read the writing of some of the South's great literary figures: Flannery O'Connor, William Faulkner, Eudora Welty, Walker Percy, and others. If you were to walk into my home, you would see sitting on a table beside my recliner a book entitled *A History of Southern Literature*.

As I reflect upon my heritage, though, I am aware now that the life I took for granted and assumed was a universal norm, a way of life I was too young and naive to question, was shot through and through with a deep racial prejudice. I still have a vivid memory of the day when I could not get an answer to a question. "Is that true?" I asked. And nobody would say yes, and nobody would say no. So I interpreted the silence to mean yes. I asked that question—Is that true?—when I was told a theory about the origin of the black race. I honestly cannot remember who told me the theory, but I do remember the theory. It was based on the Bible.

You may remember that Noah had three sons: Ham (who is also called Canaan), Shem, and Japheth. Noah and each of his sons were saved, along with their families and two of every kind of animal, when the great Flood came upon the earth. After the waters of the Flood abated, the sons of Noah, Genesis says, repopulated the entire earth.

However, this ancient story says that one day Noah had too much wine to drink and became drunk. Somehow this Old Testament leader ended up in a drunken stupor lying naked on the floor of his tent. The Law commanded (Lev. 18:7–8) that one not uncover the nakedness of his father. Old Testament theologians suggest that to "uncover" is a metaphor for engaging in sexual intercourse. So to uncover one's father meant either to have sexual intercourse with one's mother or to engage in homosexuality with one's father.[1] The story from Genesis says that the son named Ham, also called Canaan, went into Noah's tent and "saw the na-

kedness of his father." When he told his brothers, they took a blanket and walked into the tent backwards, their heads turned so
as not to see their father's nakedness and covered him with the
blanket.

Noah woke from his evening of overindulgence and learned
what had happened. And this is the outcome. Noah said,

> Cursed by Canaan;
> a slave of slaves shall he be to
> his brothers.
> He also said,
> Blessed by the Lord my God
> be Shem,
> and let Canaan be his slave.
> God enlarge Japheth
> and let him dwell in the tents
> of Shem;
> and let Canaan be his slave.

I remember the day. I was bareback, barefoot, and wearing a
pair of frayed denim shorts. "The black people of the world are
the descendants of Ham," I was told. "They are Canaan. They have
been cursed by God. That is why they are black, and that's why
they are slaves. And you," I was told, "are the descendant of Shem,
and the blacks will always be your slave."

"Is that true?" I asked, and nobody answered. Nobody said yes.
Nobody said no.

But you see, kids have other ways of getting answers, and in
time I got a clear answer. My grandfather owned a little mom-
and-pop grocery store—McClellen's Groceries. Most of his customers were poor blacks in Anniston, Alabama. My grandfather did
something grocery stores don't do today; he delivered groceries.
Can you imagine calling 7–11 and asking them to bring you a loaf
of bread and a gallon of milk? Well, that's what my grandfather
used to do. And my two brothers and I accompanied him when he
made his deliveries.

Anniston is a lovely Southern town. Quintard Avenue, the main
street through town, is shaded by towering oak trees. Azaleas and
dogwoods provide a splash of colorful beauty in the spring. If you
turn east off Quintard Avenue, you go up on "the mountain," as we
called it. It was Anniston's aristocracy. The affluent whites lived on

"the mountain." If you turned west off Quintard Avenue, you went to where my grandfather delivered groceries. It was, as I was taught, where all the sons and daughters of Ham lived.

The curse of these descendants of Ham was evident immediately. People from large cities have seen urban poverty. Folks, I have seen Southern rural poverty that you might not believe exists. Most of the unpainted houses in this section of town should have been condemned by the county health department, if anyone at the county health department had cared enough. When my brothers and I carried the groceries onto the rotting porches, we walked around the holes and the planks that appeared dangerous. The screen doors were usually missing all or part of the screen and were barely holding together. Tiny dusty yards were scattered with nearly naked children, a few chickens, and usually an old lazy dog. Inside the house you could feel the wind blow during the winter. Coal fires kept the edge off the cold. The smell of turnip greens and collards often filled the air. Three pictures hung on the walls: John Kennedy, Abraham Lincoln, and Jesus. Today I'm sure Martin Luther King, Jr., is added to that list, but he was a newcomer to the scene then.

I remember that my grandfather would make his rounds in the early afternoon on the first of the month. He tried to get there just after the mail ran, when "checks" arrived. He would go to his customers' mailbox, take out their check, place an X on the back, and then sign his name. That's the way you had to cash a check if you couldn't write. Then he would take out the amount he wanted to be paid and put the balance back into the mailbox. Today my grandfather would probably end up doing time in prison.

You know what those early experiences gave me? They gave me the answer to my question.

What can a white Southern male possibly have to say to a multiracial congregation on Race Relations Sunday when his filters have given such a distorted perception of reality? What he would like to say is that, even though white, Southern, and male are powerful filters, there is a filter even more powerful. It is the filter of biblical faith. When I began a serious study of the Bible, I discovered that racial prejudice stands under the judgment of almighty God. I learned that those who used the Genesis story about Ham, Shem, and Japheth to promote some theory of origin for the black race had severely perverted the Holy Bible. I began to read about

Jonah, who was like many of the folks in the culture where I grew up. He hated the Ninevites just because they were Ninevites. And when God showed his good pleasure to them, Jonah was so consumed with anger that he wished to die. And I thought that that must be the outcome of all racial hatred.

I read about Jesus who came to women and men equally, who loved the culturally hated Samaritans as much as he loved the Jews. He even made these people, these victims of hatred, the heroes of some of his stories. Like the story of the Good Samaritan. Jesus ends that story by saying to his Jewish listeners that if they wanted to enter the Kingdom of God they must go and do like the Good Samaritan.

Then one day Jesus broke all the rules by asking a Samaritan woman for a drink of water. You see, Jesus broke down the prejudicial barriers of gender and race. And those who follow him are expected to do no less.

This was hard for Peter. God had to tell him in a special vision, which I read to you a few moments ago as our New Testament lesson. In the vision Peter saw a great sheet held by its four corners descending from heaven upon the earth. In the sheet were all kinds of animals and reptiles and birds. These were animals that according to Jewish Law were unclean. The Law prohibited the eating of these animals.

Peter heard the Lord command him, "Rise, Peter; kill and eat." Peter being a devout Jew says, "No, Lord; for I have never eaten anything that is common or unclean." The voice of God responds, "What God has cleansed, you must not call common." Three times this happened before Peter learned the lesson God was trying to communicate.

Peter did finally understand the lesson. You see, those animals in the vision represented all the people of the world whom his religion and culture told him were unclean. That belief—that his race was chosen by God and that all others were unclean—fueled an intense racial prejudice. It's not surprising, then, that some Jewish Christians in Acts believed that Jesus' death was for the Jews only. The Gentiles and Samaritans were like all those unclean animals. But God's Word came to Peter cutting like a two-edge sword: "What God has cleansed, you must not call common." That day Peter was given a new filter through which to see life.

The Bible's teaching on race relations is summed up in Acts

10:28. Peter is speaking here: "You yourselves know how unlawful it is for a Jew to associate with or to visit any one of another nation; but God has shown me that I should not call any man common or unclean."

That is what I want our church here in metropolitan Washington, D.C., to model for Prince George's County. This is a place of worship for all people, where no person is any more or less valuable than any other person. The way of Jesus challenged Peter. It challenges us. Biblical faith challenges all followers of Jesus to rise above racial prejudice of any kind and to work for racial justice. That is the filter through which we are called to see life.

That's the Word of God for us on this Lord's Day.

NOTE

1. Walter Brueggemann, *Genesis,* Interpretation Bible Commentary (Louisville: Westminster John Knox, 1982), 90.

26. Seeking My Place in a Nation at War
Thomas M. English

Romans 8:22–28

As I was leaving the office last Wednesday at 5 P.M., the secretary said, "Your son, Mike, is on the phone." When I answered the phone, Mike said, "Dad, the war has started. They're talking about it on the radio now." Mike and I had had lunch together the day before, and our conversation was about the situation in the Middle East. He had been reading about it and watching the reports on TV. I thought he might be concerned that, if war broke out and lasted very long, he might be drafted. He said, "No Dad. I'm twenty-eight, and twenty-six would be the upper age limit." I thought, my dad was thirty-four when he was drafted during World War II.

I had decided some time ago that there probably would be a war, but I was jolted, shocked, and saddened by the news. My feelings were mixed, my thoughts confused—how to respond, what to say, what to do?

I'm saddened by the thought of the victims, destruction, and suffering this war brings to all sides; the hundreds of thousands of our men and women in "Desert Storm"; and of what is happening to the Iraqi people.

The months of preparation and talk of war did not prepare me for the first announcement that bombs were falling on Baghdad. My thoughts went back forty-seven years to when I was in the

Thomas M. English is Senior Minister of Park Hill United Methodist Church in Denver, Colorado. He received his Master of Divinity from Iliff School of Theology and has served pastorates in Utah, Wyoming, and Colorado. English has also been a high school basketball coach and high school and college basketball official.

fourth grade. My dad was drafted, trained for ninety days, and sent to Europe. We did not know where.

Shortly after he arrived in Europe, one of the teenage boys in the little town of Plainview, Arkansas, knocked on the door and handed my mother a telegram. My mother began to cry. You don't get telegrams in Plainview. She opened the telegram, which read ". . . seriously wounded." He was hospitalized in England for six months before he could be sent back to the States. Then he spent more than a year in different hospitals before he was discharged and classified "totally disabled."

Here was a man with an eighth-grade education. He had been a farmer and then became a construction worker on a dam being built, which would flood the farm that he rented. When drafted, he was a cement finisher. His body was all he had. I'm sure most of his sense of worth was tied up with his body. Now it was shattered from the waist down.

Then my thoughts went to 1968. My younger brother and his family visited us. He was on his way to Vietnam for the second time. He was thirty-four years old. The army was his life. He retired recently with thirty years of service.

Then I thought of my first appointment after graduating from seminary in 1965. I was to start a new church in Boulder, Colorado. The city became divided, split over the war. There was anger and hurt. After six years, I was appointed to the United Methodist church in Laramie, Wyoming. There were problems in the church caused by differing responses to the war. I did not want this to happen this time at Christ Church.

Earlier this week this headline was on the sports page of the *Salt Lake Tribune:* "Sports Seeks Its Place in a Nation at War." I began to think: The church seeks its place in a nation at war; a minister seeks his or her place in a nation at war. Then I thought: seeking my place in a nation at war. How do I minister to and with my congregation in a nation at war?

As I began struggling with this question, I remembered an editorial in the *Christian Century,* May 11, 1988, by James Wall entitled "Beyond Blandness in Preaching." In the editorial he said that Ralph Waldo Emerson, in his 1835 address to the Harvard Divinity School, expressed his disdain for any preacher whose sermons "had not one word intimating that he had laughed or wept, was married or in love, had been commended or cheated or chagrined. . . ." Mr. Emerson went on to say about such a preacher: "The capital secret of his profession, namely to convert life into truth, he had not learned." The "true preacher," for Emerson, was one who deals out life to his people, "life passed through the fire of his thought."

So it is. So it must be. So I try to do, especially today. What can I say to you, this congregation, during this war? What can I do that converts life into truth, life that passes through the fire of my thoughts and intersects with you?

I know I am saying something to you, this congregation. I'm saying something about what I have heard life saying to me, about what I have heard God saying to me. But I'm afraid it is somewhat muddled.

Let me share with you a notice that was sent home with some high school students.

> Our school's cross-graded, multi-ethnic,
> individualized learning program is designed to
> enhance the concept of an open-ended learning
> program on the continuum of multi-ethnic,
> academically enriched learning, using the
> identified intellectually gifted child as the agent of
> his own learning.

One parent sent back a note that read, "I have a college degree, speak two foreign languages, and four Indian dialects, . . . but I haven't the faintest idea what you are talking about in this notice." I hope I'm not as muddled and confusing as this notice.

I want to do what I believe God is calling me to do, but I'm not sure what that is. I'm really not. I know I am called by God to be a peacemaker, but what does a peacemaker do in a nation at war?

I'm strengthened and comforted by the scripture I read a few moments ago. The Holy Spirit within us prays for us in our sighs and in our groans. God's words to Moses, when he called him to lead the children of Israel out of Egypt, really speak to me: "I see affliction; I hear cries; I stretch out my arms." God sees our crying, and there has been much of it. God hears our moans and reaches out to us.

My hope is that the Holy Spirit will lead and guide as I/we struggle with how we can maintain and strengthen the connections of mutual support in a church in a nation at war.

Questions! I live with questions!

How Do We Provide a Ministry of Love in a Church in a Nation at War?

How do we provide the nurture and support we all need—support for our men and women in Desert Storm? How am I to be a pastor to and give support to those in our congregation who have family members in Desert Storm; to be a pastor to and support those in the congregation who support the war; to be a pastor to and support those in the congregation who oppose the war?

How do we love? How do we affirm the other person without requiring that he or she agree with us? How do we come to realize that if they don't agree with us, they are not our enemy? We don't have to be afraid of those in our congregation who have views that differ from ours.

I will do all that I can to see that our congregation is not split asunder over the war and our responses to the war. I've been through that. I don't want to go through that again.

How Do We Provide a Ministry of Justice in a Church in a Nation at War?

We speak out against violence, poverty, and injustice that fans war's flames. We realize that peace is not a dirty word. We realize that if we don't agree with all the decisions of our president and other leaders, we are not unpatriotic. I love my country.

I am patriotic when, at times, I call into question what is being done. I would not have the best interests of my country at heart if I remained silent and did not speak out. We must realize that those who support the war are not to be considered unchristian. I hope we don't see the slogan "Love it or leave it" on bumper stickers.

How do we keep before us what Jesus taught and preached? "You have heard that it was said, 'You shall love your neighbor and hate your enemy!' But I say to you, Love your enemies" (Matt. 5:43–44).

What we have a tendency to do during war is to demonize our enemies.

I have been outraged at what Saddam Hussein has done and is doing to Kuwait, trampled by his oppression, exploitation, and injustice. I wanted to give economic sanctions and diplomacy at least a year. I was in a small minority. As I shared with you before Christmas, the polls showed that only 8 percent wanted to give sanctions a year or more.

Now that we are at war, I want to see peace with justice as soon as possible. Then we must find something to glue us together, something to fill out lives besides fear, hatred, and vengeance.

How am I to be a prophet and a pastor? That is difficult. It always has been so, but never more than when we are at war.

How Do We Provide a Ministry of Mercy in a Church in a Nation at War?

We provide a ministry of reconciliation—reconciling people to themselves, to others, and to God. We are to be reconcilers in a culture of conflict. We need to develop and maintain the capacity to forgive and be forgiven; to accept and be accepted; to care and be cared for; to comfort and be comforted; to support and be supported; to love and be loved.

There is much anger and hostility. I saw on television a woman pointing at peace protesters and saying, "These peace protesters killed my son." There are angry protesters protesting the war, and there are angry protesters supporting the war.

How do we show mercy, forgive, and reconcile? May we never forget that God calls us to be above hate and revenge. The Christian faith affirms that the final word about humankind and the world is not one of despair but one of grace and hope.

I pray that God will be with us in our groaning and in our sighing. I pray that peace with justice will come soon and that we will begin to heal creation. I pray for God's healing—healing the earth, healing history, healing the nations, healing us, healing me. I know that doxology comes out of our groaning.

I have more questions than answers. I think they are the right questions for me and for our church at this time. I would rather have the answers, but I will live with the questions.

In closing, let me say that I may not know where I am going, but that does not mean I am lost.

V. PASTORAL

27. The Community of Faith, Comfort, and Ministry
Wayne Oates

2 Corinthians 1:3–7

The sermon I have today focuses on the large number of senior adults in our church and in our nation. This is the fastest growing segment of our population. By the year 2020, just a short twenty-eight years from now, the typical family will consist of at least four generations—great-grandparents, grandparents, parents, and children. However, when I say that we are going to talk together about the senior adults in our congregation, that picks up everybody else in the congregation, because we senior adults are grandparents of little children and teenagers. We are aging parents who agonize over the chaos in the families of our married sons and daughters with children, especially adolescents. There are people in our church who are in their fifties and sixties caring for disabled older parents who are in their eighties and nineties in the home or in the nursing homes. So we are all in this boat together in a community of faith, a community of comfort, and a community of ministry.

In a lighter vein, the age sixty-five does not tell us when we are really old. Our symptoms, our disabilities, our behaviors, and our eccentricities do. For example, you are really old when you stop saying, "While you are up, will you get this for me?" and you start

Wayne E. Oates is senior research professor at the Southern Baptist Theological Seminary, Louisville, Kentucky, and professor of psychiatry and behavioral sciences at the University of Louisville Medical School. He has served as pastor of rural and urban churches in North Carolina and Kentucky and as chaplain of general and mental hospitals in Kentucky. He has written forty-nine books and edited twenty-five in the fields of psychology and pastoral care. Recent books are *The Presence of God in Pastoral Counseling; Temptation: A Biblical and Psychological Perspective;* and *Behind the Masks: Personality Disorders in Religious Behavior.*

saying, "While you are down will you pick that up for me?" You are really not old when you absentmindedly put the telephone book in the refrigerator instead of the cabinet beside it. A mother of three young children can do that! She thinks she is losing her mind. You are really not old though until you make a habit of placing the telephone book in the refrigerator and start demanding that the rest of the family do likewise. That is when you are old. Then pain has a way of telling you when you are old, especially pain that has decided not to go away. I awakened the other morning and had no pain at all anywhere. Now, I didn't think I was younger, I thought I was dead! The presence of pain lets me know that I am still alive!

Seriously, we know that we are old when we think that life is over for us, when we have lost curiosity, a sense of adventure, and interest in those people around us. Then we are old. We can become old at any age when that happens.

I am grateful for St. Matthews Baptist Church because I don't know of a more close-knit group of people ministering to each other than I find here in this church. Older people being supported and sustained by young people; and young people being guided and inspired by older people. So let's read our scripture together again. I'll just read verses 3 to 7 at this time: "Blessed be the God and Father of our Lord Jesus Christ and the father of mercies and all comfort." That is the community of faith. "Who comforts us in all our afflictions"—that is the community of comfort—"so that we may be able to comfort those who are in any affliction with which we ourselves are comforted of God." That is the community of ministry.

Let's take those one at a time.

The community of faith in God. Yes. But not just any ordinary old god. Not just any god. Our God is a God above all gods; the Lord of Lords. This God is the Father of our Lord Jesus Christ. He is not a vengeful, storm god who willingly and willy-nilly inflicts suffering upon us. This God visited us in our human form and suffered temptation, pain, crucifixion, and the opening of the gates of a new life for us. He is the God and Father of our Lord Jesus Christ, the Father of mercies and the God of all comfort. Now that word *comfort* comes from the same word from which the name of the Holy Spirit comes. The Comforter, the Counselor, the Paraclete, the One who is called alongside us—not over against us. He is our companion in suffering with whom we can converse and who never leaves us in our loneliness. Suffering isolates you and makes you lonely. The Holy Spirit comes to us and lets us know that God is with us and that we are not alone. He never comes over against us in condemnation but always comes alongside us in comfort and companionship and in conversation. That is the kind of God we have. That is the God that we place our faith in and that is the God that draws us together here on Sunday morning and Sunday evening. This is the God of love and of mercy and of comfort who comforts us in all our afflictions.

Robert Browning, in his long poem "Saul," has David, who is ministering to him in his depression, who is Saul's healer of his despair and loneliness, say, "Saul, 'tis weakness in my strength that I cry for to God. My flesh I seek in the Godhead. O Saul, it shall be that a face like my face that receives you. A man like me thou shalt love and be loved by forever. A hand like this hand will throw open the gates of life for you. O Saul, see the Christ stand." That is our God. That is the community of faith that brought us here this morning and our faith in this Christ/God who is Jesus, lays a hand like my hand upon us to comfort us. A man like me whom we can love and be loved by forever. This is the community of faith of the God of all comfort.

Now, let's look at *the community of comfort*. This leads us to the second part of the text. This Christ-like God comforts us in all of our afflictions. God comes alongside us in *all* of our afflictions. This God does not pick out a favorite few sufferers. He said, "In *any* affliction," be it massive business failure, a divorce, cancer, perpetual pain, whatever it is, Alzheimer's disease, Parkinson's, a broken hip that won't mend, AIDS. God is no respecter of people, nor is he any respecter of their diseases or calamities. Suffering is no respecter of persons either. Some isolate us from people more than others, such as chronic schizophrenia. But, as has been said, all human beings are more alike than they are otherwise. As William James said, "There is very little difference between us human beings. But what little there is we make an awful lot of." We are more alike than we are different. Thus God, the God of all comfort, makes us a community of suffering in any of our afflictions.

Now the third community—*the community of ministry*. God does not comfort us without a purpose. He does so that we may be enabled to comfort each other by means of the comfort with which he has comforted us. We learn from our sufferings. Jesus, it is said in the Scripture, learned obedience from the things that he suffered; so we learn obedience and discipline from the things that we suffer. This becomes a set of tools for us as we become sensitive and compassionate for all people who are in suffering. Whatever that suffering is, we become a community of comfort. The main meaning or purpose of suffering is to find a new purpose in life. I don't know of any better explanation of why people suffer than that we might become a comfort to those who are in affliction.

We older people have many, many sufferings. We face, first of all, the suffering of retirement from meaningful work. Then we face the issue of rebuilding a whole new system of habits and rituals and customs whereby our life will be meaningful. We face the issues of increasing disabilities of body and of mind. We face the possibilities of falling and breaking a hip or an arm such as a dear old friend and teacher of mine did two weeks ago. His birthday came up, and I always call him on his birthday, because he was my teacher and my friend. He was nine years older than I, but he became my mentor and my friend. I have copied much of my style of teaching and preaching and ministry from him. I thought he was on vacation. I tried to call him, but he was not there. I hoped as I wrote him a letter that he would be having a nice family gathering with his two daughters and their families. But then I got a call from his wife who said that he had fallen and broken a hip and an arm and was in the nursing home. These are just a few of the sufferings that older people face. But it is not just aged persons.

This is just the dark side of aging. The bright side comes in the message of the prophet Joel, in Joel 2:28. The Apostle Peter repeats it in Acts 2:17 in which he said, "I will pour out my spirit upon all flesh and your sons and daughters shall prophesy; your young people shall see visions; and your old people shall dream dreams." The bright side of being older is that we can mingle our dreams with the visions of people younger than we and we can cease to compete with younger people and become a person who inspires them and who mingles our dreams with their visions that they will be able to accomplish that which we are no longer able to accomplish. We can become their sustaining grace as they do the work of the Lord.

Then, too, there is our role as grandparents. You remember the story of Bill Clinton, in which he told of his father having been killed in an automobile accident just before he was born. Then as a wee, wee lad he had to be cared for by his grandmother and grandfather while his mother equipped herself to take care of him and to be a nurse. Then his stepfather, whom she had married, became a severe alcoholic and was very brutal to him. But the sustaining power in Bill Clinton's life was his grandfather. His grandfather became the tower of strength in the skipping of a generation. In his acceptance speech he said, "I want you to know my grandfather." We, as grandparents, quite often have to reach past inadequate sons or daughters to get to the needs of our grandchildren. That is one of the heaviest responsibilities one can possibly have. The community of the congregation is one in which visions and dreams all mingle together across generational lines, which provides sound, nonexploitative, nonbrutal friendship in our relationship to younger people.

I remember very well when I was sixty years of age. I had a mother and father of a fifteen-year-old bring their daughter to see me. She was having a great deal of trouble. She came in and sat down in my study. She was in her blue jeans, and she crossed her legs in her chair and butterflied her knees and legs. I greeted her and thanked her for coming to see me. She said, "Well, I have one question I want to ask you." I said, "Ask on, Marsha." She said, "Why is it that an old man like you is wasting his time talking to a young squirt like me?" I said, "That is a good question. Let me think on it." I thought a little while then said, "Marsha, you are fifteen, and I am sixty, and I am four times older than you. But when I am ninety, and I plan to be ninety with God helping me, you will be forty-five, and I won't be but twice as old as you are," and grinned. "But then I will need you to come to see me because I will be an old man and people will quit coming to see me. But I need all the friends your age I can get." She leaned back and said, "Old man, you are something else!" We were friends.

I had a call just yesterday from a person whom I had met when she was ten years old. Her father had killed himself with a pistol in the bathroom. She came home from school and found him. I followed this shattered young girl for four or five years. For the first year, every afternoon at five-thirty, I either stopped by her house for a minute or I called her on the telephone, or if I was in a plane somewhere I would write her a note and say, "It is five-thirty. I am here and I wanted you to know that you are not alone." She is thirty-three now, and yesterday afternoon we got a call, and she and her mother came to see us. It was a bit of ecstasy to see her grown and effective as a social worker in Seattle. It is a community of ministry. We search through our congregation, and include other people, and this is the most authentic kind of evangelism there is: that we will reach out to other people who never darken the door of a church and minister to them in their sufferings and become a comfort to them. This is the meaning of the gospel—a community of faith, a community of comfort, and a community of ministry. God help us. Let us pray together.

O Lord, our God and Jesus Christ our Lord, grant us as older persons to use our love to bless little children; to use our wisdom to have creative fellowship with the young. Grant us grace to be good role models and mentors for young adults. Empower us as we struggle alongside each other as older people and endow each day with a sense of mission in the service of our Lord Jesus Christ. Heal us with the joy of your presence. In the name of our Lord Jesus Christ we pray. Amen.

28. A Funeral Tribute to Jimmy Marius
E. M. Sherwood

Matthew 9:13–14; 25:40

We have not met here to extol the virtues of some great man whose life the world deems notable but rather to remember a child who experienced neither the joys nor the griefs of becoming a man, although he lived among us for sixty-five years.[1] I have known Jimmy for twenty-one of those years. He knew that I was the "preacher," his pastor, yet he always called me "Uncle Sherwood." Why? I have no idea, but I'm glad I never tried to correct him. I'm glad he felt that close to me.

Jimmy was different; *unique* would probably be a better word. I'm not sure he knew how unique he was. He seemed to accept himself as he was, apparently giving little heed to the opinions of others. There were times he seemed to think we were the "different ones" and considered us rather silly. Perhaps we may conclude that he belongs in the category of the "little ones" Christ spoke of. We may even consider him as being "one of the least of these." I'm not wise enough to know how much Jimmy understood about sin, repentance, faith, and salvation. But this one thing I am sure of: Jimmy trusted the Lord Jesus Christ with all of his heart, mind, and spirit. Jesus had some harsh words for those who would reject one of these "little ones": "better for him that a millstone were hanged about his neck, and that he were drowned in the depth of the sea."

Jimmy's needs were simple; it didn't take much to please him. Three things he wanted with him at all times. He took his Bible

---

E. M. Sherwood, a native of Tennessee, served as pastor of eleven churches in his forty-nine years of ministry. While pastor of Dixie Lee Baptist Church, Lenoir City, Tennessee, he was pastor of the Marius family.

with him everywhere, even to bed. He received a new Bible every Christmas, and even though he could not read, the old one was just about worn out. The second thing he carried was a pencil, unsharpened. He preferred striped ones. One Christmas, Virginia and I looked all over town trying to find him some striped pencils, but we couldn't. The third thing was a fan. Even on the coldest days you would see Jimmy sitting in church fanning himself. It may have seemed odd to others, but he seemed to get a lot of joy from it.

Jimmy loved the church and always knew when it was time to go to worship. He looked forward to "family night"; that was when everyone brought a covered dish, and we ate supper together. One icy, snowy Sunday morning Henry was afraid to drive on the slick roads and told Jimmy church services had been canceled because of the dangerous road conditions. In a little while Jimmy heard the church bell ringing and was so distressed about missing church that Henry carried him piggy-back up the hill, across the field, through the snow to church.

Jimmy loved to sing. It did not bother him that he could not harmonize with others, neither did it bother those who sat near him. His favorite song must have been "At Calvary," the song that Ella sang so beautifully a moment ago. He requested it to be sung every time he had an opportunity.

Some may think Jimmy's life was unproductive. On the contrary he unconsciously taught us many things: to be more compassionate toward the hurting, more patient with the weak, more tolerant toward the slow, and more aware of the feelings and needs of those we look upon as being less fortunate than we. Perhaps you could add many other lessons to these I have mentioned.

We are sad because of Jimmy's death; yet we are comforted because we know that Jimmy is not "different" anymore. John, the Beloved Apostle, reminds us "it doth not yet appear what we shall be: but we know that, when he shall appear, we shall be like him: for we shall see him as he is" (1 John 3:2).

Little was required of Jimmy because he possessed little. He could not discuss the profound subjects of life, death, and eternity. But you can, and because you possess much, much is required of you. Out there in eternity you will stand before the same God Jimmy is with today.

NOTE

1. Richard Marius is director of the expository writing program at Harvard University and a contributing editor for *Best Sermons*. He writes the following about his brother, Jimmy, the subject of this sermon: "James Henri Marius was a Down's Syndrome child. My mother and father moved to a farm at a place called Dixie Lee Junction in east Tennessee in 1930 so he could grow up in the tranquility of what was then a remote neighborhood. In time my family began attending the Midway Baptist Church, which adjoined one of our fields, and Jimmy—as we all called him—became a fixture there. He had only one desire, and that was to be loved; he was much loved by the family and by the community. He died on the night of December 23, 1991, and about three hundred people turned out for his funeral on the evening of December 26. As it happened, December 26 was my late father's birthday. My brother John and I commented to each other that it was in a way a good birthday present for Dad because our family and our community had fulfilled Dad's greatest wish, that Jimmy be loved and cared for as long as he lived."

29. Write This Down: A Prescription for Ministry

David Allan Hubbard

Then I saw a new heaven and a new earth;
for the first heaven and the first earth
had passed away,
and the sea was no more.
And I saw the holy city, new Jerusalem,
coming down out of heaven from God,
prepared as a bride adorned
for her husband;
And I heard a loud voice from the throne saying,
"Behold, the dwelling of God is with human beings.
He will dwell with them,
and they shall be his people,
and God himself will be with them,
He will wipe away every tear from their eyes,
and death shall be no more,
neither shall there be mourning nor
crying nor pain any more,
for the former things have passed away.
And he who sat upon the throne said,
"Behold, I make all things new."
Also he said, "Write this, for these words
are trustworthy and true."

—Revelation 21:1–5

David Allan Hubbard is president and professor of Old
Testament at Fuller Theological Seminary, Pasadena, California. He
was educated at Lutheran College in Oakland and Westmont
College in Santa Barbara; at Fuller Seminary, from which he
received the B.D. and Th.M. degrees; and at St. Andrews
University, Scotland, from which he received the Ph.D. in Old
Testament and Semitics. He is an ordained minister of the
American Baptist Churches of the U.S.A. Dr. Hubbard has authored
thirty-five books, including commentaries on several Old Testament
books.

The command is to *write this down* (v. 5).
A stronger mandate than Scripture's typical call to
    hear,
stronger than the *hear a father's instruction* of
    Proverbs,
stronger than the *hear this word* of Amos,
stronger even than the *hear, O Israel,* of Moses'
    creed.
Write this down is a more universal charge than
the modern order of "Tape it!"
There we have to take the right player,
guard against snarls in the tape,
haul our own source of power.
With delight I watched a TV tape of an
ethnomusicologist in Tahiti, capturing
exuberant outbursts of Polynesian music.
He had three mikes waving over the heads of the
    island singers
drinking in their melodies, harmonies, rhythms.
Then his battery pack went dead.
At the peak of their ecstasy the concert
droned to a halt.
He laid down the mikes, stopped the singers,
dumped a dozen AA batteries into the pack,
crawled back into the crowd of
brown-skin vocalists
and hoped to resume the wondrous moment
of uninhibited song.
The command is not to *hear* or to *tape* but to
write this down,
A more flexible and reliable way
of capturing the irreplaceable words.

There is no call here for the punching of a
    computer
perched like a lunch box on the lap.
Words of the One on the throne are too precious
to store on a disk
where only those who know the code
can retrieve them,
where moth and rust may corrupt
and viruses break in to steal.
Besides, this message
I make all things new
needs no revising.

The command is to *write this down,*
to take reed or quill in hand,
snatch a scrap of papyrus or parchment,
dip the pen in sooty ink and
write this down.
Spelling, grammar, legibility,
all speak of taking the message into our persons,
making it our own,
absorbing it into our minds and hearts
and senses—touch, sight, hearing,
even smell if we have the right ink.

The command is to *write this down.*
Make it your own and depend on it.
That's what it means.
Write this down, as God's finger wrote the Law,
the permanent record of his will for his people.
Write this down, as Habakkuk wrote God's vision,
to carry it with you
and read it on the run.
Write this down, as Baruch copied Jeremiah's words,
to survive the wrath of Jehoiakim,
to outlast the Exile in Babylon and Egypt,
to preserve words of judgment and hope
for generations following.
Write this down.

I.

Write God's pain,
God's pain of *separation*
from people he has created and loved,
from people who have been seduced by false gods,
or plagued by persecution.
God hurts to have us with him.
That's why he ordered Moses to build
a tent of meeting for his people.
That's why he sent the Son to camp among
us in human flesh.
God hurts to have us with him.
That's why he longs for the right time to
bridge the gulf of isolation.

"Behold, the dwelling of God is with humankind."
Write God's pain,
God's pain of *suffering*.
God hates tears.
Joy is the divine good gift.
God longs to wipe away all tears:
the tears of the poor who tuck their
children into bed hungry,
who live in fear of the dangers on the streets,
who knock in vain on the doors of employment
   offices
where signs read,
"No jobs available."
God loathes the tears of rage of those
whose frustration may drive them
to loot or maim.
He abhors the tears of loss shed by those
whose homes and shops are ravaged in the riots.
God yearns to make all things new
and aches to see the old order with
its blood, sweat, tears, and death
give way to the new—
the *"all things new"* that he has promised.
And he commands us to *write this down*.
Write God's pain.

II.

Write God's work.
God's list of hurts
forms the agenda for our work.
The new day is on the way.
Because we believe that,
we seek to live it ahead of time.
God craves to reconcile the human family to
   himself.
That craving frames our priorities:
The gospel of reconciliation,
the gospel of the renewed relationship,
is what we show and tell.
The theme of our lives is the wonder that
God wants us to belong to him
and be God's people who enjoy him as our Lord,

for all time and beyond.
God delights in easing pain.
We work to wipe the tears from the eyes of
the poor,
the oppressed,
the lonely,
the misunderstood,
the neglected,
the abused.
We bring touches of the new
to mourners at the graveside,
to orphans, widows,
aliens in a strange land,
persons shunted to the margins of life.
"I make all things new":
That promise sets our agenda for life.
We can never deviate from
that consuming call.
That's why we *write this down*.
Write God's pain,
and write God's work.

III.

Write God's song.
The words are trustworthy and true;
we hear God's heartbeat in them.
The words are trustworthy and true;
we find our missions in them.
The words are trustworthy and true;
we lift our voices to sing them.
The Book of Revelation is not only an
assemblage of visions,
it is also a collection of hymns,
hymns that celebrate the triumphs of the One
who sits on the throne and of the Lamb;
hymns that herald the conquest of the *old*,
and the inauguration of the *new*.
"All things new":
Write it down and sing it.

Bill Gaither had gathered a group of his fellow
gospel singers,

country-western types, old-timers who had served
  Christ
for scores of year.
All day they sang together and told the stories
behind their songs.
With craggy yet radiant faces, they sang.
Aglow with the joy of their music, they sang.
Tears streaming from closed eyes,
uplifted faces aimed heavenward,
hands stretched to God as they traced
the rhythms and melodies
of their tunes, they sang.
Songs like this, they sang:
"My heart can sing when I pause to remember
A heartache here is but a stepping stone
Along the way that's winding ever upward.
This troubled world is not my final home.
But until then my heart will go on singing.
Until then with joy I'll carry on,
Until the day my eyes behold the City,
Until the day God calls me home."
I heard the words, looked at the lined and
furrowed faces, and thought of what they
had been through.
Raised on little farms in the hollows of Appalachia,
fighting for survival on the treeless, dusty plains
of west Texas,
They learned to pick a banjo
riding on a bale of hay in a bumpy pickup truck.
Later they drove hundreds of miles between
churches in cars that burned too much oil
and wore tires thin too quickly.
They eked out a living on love offerings from
Depression farmers who had lots of love
and little cash to offer.
And they sang all the way, bucked up by the
hope that God would make all things new.
Year after year in churches, campgrounds, and
school auditoriums they sang,
dreaming of the new day, the better way,
the victory yet to come.
They wrote it down,
and then they *sang it*.

That hardscrabble life was
made new by their songs.
Our high-tech life promises to be
no less hardscrabble than theirs.
In fact
it may be an axiom:
The higher the tech, the harder the scrabble.
People's hearts yield no more readily to Christ's
    claims
in our day than they did in theirs.
Churches take root no more rapidly
in our soil than they did in theirs.
Emotional struggle is no less painful
in our situations than in theirs.
Family tensions carry no less anguish
in our homes than in theirs.
We face our own brand of the Great Depression:
The dearth of values,
the scarcity of caring,
the shortage of love that renews.
God's heart aches at least as poignantly now as
    then.
God's work of renewal has not been made less
    onerous
by anything our modernity has fashioned.
God's song still has to be sung with teary eyes
and hands that clutch at heaven for help.
That's why we in our decade need to
write this down,
write down God's true and trustworthy words:
Behold I will make everything new.
And till then the Voice persists:
Remember my pain.
Pursue my work.
Sing my song.

30. The Doing and Undoing of Ministry
Lloyd J. Averill

Philippians 2:1–4, 12–16a

By all ordinary measures, Christian ministry is simply an undoable calling.

In fact, I want to make my assertion even more blunt: Anyone who enters upon the calling of ministry, and anybody issuing a call to ministry, should not expect that calling to succeed.

I.

Just consider the traditional roles by which Christian ministry is defined: pastor, priest, prophet. What is it, for example, to be a pastor? Surely it is to bring the resources of Christian faith to women and men in whatever conditions of spiritual distress or spiritual excess in which they may find themselves, all across the spectrum of generations from infancy to age: conditions of death and birth, grief and rejoicing, failure and achievement, pain and ecstasy, cowardice and heroism, boredom and excitement, pointlessness and purpose. Where is the individual, woman or man, who is fully adequate for that?

Lloyd J. Averill is Senior Lecturer and Director of Continuing Education, Community Relations, and Development at the University of Washington School of Social Work in Seattle. A member of the United Church of Christ, he received his theological education at Colgate Rochester Divinity School. Averill has taught religious studies and has lectured at more than 150 colleges and universities.

The demand that a minister exercise competent caring across so broad a spectrum of human need, while at the same time keeping her own sense of spiritual and emotional balance, would be undoable enough if it were that ministry's only demand. But there is more. What is it to be a priest? Surely it is to be a sacramental person, trustee of those solemn acts that may become transparencies of the divine in our midst; acts in which we meet the gracious mysteries of our faith: the mystery of forgiveness, of new birth, of acceptance and reconciliation and healing; acts mediated by water and wine, bread and book, cup and chrism. And if the priestly impresses anyone as less demanding than the pastoral, perhaps because its essence lies primarily in certain ceremonial acts that one can learn to perform with reasonable facility, perhaps even with felicity, that may be because in our worship we are more content with smooth liturgical performance than with theophany, more comfortable with an absence than with a Presence.

Yet the first time Martin Luther stood before the altar as a sacramental person, in his trembling he nearly dropped the consecrated wafer as he spoke the words of the mass, "We offer unto thee, the living, the true, the eternal God." Later Luther wrote, "At these words I was utterly stupefied and terror-stricken. I thought to myself, 'With what tongue shall I address such Majesty, seeing that all men ought to tremble in the presence even of an earthly prince? Who am I, that I should lift up mine eyes or raise my hands to the divine Majesty?'"

Luther is by no means the only one to experience radical holiness. When Isaiah first caught the vision of God in the Temple "in the year that King Uzziah died," he cried out, "Woe is me, for I am undone." Even in this unsacrosanct moment of history in which we live—perhaps especially in such an unsacrosanct moment—who among us would dare to be a sacramental person, would dare to stand where radical holiness may be met, would dare to experience not only the undoable but his undoing?

And even that is not all, for beyond the pastoral and the priestly, the prophetic waits to make its own demands. What is it to be a prophet? Surely it is to tell the truth. So Frederick Buechner

> wonders if there is anything more crucial for the preacher to do than to obey the sadness of our times by taking it into account without

equivocation or subterfuge, by speaking out of our
times and into our times not just what we ought to
say about the gospel, not just what it would appear
to be in the interest of the gospel for us to say, but
what we have ourselves felt about it, experienced
of it. It is possible to think of the gospel and our
preaching of it as, above all and at no matter what
risk, a speaking of the truth about the way things
are.[1]

Yet who among us dares really to be the prophet: to say un-
varyingly to those to whom we are called to minister, What is the
truth, the whole truth, and nothing but the truth?

So ministry is, by the measures of its classic definition as pastor,
priest, and prophet, an undoable calling. Anyone who enters upon
a calling to ministry, or anybody that issues a call to ministry,
should not expect that calling to succeed.

II.

It is not only that the tasks themselves are inherently beyond fulfillment. That would be problem enough, but the situation is
worse. It is also that, in ministry, the evidence for whatever effectiveness we may have is frustratingly elusive. The fact is that we can
never know enough to know whether or not we have, in fact, even
approached success.

How, for example, is a minister to judge the success of pastoral
care in a situation of bereavement? How often does a pastor go
away from such a situation congratulating herself on having been
adequate to the needs of the bereaved? Oh, occasionally, perhaps.
It would be arrogant for me to assume that that never happens.
But more often, I think, the pastor goes away from the bereaved
wondering. Wondering about the bereaved one, "Why him, of all
people? He just doesn't deserve this. Come to that, why me, of all
people? What have I to give in the presence of such unspeakable
need? I'm not sure I can cope with another death in this congregation."

Or how is a minister to judge the success of his priestly min-
istration? He does not command the presence of the Holy Spirit in
worship. He is merely a preparator of that Presence. Whether or
not the worship he plans works in any profoundly spiritual sense

is not his to determine. He does not control the efficacy of the sacramental mysteries given to his ministry. He is merely the steward of those mysteries. Whether or not acts of baptism and eucharist, of forgiveness and reconciliation, of prayer and proclamation actually work in any profoundly spiritual sense is simply beyond his power to manipulate. In short, as nothing that he is given to do as priest is his to withhold, neither is it really his to confer.

And how is a minister to judge the success of her efforts at prophetic truth-telling? Not, clearly, by what members of the congregation tell her as they leave the church on Sunday morning after shaking the pastoral hand in what I have sometimes called, cynically, the "perjury line." For the sake of our own psychological balance, our own spiritual health, we ministers dare not permit ourselves to believe that there is any correspondence between the niceties that are mouthed there and the degree to which our words have penetrated to the places where those nice people really live. When someone in that line says to me, after I have spoken words intended to disturb and rearrange, "That was a lovely sermon—and I could hear you all the way to the back pew where I always sit," I must suspect that no real hearing occurred. And my inner response is not gratitude for a well-intended compliment but despair at the opportunity apparently lost to truth—lost to that now-departing one and to me. More than one would-be prophet has left the congratulatory flattery of that postpartum ritual at the door of the church with an enormous sense of failure, ready to weep because it is almost impossible to know whether any who passed that way had really heard the truth she sought to speak.

So clergy and laity alike need to understand that Christian ministry is an inherently undoable calling and that the evidence even for a limited effectiveness is fugitive.

III.

And so far I have only touched on the good news! The bad news is that, however undoable it may be, and however it may frustrate the efforts of those who practice it to get even a relative fix on their effectiveness, it is nonetheless an absolutely imperative calling. Nothing is more important—nothing! Of course, other vital callings have been established in the providence of God to keep human life human and to make the human more humane. Yet with all due respect to those admirable callings, nothing is more important than mediating, in acts of imitative compassion, the reality that you and I are sought beyond our seeking, loved beyond our loving, forgiven beyond our forgiving, accepted beyond our accepting, valued beyond our valuing, believed in beyond our belief. What greater need is there for each of us, in this unrelenting and broken world, than to experience the possibilities for healing—for "wholling"—that are offered in that compassionate reality, even if it is only now and then that we experience it, and even if its pastoral mediator sometimes stumbles in offering it? Said the Italian dramatist Ugo Betti, "That's what's needed, don't you see. That! Nothing else matters half so much. To reassure one another. To answer each other. Perhaps only you can listen to me and not laugh."[2] That is what pastoral ministry comes to. Where else are we to go in the world except to that ministry, even with all its incompletenesses, not merely to know that reality but to be known by it?

Nothing is more important than naming the mystery. There is a mysterious darkness in the depths of our existence. At special moments we sense its movement beneath the external events that clutter our lives. We know that the mystery in our depth has power in us and over us; that, whatever proximate freedom we have, we are not ultimately free to order our own lives. Things happen that we have not planned, and planned things have not happened. From time to time mystery erupts in ways that baffle us, in events we cannot explain: sometimes in graces we did not know enough to choose, sometimes in tragedies we think we do not deserve. Does it have a will, that mystery at our depth, or is it merely the reflection of an unfeeling randomness at large in the universe? Is that movement within friendly or malevolent? Does it have power to heal or only to hurt? So at desperate moments we are driven to ask. And if silence should mock our questioning, then we are left prey either to superstition or despair. Christian ministry breaks the silence. Said Paul of Tarsus to those in his own time who had met the mystery, "You people of Athens are too superstitious. For as I passed by and beheld your devotions, I found an altar with this inscription: *To an unknown god.* The one whom you worship ignorantly I now declare to you and name with the Christian name. It is sovereign love that lurks in your depths, and if you would know that love and what it wills, look into the face of Jesus whom we call the Christ" (paraphrase). Naming the mystery is what priestly ministry comes to.

Nothing is more important than telling the truth. In this age of self-serving and empty rhetoric, of manipulation and disinformation, there must be at least one place to which we can go for a reality check if we are not to lose our bearings. There must be at least one place where, in all its ghastliness and glory, the truth is told—so help us God! That is what prophetic ministry comes to.

IV.

Finally, then, why would anyone in her right mind choose to do the undoable? The answer, of course, is that no one chooses ministry; rather, some are chosen by it. Anyone who presumes to choose it without having been chosen by it is likely to be of all persons most miserable, because the undoable soon becomes an undoing. When, however, we have been chosen by it, we do it not because we are compelled to but simply because we know it must be done, for all of the reasons we have just seen.

The problematic question is not why but how. How can one do the undoable? Not, let it be said at once, by following some of the counsel Paul gave to the Philippians. I suspect that more ministers have experienced a spiritually devastating burnout because they "esteemed others better than themselves" (2:3b, KJV), and were therefore unable to set limits to their ministering, than for any other reason. Jesus gave us a different model for ministry. Go back to the Gospels and see how often he said no when unreasonable demands were made. And he gave us a different standard when he called us to love others *as* we love ourselves, to value the good of others *with the same passionate concern* we show for our own good. It ought to be clear now, from the confirmation modern psychology gives to Jesus' injunction, that the ability to take ourselves seriously is the absolutely indispensable requirement for taking anyone else seriously at all.

"Do all things without grumbling or questioning," Paul advised the Philippians (Phil. 2:14, RSV). I say, "Stuff and nonsense!" Of course, ministers ought to grumble and question. After all, there is much that comes the way of a minister to grumble about and much to question, and to repress those responses is both spiritually unrealistic and spiritually unhealthy. The Jews, from the Old Testament on, have had an admirable tradition of arguing and disputing with God in prayer. That's the best place to take our complaints in any case. The example of Old Testament figures suggests that it is a great way to restore spiritual proportion, and it would be a healthy resource for Christian ministry as well.

But Paul also has some worthy counsel to give. How can one do the undoable? First, by recognizing that ministry is not ours but God's. Says the apostle, "It is God who is at work in you, both to will and to work his good pleasure" (Phil. 2:13, RSV). So it is, though in the midst of ministry's multiple demands we easily lose that perspective. We are only pastors; the Holy Spirit is the Comforter. We are only priests, not conjurers; it is God who reveals when and where God will. As prophets, we only tell the truth; it is God who persuades.

Second, we can do the undoable if we have a certain kind of confidence. Confidence enough to let God work in his own way and in his own time, of course, but another kind of confidence as well. If we never know enough to know that we have succeeded in ministry, neither do we ever know enough to know that we have failed. Ministry becomes doable only for those who have confidence in the intrinsic meaning and purpose and importance of those pastoral, priestly, and prophetic roles, whatever the evidence at the end of the day brings forth. No one who lacks that confidence need apply.

Disappointment and disenchantment often arise because we expect our own private egos to be gratified and fed by ministry, rather than practicing it out of a conviction that something useful is going on whether we know it or not, whether those to whom we minister know it and appreciate it or not. We can have that confidence because, in addition to our own working, "it is God who is at work in us both to will and to work his good pleasure."

Finally, there is a certain small miracle that makes it possible for us to do the undoable. Frederick Buechner is one who helps me still to be a Christian and a minister in spite of everything. Buechner tells us that there was a time earlier in his own ministry when he thought his faith could be secure only if God would perform at least one small miracle. So he prayed for it. But now, he writes,

> I believe without the miracles I have prayed
> for. . . . I believe because certain uncertain things

have happened, dim half-miracles, sermons and
silences and what not. Perhaps it is my believing
itself that is the miracle of my life; that I, who
might so easily not have been, am; who might so
easily at any moment, even now, give the whole
thing up, nonetheless by God's grace do not give it
up *and am not given up by it.*[3]

That's really what makes ministry doable. *We need not give it up
because we are not given up by it!* For God is at work in us, both to
will and to work for his good pleasure.

Thanks be to God!

NOTES

1. Frederick Buechner, *Telling the Truth: The Gospel as Comedy, Tragedy, and Fairy Tale* (New York: Harper & Row, 1977), 7.
2. Ugo Betti, "The Burnt Flower Bed," in *Three Plays.*
3. Frederick Buechner, *The Alphabet of Grace* (New York: Seabury
Press, 1970) 49. Emphasis added.

31. Forgiving Our Ex-Partner
Roger Fritts

Matthew 18:21–35

I am not a supporter of divorce as a solution to marital conflict. I believe that we who are married have a duty to make an effort to stay together. At their best, churches serve as support systems to encourage couples to stay together and work out their differences.

Yet I know that divorce is a complicated topic. I would never suggest that every couple should stay in a relationship, nor even that every couple with young children should stay married no matter what. Someone once said, "For every problem there is always a simple solution—and it is always wrong." I do not have a simple answer to apply to everyone except to say that if you go through a divorce, you are still a person worthy of being treated with dignity and respect.

I have a close friend who lives in another state. Several years ago his wife left him. I explained to him that I wanted to preach a sermon about divorce, but because I had never been divorced, I was not sure what would meet the need of the members of my congregation who had been through the experience. I asked him, if he were to come to church to hear a sermon on divorce, what would be most beneficial. He said, "I would find it most helpful to hear a sermon on forgiving my ex-wife. I have found that I am able to get on with my own life, to grow and move forward, only insofar as I am able to forgive her for leaving me. Inasmuch as I cannot forgive, I remain stuck."

Roger Fritts is Senior Minister at the Unitarian Church of Evanston, Illlinois. A graduate of Thomas Starr King School for the Ministry, Fritts has also served Unitarian churches in Massachusetts and Kentucky. He is completing a book on wedding services.

I decided I wanted to talk about forgiving our ex-partner. But as I started to do my research, reading and talking with people, I found that many people do not like the word *forgiveness*.

A woman said, "If you give a sermon on forgiving ex-husbands, you will hurt women more than you will help them. Telling me that I should forgive my ex-spouse, who hit me, who hit our children, and who took all our money to pay for booze, says to me that his abuse was inconsequential and unimportant. If you say I should forgive, I will get angry, feel guilty, and stop coming to church!"

A man said, "In the church I grew up in, every Sunday the minister's sermon ended with the same message. Whatever dilemma he was talking about, his conclusion was that it could be resolved by God's forgiveness. Like God, we were supposed to forgive. But when do you stand up and say that a spouse is wrong? Are there any limits? Aren't there some things a husband or a wife can do that are simply unforgivable? *Forgiveness* is such an overused word in Christian sermons that it has lost its meaning."

A woman said, "When I was a child, my parents told me that I should forgive my brother when he hit me or broke one of my toys. I said I forgave him, but deep down I was angry. Now I am an adult, and people tell me I should forgive my husband for leaving me, but I don't feel like forgiving. I feel enraged, furious, and irate. When you say forgive, I think, 'You didn't go through what I have gone through.'"

And a man said, "Preaching forgiveness is nonsense. If people take you seriously, they will lose their ability to assert themselves. People will stop setting limits with their ex-spouses, because you tell them they should forgive, and the ex-spouses will walk all over them!"

When a word has been overused, as the word *forgiveness* appears to have been overused, it sometimes helps to use another word. I want to take a step back away from the word *forgiveness*. I want to suggest that for a moment we don't worry about forgiveness. Instead, I want to talk about the word *understanding*.

I want to suggest that if we better understand our ex-partners, we may be better able to heal the pain inside us and to wrap up our unfinished business and put it behind us. In other words, we try to understand our ex-partners and our relationship with them, not as a favor to them, but so we can let go of the past and get on with our lives.

How do we understand our ex-partner? I suggest that we can look on it as a research project. We can look at the history and patterns in both our families. We can explore our memories of the relationship to better grasp what happened. We can read books about human behavior, and they may help us gain insight into our ex-partner. We can talk to friends and relatives who know us both or talk to people in the church who know us both, asking, "What were your impressions of our relationship? What do you think was going on?" If drugs or alcohol were a problem in the relationship, we can learn from attending a group like Alcoholics Anonymous or Al-Anon. We can weigh and sift through all the information we gather, trying to make sense of it.

In my own life I have discovered that I am able to understand others only insofar as I am able to understand myself. If I work hard at it, the attempt to better understand an ex-partner becomes an attempt to understand all the mixed-up thoughts and feelings inside me. I have to breathe deeply and let my feelings of anger and fear come to the surface. I have to write or talk about those feelings. I have to explore where those feelings come from in my history. I look again at my relationship with my parents, my brother and sisters, my friends, my teachers. The better I am able to understand myself, understand the sources of my feelings and my motivations, the better I am able to understand others.

As we understand more about what is going on inside us, we are better able to use our imagination to put ourselves inside our ex-partner and try to experience the world the way she or he does. With this understanding we are less likely to repeat the same patterns in a new relationship.

If we work on gaining self-understanding and if we use that self-understanding to better understand our ex-partner, it may be that somewhere down the line we will be able to write a letter or say face-to-face to our ex-partner, "I realize you tried to do your best in our relationship." I suggest that we might define this statement, "I realize you tried to do your best," as forgiveness.

In calling this forgiveness I am defining forgiveness differently than it is often defined. To explain how I am using the word, it helps to say clearly what forgiveness is not. In a book called *Forgiveness,* Suzanne Simon and her husband Sidney Simon give a list of what forgiveness is not, which I have put in my own words:

Forgiveness is not forgetting. Memories of the past and even the pain they cause have a great deal to teach us, so that we do not repeat the same pattern in our next relationship.

Forgiveness is not endorsing. By trying to understand our ex-partner, we are not saying that their actions were acceptable. True understanding cannot occur when we are in any way denying, minimizing, justifying, or condoning the actions that harmed us.

Forgiveness is not pardoning. When we try to understand our ex-partner, we are not exonerating them of responsibility for their actions.

Forgiveness is not a form of martyrdom. In truly trying to understand our ex-partner and what happened in the relationship, we do not repress our emotions. We try to get in touch with our feelings and learn from them.

When I say forgiveness I do not mean forgetting or endorsing or pardoning or martyrdom. I mean understanding.

Imagine saying to a man or a woman that you once lived with and tried to love and now are separated from, "I realize you tried to do your best." Being able to say this without the words getting stuck in your throat is what I call forgiveness. Some of you may be thinking: "I have studied my ex-partner. I know that he did not do the best he could. I know he could have done better."

Try thinking about it this way. Going through a divorce is a process of grief. What are you grieving? The loss of your wife or husband as your partner? Let me suggest that what we lose in divorce, and what we grieve, is not the wife or husband. What we have lost and what we grieve are the expectations we had inside us. We expected this person to be different than they turned out to be. We imagined that they would be more reliable, more reasonable, more trustworthy. When you say, "I know he or she did not do the best they could," perhaps you are really saying, "I refuse to let go of my expectations!"

The goal is to understand ourselves and our ex-partner well enough that we are able to let go of the expectations we had for the marriage. I am suggesting that when we say, "I know that she did not do the best she could," we are really saying, "I expected her to be a different person than she was."

When we study the life of another person, as we learn more about them, as we learn more about their relationships with their parents and their brothers and sisters, we gain greater understanding of who they are. Gradually, our expectations are replaced with an understanding that is closer to reality. I think this is a goal worth working for: to understand our ex-partners so well that we are able to look at them and say with sincerity, "I realize you tried to do your best." When we have reached this point, we are better able to move into a new relationship with someone else, having learned from the past. We are ready to risk love and intimacy again, without carrying inside us the baggage of anger and disappointment from a previous relationship.

I am a strong believer in marriage. But if you have gone through a divorce, know that here you will be treated with the same dignity and respect with which we treat everyone else. We work hard to make the church a support system for marriages. But if your relationship ends in separation, we will not make you feel guilty.

In a community where we are treated with dignity and respect we feel stronger inside. Feeling stronger, we are better able to try to understand ourselves. As we grow in knowledge of ourselves, we are better able to understand our ex-partners and our relationship with them. As our understanding grows, we may at some point be able to say to them, "I realize you tried to do your best." This, I think, is forgiveness.

32. Struggling with Our Mortality

Donald W. Musser

James 4:13–16

When we are young, we live as though we are immortal. We act as though we are without limits. We dream of breaking through impossible barriers, streaking beyond the established norms for humankind. Anything is within our reach. We believe that if you dream with desire, if you want it hard enough, if you work hard enough, if you concentrate your energies enough, you will achieve your goal, you will reach your destiny. A bookshelf of self-help manuals undergirds our belief. A dozen health-and-wealth preachers inspire us to press beyond our limits to become winners. Wily entrepreneurs sell us $29.95 videotapes containing an assured formula to guarantee material immortality.

And then, when we are lounging in our Lazyboy recliner, guzzling a can of RC Cola and munching on boiled peanuts, watching Robert Tilden's "Success for Life," a phone call explodes our very American myth into a thousand pieces. Oh, it may not actually be a phone call. But something awakens you from a deep slumber of innocence and naïveté to news that changes you forever: news of twisted wreckage and mangled bodies, a chilling message that a heart attack has slain a friend, or the agonizing announcement that

Donald W. Musser is Sam R. Marks Professor of Religion at Stetson University in DeLand, Florida. A member of the Cooperative Baptist Fellowship, Musser is a graduate of the University of Chicago and the Southern Baptist Theological Seminary. He is a chaplain in the U.S. Air Force Reserve and his sermons have appeared in *Pulpit Digest, Criterion,* and other publications.

your parents or children are parting in divorce. News that ties your stomach in knots and sets your heart pulsating out of control.

I vividly remember the day twenty-five years ago that I awoke to my own mortality. Having received a dramatic call from God to turn away from a career as a chemical engineer to prepare myself for the teaching and preaching of the gospel, I had resigned from a lucrative job with the Exxon Corporation and U-Hauled with my bride of less than a year to the mother of all Southern Baptist seminaries. (A Yankee by birth, I went to Southern Baptist Theological Seminary by the grace of God.) Shortly after completing my first year of study, and on the day after my twenty-third birthday, I entered Kentucky Baptist Hospital where a clavicular biopsy and a battery of blood tests revealed that I had lymphoma, an inoperable cancer of the lymph glands. Innocence and naïveté and unbridled idealism died that day. The ancient words of the writer of James became for me a personal and existential reality: "You are like a puff of smoke, which appears for a moment and then disappears" (James 4:14b). I have not disappeared yet. I learned in that valley of the shadow how fragile life is. Daily, I give gratitude for the chemotherapy that killed the cancer cells and to the Grace that has kept the smoldering invader in remission for a quarter century. To be sure, the illusion of immortality beckons me no longer.

All of us, some early in life (like the passionate teenagers who find themselves pregnant at sixteen) and others later (like the privileged and pampered college freshman who has never washed or ironed her own clothes) awaken to the fact that we do not command the universe. We live in an imperfect world where the threads of drudgery and sorrow are woven into the fabric of life. We learn that reality is laced with tragedy; that the powers of death fester in every human achievement, threatening to swallow every breath of life.

How do we live in a world that bears within it the dissolution of every achievement? How do we cope when we set our sights high, only to have some inane, unplanned catastrophe dash our hopes? How do we understand our mortality? At least three paths are open to us: the path of illusion, the path of despair, and the path of the gospel.

The path of illusion effectively denies our mortality: We live as though we will never die, as though we can't die. Nothing illustrates this more clearly than the cult of youth that pervades our culture. Teens believe they are immortal. If they were honest with us, every teen in this congregation could tell us of harrowing experiences within the past month where they could have been maimed or killed or had their reputation ruined. But adults should not agree with this assertion so smugly. On every hand adults battle the aging process. We hide the gray with Grecian Formula; we gulp megavitamins; we sweat with Richard Simmons; we eschew biscuits and gravy and gnaw on carrots and broccoli. If we are affluent, we spend thousands to streamline the wrinkles in our faces and to suck the celluloid from our thighs and buttocks. We groan our way to the spa wearing a T-shirt that announces, "I may grow older, but I'll never grow up."

The denial of our mortality appears prominently in the pseudo-sophisticated subtleties that characterize the New Age that has been embraced by young and old in middle-class America. For New Agers, mortality is an illusion. Your mistake is that you think you will die. Actually, you have immortality within you: Like Jonathan Livingston Seagull, you can find within yourself intimations of immortality and the energy to ascend to new realities far beyond your imagination. Just believe it; just do it. You are without limits.

Unlike Jonathan, who flies freely and unhindered into fantastic new worlds created by the imagination, some of us choose the path of despair. A dark realism enfolds us. We refuse to commit ourselves to any large and distant goals. We choose not to throw ourselves into life because we fear we will be trampled by intruding evil. Our model is not Jonathan but rather Albert Camus's character Sisyphus, who pushes a boulder up a mountain, only to have it thunder down the other side. And he plods dutifully down the mountain to push it up again, endlessly repeating a meaningless task. Life for the despairing is but cycles of mundane activities. We live in a gray fog where nothing ultimately matters, where no truths exist, where no morals subsist. Therefore, we set no goals, strive for no ends, plan for no contingencies. We have no sense of who we are or who we ought to try to become. Illusion and denial are not our lot: despair and apathy are our cup of ashes. Ecclesiastes is all the Scripture we have: "Vanity of vanities, all is vanity," we cry out. Our valley of shadows has no exit. Some of us anesthetize our despairing souls with alcohol or hype ourselves momentarily with marijuana or crack cocaine.

The Bible challenges both the paths of the limitless immortality of Jonathan Livingston Seagull and the meaningless despair and apathy of Sisyphus. When Jonathan concludes that divinity is ours, and from the myth of our unlimited illusions we think we are masters of our own fates, declaring that "today or tomorrow we will travel to a certain city, where we will stay a year and go into business and make a lot of money," the Bible rages back: "You don't even know what your life tomorrow will be!" When, on the other hand, we slouch into despair with Sisyphus and grouse about what a bummer everything is, the Bible reminds us that a gracious God loves us. When we have given up all hope, a touch or a smile or a card reminds us that some kind Power beyond has touched us.

The Bible provides us with a third path to life: a way between an illusory utopia that resides only in our imaginations and a senseless existence that reduces us to couch potatoes, drowning out reality with reruns of the "Andy Griffith Show." The Bible provides a vision of a middle way between illusion and despair. It declares that life has limits, while at the same time affirming that marvelous possibilities lie within ourselves and the world. It pronounces that life has focus and purpose when seen from the point of view of God, though not without tragedy and misfortune. The gospel finds a place for a life full of laughter tinged with a cup of tears, for ecstasies that touch eternity and despondency that occasionally knows no solace.

The way of the gospel begins with the admonition of James that "what you should say is this: 'If the Lord is willing,'" we will accomplish this or do that. The writer emphasizes the claim that we are dependent creatures of a Creator God who has made us. We did not will our lives; we had nothing to do with our coming into being: We are by the gracious gift of a Power beyond us. Life has been given to us as a gift. It is not our own creation. We do not own it or deserve it or control it. We are but stewards of life. Not only is life a gift; it is also a mystery. Like the Spirit of God, life comes into being and flickers out at times that we cannot calculate precisely. God is the giver of life and the taker of life. And life is fragile. In a moment it can end like a mist that evaporates into the atmosphere.

The Christian model for life is not found in the fantastic illusions of Jonathan Livingston Seagull nor in the gloomy despair of Sisyphus, but in the realistic hope of our Pioneer on the path of faith, Jesus the Christ. In his teaching about the Kingdom of God he gave us a pattern for living triumphantly in a world that sometimes smiles upon us and sometimes slaps us up the side of the head. In the grotesque and twisted pain of the cross, he enabled us to see that God is with us in a world ridiculed by grievous trials and agonies. And in his resurrection from the dead, God has sanctified the Christ-like way as a path for us.

We often struggle with our mortality by either creating the illusion that we are immortal or by throwing up our hands in despair and renouncing any meaning or hope in life. In the gospel we find a third path. On the gospel path we follow neither Jonathan Livingston Seagull nor Sisyphus but rather Jesus, whose crucifixion recognizes the cruel horrors of life and whose resurrection declares the victory of God over death.

Can we walk the path of Christ today? Can we crucify our mortal struggles and surrender our pride, apathy, and self-delusion, and walk in the hope of resurrection faith with him? These are the questions that face us in our struggle with mortality. The answers are ours to give. And the answers will make all the difference.

VI. DEVOTIONAL

33. On Stage with Thanksgiving

Overton C. Parrent

Ecclesiastes 2:20–3:15; Matthew 25:14–30

This coming Thursday is a special time for us in this nation. We will gather with family and friends to offer thanks for what we have been given individually and as a nation. But rather than the cursory "thank you for the big meal, day off, and shopping opportunity" approach to Thanksgiving, I want us to consider what we here might have to be thankful for. And I want to do that from the Ecclesiastes view of a world full of emptiness and from a current view of a people who may be losing interest even in themselves.

In our Old Testament lesson, we heard those familiar words about "a time to live and a time to die; a time to plant and a time to harvest; a time to seek," and so forth. That section of text, however, is drawn from a larger section that concerns the emptiness of all of our endeavors. Here are words from the initial parts of the first chapter of Ecclesiastes; just listen to this gloomy picture of life:

> Emptiness, emptiness, all is empty. What does man
> gain from all his labor and his toil here under the
> sun? Generations come and generations go, while
> the earth endures forever.

Overton C. Parrent was born in Frankfort, Kentucky, and educated at Eastern Kentucky and Vanderbilt universities and at the Universities of Maryland and Southern California. He is a Presbyterian elder. He is currently employed as principal system safety engineer and head, systems design branch, Naval Surface Warfare Center, Silver Spring, Maryland, and is the U.S. Navy representative to various national, international, and NATO organizations.

The sun rises and the sun goes down; back it
returns to its place and rises there again. The wind
blows south and the wind blows north, round and
round it goes and returns full circle.

All things are wearisome. The men of old are not
remembered and those who follow will not be
remembered by those who follow them.

That is a view of a life that is boring, colorless, routine, mind-
lessly repetitive, and lacks an affinity for or an interest in what
predecessors of generations past have done.

If that was the psychological condition of one of our acquain-
tances today, we would probably encourage them to seek mental
health counseling for their depression.

But that view isn't far off from the view of people in more
recent times, at least as far as has been interpreted by some artists
and writers.

A few weeks ago in Brussels, Belgium, I went to see a famous
painting by the sixteenth-century artist Peter Bruegel entitled
"Landscape with the Fall of Icarus." You may remember the Greek
myth about Icarus who, in escaping from prison, rose into the sky
by means of wings made of wax and feathers. He flew too near the
sun, the wax melted, and he drowned in the sea.

Well, in the painting by Bruegel, such a monumental accom-
plishment is reduced to two tiny legs disappearing under the water
within a majestic maritime scene with visual emphasis on a laborer
plowing his field, a shepherd, and a fisherman—none of whom are
paying any attention to the fall of Icarus. This is purported to be
an expression of the indifference of the world in view of the fate
of the individual, however exceptional his acts may be.

That was a view from the sixteenth century. More recently, Saul
Bellow, the Nobel prize–winning novelist, addressed the emptiness
in our contemporary lives by saying that people are losing interest
even in themselves or at least are not taking their lives seriously
because of the intrusion of mass media in our lives.

I ask you to think for a few moments of the emptiness discussed here in an analogy with a stage in a large concert hall or
theater. Well before the performance, the stage is barren and dark,
no lights, no movement, quiet. You can see the backstage structure
and catwalks above. The curtains are open to the vast emptiness of

the auditorium. You imagine the possibilities of how this stage could be set for a play or a concert, awaiting the actors or performers who would come to bring life and value and nourishment for those who will come to see and hear.

I want to use this image of the empty and dark stage as a setting as we go back to Ecclesiastes for a further look. As you recall, after the rather joyless discourse on life, the writer acknowledges that we can and should enjoy the fruits of our labor *because God has given us the gifts of wisdom and knowledge and the ability to do so*. Now that begins to put the matter in a different perspective. God's gifts to us of wisdom, knowledge, skills, abilities—our talents—are what we must use to bring meaning and joy to our lives and to truly enrich the lives of others. Using our analogy of the empty stage, we have to bring the light, music, and drama of living to the stage that life has set before us. We do that with the gifts God has given to us.

In our New Testament lesson, the parable of the talents, the issue was that the servant who had been entrusted with just one gift had done nothing with it, while the other servants, who had been given several gifts, had multiplied their holdings on their own initiative, were praised by their master for being good and faithful servants, and were entrusted with additional assets.

Through God's grace, each of us has been entrusted with valuable gifts and blessings. And just as for those servants in the parable, we are expected to use those gifts, enjoy the fruits of applying them, and be able to account for our stewardship of them.

As Dean Hoge discussed in this pulpit in September, Paul, in the twelfth chapter of 1 Corinthians, uses the analogy of a complete body to illustrate how God gives each member of the body a variety of gifts, a variety of service, and a variety of work. Let me extend that analogy by suggesting that, just as blood and nerve pulses flow to each member of the physical body, the Holy Spirit is infused in each one of us, the members of the holy Body of Christ, to accomplish some useful purpose through the gifts we have been given. And when life is well lived, the Holy Spirit blends and coalesces the sacred and the secular aspects of our lives much like hydrogen and oxygen are blended to form water.

If, for example, through the power of the Holy Spirit a person has a gift for wise speech or can put the deepest knowledge into words, he or she can use those abilities for secular and for sacred purposes, and we can thank God for that. If through the power of the Holy Spirit a person has a gift for healing or a gift of prophecy or of interpreting the Word or of singing or playing an instrument or mothering or any other gift, we can thank God for that. Now we have the opening lines of the play or the leitmotif of the opera for the performance on our vacant stage—we can thank God for the power of the Holy Spirit working in and through us in one or many ways.

Commander Everett Alvarez, Jr., was the first American pilot shot down over North Vietnam; he was a POW for nearly nine years. Against seemingly insurmountable odds that tested his faith in himself and his religion, he set a standard for all other POWs to follow. In a recent talk, CDR Alvarez said that he and his fellow prisoners of war knew that the gift of freedom to be who they wanted to be and to do what they wanted to do was what they had fought for. And they thanked God for that.

In September, I attended a talk by Mr. Jim Brady who was wounded in the assassination attempt on President Reagan. As you know, Mr. Brady was severely disabled and is still having to relearn how to talk and move. But even with those severe injuries and bodily limitations, he is using his gifts and inner strength to actively lead a national effort to encourage the employment of the disabled. He is using the abilities he has left—especially his acerbic wit and his knowledge of political maneuvering—to enrich the lives of others, and he thanks God for this additional mission in his life.

Do you remember that old hymn "Count Your Blessings"? "Count your many blessings name them one by one; Count your many blessings, see what God has done." Well let's do a little counting of some things we can be thankful for here at Takoma Park Presbyterian Church.

First, let me say that I can't talk about the blessings of this congregation without thinking about all those who have gone before us as founders, builders, leaders, and members of this congregation. People who have given generously of their time, talents, and money to establish and maintain a magnificent place of worship and fellowship and Christian education and singing and eating and rejoicing and mourning and doing all the other things we do here as a community of believers who happen to subscribe to and observe a Presbyterian form of worship rich with its traditions of doing things decently and in order.

Just in my time here of nearly thirty years, I come into these buildings and I think of people—people who have been just like you and me and have given so much. I think of Elsie Reed, Martha Bovard, Myrtle Minton, Helen Hall, Evelyn Ferry, Elizabeth Jackson, John Hall, John Scoltock, Ed Henderer, Lloyd Reed, John Magness, Harold Flickinger, and many more that most of you here don't remember and many more that I don't remember. But they were here just as you and I are here now, and we can all be thankful for their lives and contributions here.

But what about more recent "people" blessings? Were you here the Sunday we said our official farewell to our pastor, George Taylor? Do you remember former member Ann Kearns thanking the congregation for the spiritual nourishment we gave to the Kearns and their children while they were members here? Recognizing the Christian love and leadership that family brought to us, I wonder who nourished whom.

There are many others in our congregation today who give the gift of themselves through love and kindness and vigor and knowledge and friendship and concern. I am going to mention a few names. I ask their indulgence and in no way do I want to embarrass them. It is just my way of bringing a point into one specific focus.

If you know anything at all about this congregation, you know that Clayton Hardison and Harry Yehnert and Jim Barclay have given unreservedly of their time and energy in trying to keep this wonderful, big, aging facility in a respectable state of repair. And for years they have been founts of wisdom and strength for essentially every significant aspect of our corporate life as a worshiping body as elders, trustees, deacon, choir member, Shepherd's Table leader, adult study leader, budget protagonist, Sunday offering tellers. Their gifts are blessings to this congregation. They nourish what is of value to them through the powers given to them through the Holy Spirit. And notice something—there is no expectation of appreciation on their part.

Then there are Selma Whitney and Jo Hoge and Alice Keith, who have established communication links within our congregation and the neighboring community that rival a CIA spy network. They keep us informed, and they spread a vital personal level of care and concern. Selma brings flowers to grace our sanctuary and sees that they get to some member or friend who is confined at home or in the hospital or perhaps has undergone some loss. Jo contributes vigor and enthusiasm into making contacts especially with families with children and into checking on those we haven't seen in a while. Alice visits our members and friends who have a hard time getting out to come here to be with us physically; she carries the spirit of our fellowship to them in their homes or hospital room or nursing home.

Again, these are examples of people using the abilities vested in them by the Holy Spirit to help make us be a viable community of faith in this area. They bring color and live action to their stage setting by using their gifts but with no expectation of appreciation being expressed to them. And we can thank God for that.

I've used that phrase twice—no expectation of appreciation. That's not to say that we should not constantly be thanking all of these dedicated people; it's just that they aren't doing the things they do to derive some expression of appreciation from us. They are providing ordinary, everyday examples of how I believe our faith instructs us to use what we have been given—to use our *gifts* as offerings of our *thanks*.

I believe God's gifts to these people are being used as were those of the good and faithful servants in the parable of the talents. In my scenario, their offerings of thanksgiving are the plays, concerts, symphonies, and operas that they are acting out on the stages of their lives. And we can thank God for that.

We have this congregation with its friendships, concerns, interests; a congregation in which we have opportunity for corporate worship where we can share the sacraments and renew and strengthen our faith, where we can hear the Word of God for us and learn to apply his words in our everyday lives. And we can thank God for that.

We have the gifts of our lives, brains, imaginations, of art, music, knowledge, freedom, food, health, and family. And we can thank God for that.

We have work to do, services to render, care to give, love to share, bodies to heal, anger to overcome, losses to mourn, and nature to awe. And we can thank God for that.

We have God's gift of eternal life through Jesus Christ, and we have the Holy Spirit living within us distributing to each of us varying gifts and ministries. And whatever else we know about God, we know that he is everywhere, on stage with each one of us, trying to communicate with us and, by the power of the Holy Spirit, through us to others. And we can thank God for that.

Yes, as the lesson this morning says, there is a time for every matter under heaven. The curtain of life is up, the lights are on, the orchestra is playing, we *are* on stage. But in the view from my stage, it is not a time of boring, colorless routine that disregards what acts have gone before us. It is a time for thanksgiving, for counting and acknowledging our many blessings, for building on what our predecessors have built for us, for nourishing and strengthening the faith of those around us, and for otherwise demonstrating our stewardship of the gifts God has given to us today.

In Jesus Christ, God has joined us together in the family of faith that is his Church. Through our baptism with the Holy Spirit, we are members of God's household with talents and gifts he has given to us through the Holy Spirit so that what we say and what we do on the stages of our lives may be his Word and his work.

And we can thank God for that.

34. I Am Sending You
James Ayers

> It was the evening of the first day of the week. The disciples had
> locked the doors because they were afraid. Then Jesus came and
> stood among them and said, "Peace be with you!" After he said
> this, he showed them his hands and side. When the disciples saw
> the Lord, they were overjoyed.
>
> Again Jesus said, "Peace be with you! As the Father has sent
> me, so I am sending you." Then he breathed on them and said,
> "Receive the Holy Spirit. If you forgive anyone's sins, they are
> forgiven; if you retain anyone's sins, they are retained."

—*John 20:19–23*

Long, long ago, in a universe far, far away, once upon a time, there
was an adventure. A quest. A decision was made, a goal was set—a
high and lofty goal, fraught with danger, yet offering such a wondrous reward. And so the adventure began.

It was a quest to rescue the people who lived in a distant kingdom. This kingdom had many names; it was sometimes called the
Land of the Shadow of Death. That was because death had captured the kingdom, had taken it over, had declared that he, death,
was the real king of that land. He wasn't, of course, and the people
knew that, but his shadow seemed to stretch everywhere across the
land, touching everything, nibbling at the edges of everyone's lives.
You could never quite ignore the shadow of death. They knew, like
a distant memory buried deep in their souls, sometimes nearly
forgotten yet still there, that they were not created for death; they
were created for life. And yet still the shadow of death hung over
their land and over their lives, and no one could escape from its
sadness and despair. And sooner or later death himself would

James Ayers is pastor of First Presbyterian Church in Waltham,
Massachusetts. He received his master of divinity degree from
Gordon-Conwell Theological Seminary. Ayers is well versed in seven
languages and has held many teaching and pastoral positions. He
was a first place winner in the competition in *Best Sermons 4*.

come personally for each individual, and there was no escape from him, either.

In the wisdom of the great king—the king of the universe and the true king of the kingdom that was now called the Land of the Shadow of Death—in the wisdom of the great king, a hero was chosen to rescue the people. This hero would have companions at certain points during the adventure, but there would also be moments when the hero would have to stand and do battle alone.

And so the great king sent his son into the kingdom. He sent him secretly; by the great king's great power he had him born as a baby. There was risk in this, for while he was a baby he would have no knowledge that he was actually the son of the great king. Even as a child he would only have a few clues. What if he misunderstood his mission? But the child grew, strong and wise and brave. He read the ancient books, which told of the love of the great king for the people of the land and which told that one day the great king would send an anointed one, a messiah, to tell the people of his love and to set them free from the power of death. And sometimes the boy would climb up on top of the hill at the edge of town, and he would listen for the voice of the great king.

The boy's name was Salvation. That was the name they gave him when he was born. In the language the people of his village spoke it was Yeshua. It was not an uncommon name, in that time and place, but sometimes he wondered whether it might mean something more in his case: he wondered. For he thought that he had actually started to hear, sometimes, the whisper of the great king: "You are my son. I have sent you for a purpose." That would be a wondrous thing, the boy thought to himself. But sometimes he asked himself, "What if you're mistaken about all this? What if you've never really heard the voice at all? What if you go marching off to look for the purpose of the great king and accomplish nothing? Perhaps it's better," he told himself, "just to stick to my woodworking, to do my job, to mind my own business. Son of the great king! What a fantasy. Here we are in the Land of the Shadow of Death, and you'd better do your job and earn your living, because the end of your living comes all too soon."

If that had been the final thought the young man had on the subject, there would be no story to tell. But he continued to listen for the voice of the great king, and the conviction grew within him that the words he had heard were true. And he began to preach, and people listened, and a small band of followers gathered around the man whose name was Salvation, for they believed him.

And he taught them that, although they lived in the Land of the Shadow of Death, the great king was the true king of the land, and that he had a purpose for them. He taught them about how to live with one another. And he taught them about himself. I am the Messiah, he told them: I am the one who the people have believed would some day come to set everyone free. I am the Light of the World, he told them: I am the one who gives light and understanding and freedom to those who walk in shadow and darkness. I am the Bread of Life, he told them: I am the one who comes to nourish your souls. I am the Good Shepherd, and I have come to lay down my life for all the lost sheep in this lost land. I am Teacher and Lord, and I give you an example of how to love one another. I am the True Vine, and like branches in the vine you find your life and sustenance flowing from me. How can I say all these things? Because, before Abraham was, I Am; I Am the I Am. I am the son of the great king, and I am here to set you free.

Ah, how they loved him then. They wanted to hear every word; they wanted to follow him always, to be faithful and loyal no matter what. But death was angry, and death reached out an angry claw to strike him down. His companions tried to be brave, but their courage melted away as death drew near, and they ran. And only the man whose name was Salvation was left, face-to-face with death.

And death laughed. Death laughed as the man whose name was Salvation was dragged through the mockery of a trial, as his head was crowned with a crown made not of gold but of thorns, sharp and cruel, with blood running down into his eyes. Death laughed as the man's arms were nailed onto a wooden beam: Take that, carpenter! Death laughed as the man prayed, "Forgive them, for they don't know what they are doing," because even if they didn't know, death knew. Death knew and death laughed. "So your name is Salvation?" death mocked. "And you're the son of the great king! But this is my land, the Land of the Shadow of Death. I am the king here. And you're dead." And death laughed, as he reached in and ripped the soul free from the bloody body, leaving it lifeless, cold, dead.

And then there was silence. The day turned dark. Night fell. The sun came up the next day and went down again at night.

Nothing had changed in the Land of the Shadow of Death. Some of his followers had crept back together, but there was nothing they could think of to do, nothing they could say. Death was still the king, and death would always have the last word. So they sat and watched the shadows grow darker and felt the chains of fear wrapping around their hearts, tighter, heavier. And in the midst of the silence, all they could hear was the sound of soft laughing.

The laughter began to grow louder. It grew in intensity, too. There was something in how it sounded that they could not quite recognize, and they did not know what it could mean. It was different, different from all the laughter they had ever heard before; it was ringing laughter, ringing with joy, shining joy and exultant gladness. And along with the laughter they could hear the sound of a thousand bright trumpets and the singing of legions of angels. And suddenly there he was, the man whose name means salvation, right in front of them. They had locked the doors, even though a locked door would not protect them against death, but they had locked the doors because people gripped with fear do desperate things. But locked door or not, there he was, the son of the great king, standing right in their midst, filled with laughter and victory and peace and glory. And he laughed, a laugh that sparkled with such purity, such wonder, such splendor, a laugh filled with goodness and love. In that moment they felt the cold chains around their hearts fall away as their fear melted and their despair turned to wonder. And they laughed, too.

Then he explained to them that the power of death had now been broken and that the land would no longer be known as the Land of the Shadow of Death; now it would be called the Kingdom of God. They had thought their hearts were as full of joy as anyone's heart could ever be, but when he said that, when he said that the new name of the land would be the Kingdom of God, it seemed so wondrous that they could hardly bear it.

And then, then he explained to them about the plan of the great king. He explained to them how a hero had been chosen. And he looked into each one of their faces with a searching intensity, and he said to all of them and to each of them (and because he is the son of the great king, he could even look down the long stretches of time to see you and me, and to say it to each one of us), he said, "You are the hero that I have chosen. As the Father has sent me, so I am sending you. You are the hero, chosen according to the plan of the great king, and your quest is to tell the people this great news. For even though death's power has been broken, he will still lie to people and tell them that he rules. From now on, those who die will simply leave this land and come to live with me; but death will lie and will tell people to be afraid, and he will tell them that he is the final answer and the only real power. But you [that's right, you; across the centuries he looked, from then till now, the man whose name means salvation looked, and he saw you, face-to-face], you are the hero I have chosen. You will make the difference for them, because, in spite of your questions and in spite of your fears, you will show them and tell them that the message is true, that death has been defeated. As the Father has sent me, so I am sending you."

And we, the gathered disciples, the friends of Jesus, the one whose name means salvation, we can scarcely take it in. This is a great and noble task we have been given, worthy of our greatest efforts; but we hardly feel worthy of such honor. We hardly feel capable of such responsibility. Perhaps he should send someone else.

Somehow the voice of our hesitation must have carried back along the corridors of time, for the son of the great king responds to our uncertainty. "On your quest," he tells us, "on your adventure, you will have companions who will help you and encourage you. There will be moments, however, when you will look around and see no one, and you will have to choose to stand for the truth even if you have to stand alone. Yet because you are the hero I have chosen, I know that you will not fail."

And he tells us this: "I will give you two gifts that you may use in the midst of the conflict. First, you will have the Holy Spirit; he will dwell within you to empower you, to give you courage and wisdom. Live your life in obedience to the Spirit's voice, and the Spirit's holiness will shine in you for all to see.

"And second, I give you the power of forgiveness. If you forgive the sins of anyone, they are forgiven; if you retain the sins of anyone, they are retained. Because they know the guilt of their own sins, people will believe death when he lies to them and tells them that he will have the final word, that in the end he will have them. And when they believe what he says, it will wrap chains around their hearts, chains just like the ones you have felt. But I have given you the power of forgiveness, and when you tell them how their sins can be forgiven, they will be set free."

And here we are, the unlikely band of heroes selected by Jesus. The task seems daunting, yet he has chosen us. We feel timid and inadequate, yet we are the ones he sends.

We have the gifts he has given us: the power of forgiveness, to set people free from the burdens of the past, and the presence of the Spirit, to transform their lives for the days to come. We will use these gifts, and we will use them well, and people will be set free, and their lives will be transformed.

There will be risks. There will be setbacks. We will stumble over our own uncertainties. "Yet despite it all," says the man whose name means salvation, "you will accomplish this quest I give to you. I have chosen you, and you will not fail. You will fulfill the purpose of the great king. As the Father has sent me, so I am sending you."

35. God Depicted in Scars and Beauty

John N. Jonsson

Acts 13:15–16, 26–33; Revelation 7:9–17; John 10:22–30

Today is Mother's Day, so I wish to pay special tribute to my own mother. I well remember when our daughters Lois and Sylvia were leaving home to further their studies, they said to Gladys, my wife, "Mom, thank you for never betraying us." They knew their mother was a confidante when they were in trouble or when they needed to share the secrets of their hearts. I recall when I was a young man in my student days, at times having to wear an army uniform and being attracted to and by the beautiful young ladies in the city life. I would look at them and say to myself, "Can I take them home to meet mother?" Decision made!

We have all heard the story of the mother who had ugly scarred hands. Her young son once asked her why her hands were so ugly. She told him of the fire in their home when he was a child and how he was trapped in the flames, and risking her own life, she plucked him from the flames. The boy was silent for a while, and then he took hold of his mother's hands, looked into her eyes and said, "Mother, you have beautiful hands."

We have heard of the account of the scorched body of the hen in the blazing barn. When it was lifted, out scuttled one or two chicks still alive. We are reminded of Jesus as he looked with sor-

John N. Jonsson was born in South Africa of Swedish missionary parents. He was educated at Spurgeon's College, London, the University of London, and the University of Natal, from which he received the Ph.D degree. For several years he was professor of Christian missions and world religions at the Southern Baptist Theological Seminary. He currently teaches at Baylor University in the field of world religions.

row and anguish over Jerusalem and sobbed, "O Jerusalem, how often I would have gathered you as a hen gathers her chicks under her wings, and you would not." No roosters around, they had fled in fear to safety. But mother was there to risk her life because of the incomparable life of her children.

"Mother, what beautiful hands you have!"

Today as we once again seek to bring into focus the meaning and message of the lectionary scriptures incorporated in our morning celebration, we depict God in scars and beauty. Paul and Barnabas, as they arrived in Antioch Pisidia, Asia Minor, were asked to say something in the synagogue, if they had anything of encouragement to say, and so Paul takes them down to the tomb of Jesus (Acts 13:15–16, 26–33) with the scars of death, as the context in which the beautiful Shepherd gives us "eternal life" (John 10:22–30), and no one can pluck us out of his nail-pierced hands. The Good Shepherd is the beautiful Shepherd.

Scars are identifications of those who at great risk rescued us from the deadly dangers and precariousness of our life situations. They did so because of the inestimable value they put on our lives, lives that were not designed to perish. Even in visions of heaven in Revelation, the subject of veneration and worship is "the Lamb on the throne that had been slain!" The scars of God persist for eternity as the witnesses to our pride of place in his estimate of us for our salvation.

There is an early account of one of the early saints who, in a time of meditation, had a mystical, psychedelic experience of the Risen Lord appearing before him in all his glory. He was about to worship the apparition, when he cried out to see the "nail-pierced hands" of the Savior. Immediately the apparition disappeared, and he knew he had been hoaxed.

The Scriptures often depict God as good, *God as beautiful*. As the people of Judah celebrated their faith, they expressed their desire "to behold the beauty of the Lord and to enquire in his temple," (Ps. 27:4), for "strength and beauty [were] in his sanctuary" (Ps. 96:6). When God created the world and all its environment and living beings, as recorded in Genesis 1, God exclaimed how beautiful creation appeared to be and how superbly beautiful people human beings were. That is why, when people destroy life and the environment, we declare them to be ugly monsters and evil tyrants.

The problem within the life of the Church is the extent to which we romanticize life and extract from reality the austerity, despicableness, depravity, dereliction, and the damnableness of the ugly in life. We gloss over the stern realities of the chaos and absurdity of life in the raw within the secular world of hurts, horror, and death. That is why the French and Norwegian Expressionists in their drama and art forced their audiences to wrestle with human contexts where there is a constant tension of beauty and the beast, between the sublime and the ridiculous, the sacred and the profane, the good and the bad, the just and the evil, the beautiful and the ugly.

The dilemma in which we find ourselves when we are forced to face the dichotomies of these existential contradictions in our lives and in human societies is the stark awareness that God is implicated in this mess. It is not without significance, therefore, that in many of the religions of the world, God is depicted as being implicated with evil. In the ancient Persian religion, Zoroastrianism, the high god Ahura Mazdah is depicted as being both the good spirit and the evil spirit. This shock is felt also in Hindu philosophy, which implicates God in human providence (Vishnu) and in societal destruction (Siva). In Native American religions the Eternal Spirit is also the Trickster in human life. Even in Islam, Allah is depicted as being the super deception that outdoes all our worst deceptions. Job in his holocaust experience had to implicate God not only with the good we get but also with the bad.

Within the realism of human life and our societal existence, God appears to be the author of good and evil. The theological theorists, within the rationalizations of their detached metaphysics, have to speak of the problem of evil, but they rarely if ever speak of the problem of God. Their arguments are for God's existence. But when we wrestle together within the dilemma in which secular people find themselves, their problem has to do with the character of God. Their concern is not whether God exists; their anger, confusion, and bewilderment has to do with "what kind of God is this who allows these heinous events to transpire within our lives?" Job in his dereliction is angered by the slick rationalizations of his friends who have all the answers to account for his complaint. Jeremiah in his pit of despair (Jeremiah 20) accuses God of having raped him, of opening him up to rape by others, with the slur that every time he talks about God, people treat him as someone to be kicked. God appears to many, and in many situations, to be ugly, because the scars of suffering and death are so bewilderingly ugly and hurtful.

One of the grave concerns about the death penalty as a means of maintaining law and order in society is that we do not know how to handle the beast in society, so we put people away to get rid of them; we eliminate them from society to remove them as far as possible from our view and memory. At worst, punishment is viewed as making an example to prevent others from committing a crime, or a kind of retribution of an eye for an eye. At this rate we will all soon be blind! At best, it is a kind of restitution to those who have been wronged, but even then it is only the ugly in us that is vindicated. Rarely is there any thought of punishment being rehabilitative—an attempt to change the person and the situations that contribute to the crimes. And that's the bad news.

When I was a student, a man came to a Baptist pastor and confessed that he had murdered someone twenty-five years earlier. The minister took the matter in hand, only to find from the authorities that someone else had been executed in his place, making him a free man. Case closed. My minister used this incident in a sermon to illustrate how Jesus had died in our stead. He saw it as good news. I differed, feeling it was bad news that the process of law enforcement had necessitated finding a culprit for the crime to close the file. To me it was a warning how systems of law can default in seeking to rid society of what is considered to be a scourge to society. And that is what they did to Jesus—they had him killed, took him down from the tree, and laid him in a tomb. That's the bad news (Acts 13:29).

The good news, Paul tells us, is that God keeps promises made and raised Jesus from the dead; therefore "we bring you good news of God fulfilling promises made" by raising Jesus (Acts 13:30–33) and adopting us as children of God (Psalm 2).

Whenever we talk of the Resurrection there is the dark, dismal dereliction of the cross; the ugly, the cruel, the despicable, the horror of the Skull. That's the bad news. But when we speak about the gory cross, it is always to be seen in the promises of God within the morning glory of the Resurrection. That's the good news. The scars and the beauty belong together.

Whenever the theological theorists speak about the cost of our salvation, they are inclined to restrict it to the courtroom scene, where God the judge imposes the penalty on unjust sinners and then promptly, in Jesus Christ, comes off the bench of judgment and stands by us and pays the price of our crime. Within the realism of life, however, the human dilemma is more that of a battlefield, where we find ourselves being threatened and awaiting the deathblow of the enemy. This is the deadly situation in which we find ourselves, and salvation spells the ransom paid by the Christ of cosmos who slays the enemy, delivers us from death, but in the process is mortally wounded in death on our behalf. The courtroom scene arouses grave questions as to the character of God as judge. The battlefield transfers the tyranny of God to the enemy of humankind, the enemy whom the God-person came to slay (Heb. 2:14–18). The battlefield scene of human existence, and the lifeblood it cost God for our ransom, highlights how highly God prizes our humanness and personhood, and as a consequence how beautiful the scars appear to us, for they are the witness of our salvation. The good news is that we are of infinite worth to God. The battered scars we carry on the battlefield are matched by the the wounds of the Savior of humankind.

In the light of the magnanimity of Jesus, we reject the hidebound logic that the scars of human suffering are the just deserts of our guilt and are as a consequence the punishment of our sins. The message of Job is witness against that. Job had always believed that "your sins will find you out," until calamity and disaster came his way. Now humanly bankrupt, physically diseased, and mentally destroyed, Job has to disagree vehemently with his three friends who jibe him, torment him, and accuse him of being secretly responsible for his calamity. Job protests that he has done nothing so dastardly as to have earned the severity of this kind of treatment from God. For God to be responsible for such heinous treatment of Job brings the integrity of God's character very much into question. And we feel the same about our misfortunes in life. We have not done anything of this proportion to merit the judgment of God.

William Barclay, the Scottish professor whose expositional writings of the New Testament have enthralled the world, has all too often been labeled a rank liberal by the fundamentalists. I am proud of the fact that the Baptist World Alliance has sent many hundreds of sets of volumes of William Barclay's works to Baptist leaders across the world to help them in their understanding of the

Bible. William Barclay's daughter, a young teenager, was very tragically drowned in an accident off shore. He received a letter from
one of these fundamentalists who wrote saying that he hoped William Barclay had come to realize that this tragedy in his life was
God's judgment on him because of his liberal theology. It took a
long time for Barclay to reply, and when he did it was in this vein:
"My dear misguided brother, I think the problem is that the one
you consider to be your God is the one I consider to be my devil."

We reel in anger against the suggestion that our human scars
are tokens of the judgment of God. We equally react against sug-
gestions, however, that the good news means that we hope for a
future happiness that will eliminate all scars and stress. We are not
attracted to John Hicks's futuristic eschatology that views heaven as
some kind of frictionless existence. What kind of God is this that
pounds us to pulp in this life in order to give us some reward of
a frictionless existence?

A young person in my church in Pietermarizburg, South Africa, had run the sixty-five-mile Comrades Marathon to Durban
along the seacoast. As a reward he ran across the beach sand and
dived into a wave in the sea. Unfortunately, his head hit a hidden
sandbank, and he has been paralyzed neck down ever since. Who
wants this kind of frictionless heaven?

Dr. Boreham was once walking with a naturalist along a beach
in Australia. They came upon a jellyfish (a medusa) sprawled on
the damp sand. As they examined the flabby substance, the naturalist pointed out that effortlessly the medusa absorbed its sources
of energy from its immediate environment. Dr. Boreham was quick
to remark that he would like to live a life in which it was not
necessary to exert oneself to get one's food. The naturalist replied
in turn, "But then you must remember that the jellyfish is among
the lowest forms of life." Who wants heaven like that?

There is an old Scottish remedy for toothache. Keep rubbing
your fingers on the rugged edge of a rock, and soon the toothache
will disappear!

Possibly, the most exasperating characteristic of so-called spiritual people is their determination to account for everything as the
will of God. When our son David was tragically drowned in an
African river some years ago, we were bombarded with all sorts of
explanations as to why it was the will of God that David should
have died. One bears repeating. We were told a story of a mother

who prayed to God to heal her dying son at all costs. God answered her prayer, so we were told, but the boy grew up to be a murderer. And so the insinuation almost went without saying, but we still had to listen to the enraging application to our son's death, that God had spared David from becoming some kind of disgrace to his family. All we were concerned about was, "Is it well with our David," and we were encouraged by the hugs of friends and relatives who had no answers but who shared beauty for ashes.

When I was a young boy in southern Africa, my sister Elsa was involved in an accident and broke her back. My father had just left for Sweden, which was a three-week journey from where we lived, and post took just as long to get the message of her deteriorating state of health to him. Our mother, Sarah, was at home with us children. Elsa was in great pain. We prayed for her healing. The journey seemed to be getting more difficult for her. We started praying that God would do what was best for Elsa. Her journey seemed to change. On Christmas Eve, when normally we would have joviality around the Christmas tree, it turned into sorrow and sadness as Elsa lay dying, saying she was going home to Jesus and that we should not cry. The family recounts how she stopped breathing, and it seemed as though she had been transfigured into an angel. A minister in the area spoke with sorrow to my mother about Elsa's death but then added that, if my mother had had more faith, Elsa would not have died. That was a scar my mother never seemed to be able to live with, and she would sometimes sob by the graveside. A tragic, ugly scar. But then there was the pharmacist in the town who asked my mother, "Mrs. Jonsson, how can you believe in the love of God when tragic things like this happen?" My mother was able to reply through her tears, "We never as a family knew what the love of God was until this happened to us." What beauty!

The scars of God are reflected in the beautiful Shepherd. In the Gospel according to John, Jesus is depicted as the beautiful Shepherd because of his vigilance, because of his vicariousness, for the beautiful Shepherd lays down his life for his sheep, and he gives them eternal life, and no one can ever pluck them out of his hands (John 10:22–30). He sees in each of us inestimable worth. We are gems in his hands.

Dorothee Soelle, in her book *Christ Our Representative,* expands on how modern science has made God redundant. Human scientific progress is now able to do what previously it was believed only God could do, only it is able to do it so much better. She then goes on to show how our new technology is making human beings dispensable. Computerization has outsmarted the human in the labor force of industry. People are being replaced by highly sophisticated robots. We are becoming redundant utilities. This is why Jesus Christ comes, not to resurrect the old perceptions of God, but to bring into focus the one and only true and living God. He not only represents the living God, Jesus the incarnated God-person comes into the human scene of shattered hopes, of broken promises, of twisted minds, of distorted views, and of unholy practices of injustice in society. He declares that people are indispensable and must be treated with respect.

I came home from school one afternoon when I was a young teenager in South Africa. My mother was nowhere to be found. She was always there to meet me when I arrived home from school. I found her on her knees in an Episcopal church behind our home. She was crying. I went down on my knees beside her. "Why are you crying, Mom?" I asked. "John, we are very discouraged at the way we are being treated by our white neighbors. We are trying to educate the blacks towards self-subsistence, but this is felt to be a violation of our place in society, for the blacks need to be kept in their place." With my youthful exuberance I retorted, "Don't worry, Mom, you will one day get your reward!" After all, I thought to myself, isn't that why we do everything anyway? My mother replied, "But that is not why we are doing all this." I was a bit astonished and somewhat taken aback. "Well, why are you doing all this and being hurt by those who ought to know better?" My mother replied quietly but deliberately, "We did it all because we know it is the right thing to do." What scars, what beauty.

We used to sing as children, "All good things around us are sent from God above." The encouragement from the tomb is that God's scarred hands make everything beautiful and good. And that is why when we destroy people and treat them as cheap ware to be sold at cut prices at the scrapyard, we are nothing but ugly. That is why when we are part of the processes and programs that are raping our countryside and polluting our water we are nothing but ugly. That is why when we are racists and child abusers we are *ugly!* That is why when we in a masculine society intimidate women and humiliate them to inferior roles even in the ministry, we are just plain ugly. There is no beauty in such ugliness.

But the scars of God at the cross and the tomb are not ugly. God raised Jesus from the dead, and there is beauty in the ashes, and there is hope for the beast to change and become beautiful. Your scars can also become beautiful, if they are scars that see such worth in others that there is no extent to which you will not go to save what is inestimably precious in others.

And so among the scars of life we salute our beautiful mothers. Mothers who gave birth to children in our families. Mothers who never gave birth physically to any children but have mothered the people of God in our churches and societal communities. We stand and salute you all and say with deep conviction, "What beautiful hands you have, Mother."

I was in a ministers' fraternal meeting. We were discussing the merits of the different translations of the Bible. We all had a turn sharing what was our favorite translation of the Bible. "Well, what is your favorite translation of the Bible, John?" someone asked me. I replied, "I like my mother's translation."

36. Night Fishing
Roger Lovette

John 21:1–8

The story is found in two Gospels, Luke and John. Early in Luke's Gospel, Simon and his companions had fished all night and caught nothing. In John's story the account appears at the end of that Gospel after Easter. So much had happened since Jesus first encountered those fishermen by the seashore, and yet so little had changed. Simon and six others fished all night and caught nothing. We find the story at the beginning of Jesus' ministry, and we find it cropping up again after Easter. For night fishing is embedded in the heart of the gospel message.

It is an old story—as old as time itself. The disciples used all their expertise and talent and know-how and nothing happened. They fished all night and caught nothing. It sounds like a page out of the life of every pastor I know. The letdown periods. When the dust has settled, and the reception is over, and the search committee has gone back to their jobs, and it's just you and her and the dog and two homesick kids and boxes and strangeness and four hundred miles from any friend you have. It is more than a little scary. The Scriptures say they were Simon Peter and Thomas and Nathaniel and the sons of Zebedee and two other disciples. I wonder who they were, those other two. They are not named, yet I have a hunch that it is your name and mine that should be scratched into the story. We're there too, aren't we?

Roger Lovette has served as a pastor in South Carolina, Kentucky, and Tennessee. He is a native of Columbus, Georgia, and a graduate of Samford University (B.A.), the Southern Baptist Theological Seminary (B.D.), and Lexington Theological Seminary (D.Min.). He is the author of *For the Dispossessed, A Faith of Our Own, Questions Jesus Raised,* and *Come to Worship.* He is currently pastor of Church of the Covenant in Birmingham, Alabama.

Who has not known some defeat so painful you didn't think you could stand it? From the boys who never would ask you out to the football team you never made to the rejection slips that kept coming to the dreams that never came true—raisins in the sun—to the churches somebody else always got, our names are there, too.

In these verses, I have discovered my name. Three and a half years ago I left one place and moved to a new charge with hope and promise. I brought along my fishing lines and plugs and spinning reels and nets and tackle boxes. And three and a half years later I resigned one sad December Sunday morning. It had not worked. I had done my share of night fishing. And from the beginning to the end the story was mostly the same.

But the text says this was not the end in Luke or John. And I am painfully learning this is not the end of my story either. For I have come back from a fishing expedition of three and half years to talk about some of the things I have learned. Out there where the choppy waters swirled and the waves lashed and the wind blew and I wrestled with the taut lines, I wondered if I would ever make it back to the mainland. Fishing in the darkness I have come upon some powerful lessons.

I.

I am learning something about myself. For Simon Peter and the other disciples, this difficult experience was a watershed. From that post-Resurrection moment on, Simon really would live up to his name of Rock. He learned something about himself and failure and the demonic and faith. The record shows that Simon Peter carried with him as long as he lived the painful memory of what he learned out there fishing in the darkness.

I have learned something about limits during this time. For I used to think that work alone would do it. And how wrong I was. From James Glasse in *Putting It Together in the Parish* I came to believe that, if you really do pay your rent and work hard on sermons and proper worship and visitation and dress right for success and follow all the roadmaps, it will happen. Work alone is not enough.

In Luke's account they tell the Lord, "We toiled all night and nothing happened." The Greek word *kopos* is interesting. It means a "weariness as though one had been beaten." The meaning of toil here is exertion, tiredness caused by too much work.

Studies of troubled pastors report that they worked 25 percent harder than the usual minister. This is practical atheism carried to its furthest conclusion. Paul Minear has said that the Lukan passage is a classic example of an experience of failure apart from Christ's presence. We professionals sometimes think we can do it all. Nothing could be further from the truth. Painfully, I have learned work is not always enough. Sometimes you just have to hang it up.

Something else I am learning from the dark waters is that I am becoming less judgmental. Don't you think it happened to brash, impetuous Simon? He bragged, "I will never betray you. I will be there until the end." But later, much later, in 1 Peter he tenderly tells the troubled church, "Beloved, do not be surprised at the fiery ordeal that is taking place among you to test you, as though something strange were happening to you. But rejoice insofar as you are sharing Christ's sufferings, so that you may also be glad and shout for joy when his glory is revealed" (1 Peter 5:12–13). So unlike the early Simon and so unlike us. And so like God.

I remember standing by a South Carolina lake over a year ago with one of my best friends. As we threw stones into the water, I distinctly remember telling him, "You know, I used to be smug when pastors got into trouble. I always wanted to know what they did wrong. What was their problem. I don't judge quite as quickly now." I hope I remember those words. When I sit in the counseling room and face someone who has all the lines down, I hope that I will listen and care without judgment. And when the gossip comes about somebody who was dismissed, I hope I will suspend my usual judgment and whisper a prayer for support and love.

Another thing that I am learning is that my old yardsticks have to be discarded. Painfully, I am beginning to learn that what seemed so important is less important and things that mattered very little have taken on enormous importance. For a boy who was raised in a mill village on the other side of the tracks needed desperately a big house and beautiful furnishings. Status and success and growth and a good name were everything. I have discovered the emptiness of the outward trappings of success.

Consequently, I ran after success; I have spent more time on work than I should have. I resonate with Hudnut's book *Church*

Growth Is Not the Point. Perhaps the managerial approach to church has not produced what we intended. As I hear words like *user-friendly church,* I remember back to that solemn admonition in the Book of Psalms: "And he gave them their request but sent leanness to their soul" (Ps. 106:15). We must learn to live from the center out.

The outward props that meant so much to me have lost their power. The little things, the graces of life are meaning more and more to me. These are the things that kept me going. A counselor that held my hand and nudged me on. Colleagues that whispered hope. Members of the church where I served that held up my hands. Holy Scripture, especially the Psalms and Second Isaiah and the Corinthian letters. A big bear hug every Sunday from a little nine-year-old I had baptized. I have found strength in work and exercise and prayer and prayer and prayer. But most of all, the grace has come from a wife who believed in me and two kids and a new grandchild. These and so many other things kept me going.

I am also learning how to forgive myself and not be so hard on me. For years and years I have been my own worst neighbor. I would treat everybody, even enemies, much better than I would myself. I do not know why this is true. During this ordeal with my church, search committee members of the church I served have come by, with tears in their eyes and said, "Will you forgive me?" And I have told them that is not the question. They did not know how troubled their church was. No one knew. I told them the question is, Can you forgive yourself? This is the burden of my life right now. Can I forgive myself for calling a wrong shot? That's the question. Sometimes, Arthur Miller says, one must take one's very self in one's own arms. I am trying to forgive myself, and there is healing in this exercise.

II.

The second thing that I am learning from night fishing is something about failure. Simon and his colleagues had to learn a hard lesson. There are nights, sometimes many nights, when the fish just do not bite. There are times when we all fail.

In all my years as a minister, I have never really failed. I have had my trials and tribulations, but I have never walked away from a place and said I cannot do this any longer. Many people have told me that I have not failed at all. But it feels like a failure to me.

The Bible talks continually about failure. Moses did not make it to the Promised Land after all those years of leadership. David with all his power could not build the temple of his dreams. And neither prophet nor people could hold back the Exile. And old gloomy Joel records the sadness when he talks about the years that the locusts eat everything in sight. And then Third Isaiah writes about the people who came back to dust and rubble and years and years of nothing but hard, tedious work. And if that were not enough, there was no room in the inn. We find Jesus born to the wrong people on the wrong side of town. His own did not receive him. His brothers and sisters turned away, not understanding. The longer he preached, the fewer they came. Simon and all the others save John, one by one, forsook him and fled. Until we are left with the heart of it all—a towering cross—bearing our sorrows and carrying our griefs.

So I have learned that part of the story for any of us risk-takers is failure. But I am beginning to learn what every pilgrim must finally face. Failure need not kill you. Failure is part of the journey.

III.

Night fishing has taught me something about evil and the demonic. We moderates don't talk much about this. We leave Satan to the fundamentalists and to the "church lady" on "Saturday Night Live."

But evil is very real. We all encounter dark and light and many shades of grey. A search committee asked me weeks ago, What went wrong? As if there was something that one could name. Life is never clean cut. There were many layers of problems. There were many things going on. Nothing is simple. This is what I have learned from night fishing. None of our motives are ever pure— mine or theirs or yours. Like Paul, all the things we would love to do we wind up not doing, and all those things we say we will never do—we do them. Who can explain this mystery?

But I have come to know that I have seen the face of the demonic, and it has been frightening. For there has been a destructive side to all of this hurt and pain and abuse that is scary. I have felt it personally, and I have seen it institutionally. The last Wednesday night that I was pastor, I told the congregation that we all got caught up in something much bigger than any of us knew. Nobody won. Everybody lost. And sometimes when that happens the best you can do is to just walk away.

Do you remember that wonderful point in James Goldman's *The Lion in Winter*? Eleanor of Aquitaine and her three sons wrestle for the right to succeed King Henry. As they meet at the castle of Chinon, France, and begin to plot for the prize, John says, "Richard has a knife." And Eleanor answers,

> Of course he has a knife. He always has a knife.
> We all have knives. It is 1183 and we are
> barbarians. How clear we make it. Oh, my piglets,
> we're the origins of war. Not history's forces nor
> the times nor justice nor the lack of it nor causes
> nor religions nor ideas nor kinds of government
> nor any other kind. We are the killers; we breed
> war. We carry it like syphilis, inside. Dead bodies
> rot in field and stream because the living ones are
> rotten. For the love of God can't we love one
> another—just a little. That's how peace begins. We
> have so much to love each other for. We have such
> possibilities, my children. We could change the
> world.[1]

Sometimes the darkness does prevail for a season.

IV.

In the middle of night fishing, Simon or his companions came to believe that failure had the last word. But those fishermen learned a profound message. This, too, I have discovered. *I am learning something I never knew about faith.*

After the fishermen had fished all night and caught nothing, Jesus called them. From mending nets to mending hearts and a broken world. Cast your net yet again, Jesus said, and see what happens. And it was a wonderful sight. And in John's last chapter, after toiling all night, dead-tired he told them to throw the nets yet another time. The night was passing. The daybreak was coming on. They threw the nets back out. It was a fisherman's story that they would retell for the rest of their days. "Remember," old watery-eyed fishermen would say, "Do you remember that night on the sea?" When I was boxed in and did not know what to do, and everything was out of control and nothing worked—grace came. And I discovered there is a more powerful word in the gospel than failure.

One of the wonderful gifts that have come out of this hard year came last October. The first church I served in western Kentucky had finally moved from the old highway two miles down the road to the new highway and built a new church. They invited me back to their first revival in their new building. As I left, they gave me a videotape of the last service in their hundred-year-old church building.

The last service was a Sunday night. They gathered one Sunday evening last June to tell stories about what their old church had meant to them. They filled the church house that night. In the tape the church had changed little. The video began by showing the tiny, white clapboard church. There was the steeple with a bell that rang every Sunday. As the camera moved inside, you saw they had bought another church's pews that did not quite match the rest of the decor. There were two very large Warm Morning heaters that kept the place too warm or not warm at all. In the gothic-shaped windows bits and pieces of colored glass had been knocked out and replaced through the years by other glass pieces that did not quite match. In the center at the front stood the pulpit with the Bible a mother had given to honor her oldest who had been killed in an automobile accident. On the right was the little Hammond organ. On the left was the spinet piano. Behind the pulpit, centered, was the old, yellowing, crocheted, framed piece of the Lord's Prayer that some member had made seventy-five years before. To the left of the pulpit was the choir on a landing back of the piano.

Different members stood that night and told what had happened to them in that special place. They remembered their own baptisms and when their children had been dedicated at the altar. Someone told about their bout with cancer and how the church gathered around them and loved and prayed. They remembered revivals and Vacation Bible Schools and losing jobs and coming together after a hard week in the fields. Mostly, it was personal stuff. In that little frame church on a side road, they found something that kept them going and carried them through the years.

Is it any wonder that when the early church put the record together, Luke would begin his Gospel with a story about fishing all night and how Jesus came and made it right? Telling them, tenderly, to cast the nets out again in the same swirling waters. And John, there at the end, after Easter, would include this same moving account of failure and faith. And in the daring risky act of trying yet one more time, those believers discovered they were not alone. He was there after all.

No wonder old exiled Isaiah wrote of the treasures of the darkness. For the prophet discovered in an exiled land what I am just beginning to learn. In the heart of these two stories I have found my name. Sometimes, through the grace of God, we learn more in failure than we can learn at any other time. The night passes. Thank God. And just as day breaks, you cast the nets out again, and grace does its work once more.

No wonder the church has sung the words for two thousand years:

> Thou, in the darkness drear,
> Their one true light.
> Alleluia! Alleluia![2]

Your name, my name, everybody's name. Even in the darkness! Alleluia! Alleluia!

NOTES

1. James Goldman, *The Lion in Winter* (New York: Random House, 1966), 55–56.

2. William W. How, "For All the Saints," *The Baptist Hymnal* (Nashville, Convention Press, 1991), 355.

37. Cain and Abel and What It Means to Be Human

Glen H. Stassen

Genesis 4:1–16 (NIV)

Does the drama of Cain and Abel cause you to puzzle?

"The Lord looked with favor on Abel and his offering, but on Cain and his offering the Lord did not look with favor" (Gen. 4:4).

What can this mean? God is not unjust. God is compassionate. God is fair and just. What can it mean that the Lord looked with favor on Abel and his offering, but God did not look with favor on Cain's?

Many of the best Old Testament scholars say they don't know.[1] But I think we can figure it out.

Who told this story? It can't be Abel; he didn't live to tell. It has to be Cain. Who was Cain? A farmer in the ancient Near East, before the time of Abraham or Moses. What would it mean for Cain to say, "The Lord did not look with favor on my offering?"

When my wife and I taught at Berea College, we grew our own vegetable garden. There never was a year when the Lord looked with favor on our watermelons.

I blamed it on the sun: The Kentucky sun wasn't right to grow watermelons. But others grew good watermelons. Why not us? We were always too busy getting our grades turned in to get around to planting until the middle of June—too late for the watermelons

Glen H. Stassen was born in St. Paul, Minnesota, and was educated at the University of Virginia and at Duke and Harvard universities. He has taught at Duke University and at Kentucky Southern and Berea colleges. He is currently professor of Christian ethics at the Southern Baptist Theological Seminary, Louisville, Kentucky. His many publications include his latest book, *Just Peacemaking* (1992).

to get ripe before August, when it was always hot and dry. But watermelons need water; they aren't called watermelons for nothing. So our watermelons never found favor in God's eyes.

But our pumpkins found too much favor! Now seventeen years later, we still have pumpkin in our freezer.

The people of the ancient Near East who passed this story on knew what it meant not to find favor in God's eyes. Their agricultural technology said you should sacrifice to the gods so your crops would grow well. When the crops didn't grow well, it meant you had not found favor with God. From Cain's perspective, *his* crops were not growing well, but Abel's sheep were multiplying.

And what was multiplying in Cain was envy and resentment.[2]

You and I know what it means when life is going against us. Sometimes it's because I am not doing it right or don't know how or am too proud to ask somebody to teach me. And sometimes it's because of the sin and injustice in our society. When we ourselves experience injustice or identify with those who do, we get resentful. The rich get a lot richer and the poor get a lot poorer. And what we get is jealous and full of resentment. The economy has problems, and people's income is threatened. There are two million people in our land who are homeless; thirty-seven million without medical insurance; I don't know how many addicted to drugs or how many feel alone or abandoned. Or how many don't feel life has hope, joy, and purpose. I know I have felt that way. And then I feel resentment building up in me. I walk down the street muttering, "Get off my back!" Have you ever heard yourself, out loud or not, talking resentment to yourself?

I first preached on Cain and Abel in East Germany just after the Wall had opened up. The people had lived over forty years under a rigid and authoritarian ruler. They had tried to push for freedom but had been crushed. They knew the experience of discouragement, despair, and depression. Now freedom was breaking out. They were experiencing euphoria. But the story of Cain and Abel caused me to have to warn that they would experience discouragement and resentment yet again. The biblical warning came true sooner and harder than they or I had expected.

Martin Luther King has written of the dark night of the soul, when nothing is working, there is no way forward, and despair reigns. The dark night of despair, he says, always seems to come before the dawn.[3]

> What does it mean to be a human?
> It means we have times when things aren't
>   working out.
> When resentment and envy are crouching at the
>   door.
> When things are unfair and unjust.
> When those closest to me don't seem to care.
> And I feel lonely.
> When it must be that God is against me.
> When others are succeeding, but I am not.

"So Cain was very angry, and his face fell" (Gen. 4:5).

The temptation is to blame others or to blame God. To live with resentment, and let it turn into hate and anger. Or to stuff the envy and anger down inside, and let it feed on you. Then you get depressed, and you don't care anymore.

Depression is dangerous. It has no room for hope and love. Not caring anymore is dangerous. It takes away the energy to join together with others to make justice happen. And when people don't act in hope and caring to make justice happen, injustice rules. Injustice causes the envy and resentment that we see in Cain, the envy and resentment that lie crouching at the door, tempting us to do violence. It's a vicious cycle.

> What does it mean to be human?
> It means we have times when things aren't
>   working out.
> When resentment and envy are crouching at the
>   door.
> It means envy, resentment, anger, hate, depression,
>   and apathy are part of our life.
> They lurk at the door like a lion about to spring
>   on us.
> They portend danger.

"The Lord said to Cain, 'Why are you angry, and why has your face fallen? If you do right, then you can look up. If you do not do right, sin is crouching at the door; its desire is for you, but you must master it'" (Gen. 4:6–7).

The Old Testament scholar Gerhard von Rad says,

> Hot resentment had risen in Cain, which had
> distorted even his body! He envies God's pleasure

in his brother. God warns him about this change
of his being and the danger of this sin seething in
his heart. . . . The comparison of sin with a beast
of prey lying before the door [means] . . . it is only
a very short distance from the inner emotion to
the act. The statement . . . shows sin as an objective
power which, as it were, is outside the man and
over him, waiting eagerly to take possession of
him.[4]

But von Rad also says,

It is a fatherly address that wants to show the
threatened man a way out before it is too late.
One sees that Cain was not completely rejected. . . .
Especially urgent is the appeal . . . "If you do well,
you are able to lift it up."

And Walter Brueggemann comments,

This suggests we can choose and act for the good.
Cain is free and capable of faithful living. But sin
is waiting like a hungry lion ready to leap. Sin is
lethal. There is danger to Cain in how he handles
his rage and depression. Sin lusts after Cain. Sin
crouches like a beast of prey. The danger of
destruction is nearby. But you can do right.[5]

How can we do right? Jesus must have been thinking of Cain
and Abel when he said in the Sermon on the Mount,

Every one who is angry with his brother shall be
liable to judgment. . . . So if you are offering your
gift at the altar, and there remember that your
brother has something against you, leave your gift
there before the altar and go; first be reconciled to
your brother. (Matt. 5:23, RSV)[6]

Here Jesus is talking about two brothers like Cain and Abel,
who have envy or anger between them, and one of the brothers is
offering his gift at the altar of worship. He warns that it can lead
into danger and destruction if they do not do right. And he spells
out what it means to do right: "First go and be reconciled to your
brother; then come and offer your gift."

So many people sweep their anger and envy under the rug. Under the rug it doesn't go away; it builds up, and eventually it trips you up.

Jesus doesn't just say, don't do wrong, but do right: Go talk and seek to make peace. Take an initiative. First you talk before you walk.

In East Germany, church leaders and demonstration leaders knew Jesus' teaching: go talk with your brother and seek to make peace. They had talked several times with government leaders, including even Egon Krenz, the chief of the hated national security police. They spoke to him with respect as a brother, explaining their own nonviolence and urging how important it was for the police to be nonviolent.

Then one month before the Wall came down, the people were about to conduct a massive nonviolent demonstration. The rigid East German dictator, Erich Honecker, had just praised the Chinese leaders for stopping the demonstration in Tiananmen Square by using massive violence. He was threatened by the demonstrations in his country, and he was angry. He ordered the national security police to arm themselves with lethal weapons and shoot the demonstrators, just as the Chinese had. The police got the weapons. Hospital personnel got orders to prepare for a carnage. But the night before the demonstration, Egon Krenz, the head of the hated security police, whom the demonstration leaders had gone to talk with, went to Leipzig and countermanded Honecker's order. He ordered the police not to shoot but to be nonviolent. It was a daring act; it risked his career and his life. Honecker was a desperate and ruthless dictator. To countermand his order would incur his wrath. But there was no violence the day of the massive demonstration. It became the day of "the turning," from violence to nonviolence.

The next day in the Politburo came the showdown between Honecker and Krenz. The very leaders the demonstrators had dialogued with turned against Honecker and ousted him. East Germany turned toward freedom.

We have got to learn to talk it out. Not to let envy and anger build up into violence, but to talk it out.

"One American male in every forty dies a violent death sometime between his fifteenth and thirty-fifth birthday," from murder, suicide, or an accident. Men in their twenties are four times more likely to die a violent death than young women are. The United States has the highest murder rate of all developed nations. We also have the highest number of guns.[7] Over one third of adult women are battered by their husbands or men friends.[8] One out of three women are victims of rape or attempted rape during their lifetime, mostly by persons they know.[9]

What does it mean to do right? It means to go talk and seek to make peace. I can do something about your anger and my anger. I can talk it out. Many churches and schools are now teaching skills of conflict resolution. It is making a big difference.

Recently, I attended the annual meeting of leaders of the largest part of the U.S. peace movement—Sane/Freeze: The Campaign for Global Security. The most encouraging news came from those who are teaching conflict resolution in schools, reporting how children are learning to stop fights and to get their peers to talk it out. Now the kids are spreading the skills of conflict resolution to their parents.

They need to spread to governments. Not too long ago, the leaders of Iraq and the United States did not get together to talk through their problems. The result is that over 200,000 people are now dead, and the suffering goes on. We have got to learn to do right, to talk with our brothers and sisters and seek reconciliation.

It is true of families. Resentment within families does not always lead to physical violence, but it kills spirits. We have got to learn to do right, to talk with our spouses and brothers and sisters in a way that can seek honest confession, forgiveness, and reconciliation.

> What does it mean to be human?
> It means we have times when things aren't
>   working out.
> When resentment and envy are crouching at the
>   door.
> It means we need to talk and seek to make peace.

"Cain said to Abel his brother, 'Let us go out to the field.' And when they were in the field, Cain rose up against his brother Abel, and killed him. Then the Lord said to Cain, 'Where is Abel your brother?' He said, 'I do not know; am I my brother's keeper?'" (Gen. 4:8–9).

Cain does not do right. He does not take an initiative to make peace. He takes out his anger by killing his brother.

God confronts him.

He answers, Am I my brother's keeper?

Yes, we are—we are responsible for love, justice, and solidarity with our brothers and sisters. We are responsible for one another.

Some have turned the meaning of the Cain and Abel story on its head, so it turns brothers and sisters against each other. They have made Cain stand for one group of people: In Germany, they did it to the Jews; in the United States, they did it to African-Americans. Instead of teaching brotherhood and sisterhood, they used this very story to teach that we have no responsibility for our brothers and sisters.

This is not a story about one group of people, about one race. It is a story about all of us, about the human race.

The early part of Genesis is all about what it means to be human: Adam and Eve, Cain and Abel, Noah and the Flood, the Tower of Babel, all stand for the human race.[10] Many other ancient cultures have similar stories about two brothers who are sons of the first humans, who are jealous, and who fight and kill one another. These are all about what it means to be human, not about one group of people.[11]

> We are all potential Abels, and we are all potential
>   Cains.
> It ain't just Abel; it's us.
> It can't just be Cain; it's us.
> It's not just Cain and Abel, it's you and me,
>   brothers and sisters, all of us together.
> We all have times when things aren't working out.
> When resentment and envy are crouching at the
>   door.
> We all need to talk and seek to make peace.
> We are our brothers' and our sisters' keepers.

"The voice of your brother's blood is crying out to me from the ground. And now you are cursed from the ground, which has opened its mouth to receive your brother's blood from your hand. When you till the ground, it shall no longer yield to you its strength" (Gen. 4:10).

By our greed and violence, the ecology is ruined. Many other ancient cultures have a similar story-of-origins connecting human violence and the polluting of the earth.[12] They knew what we try to deny. Injustice, violence, and the destruction of the creation are tied together. So are justice, peacemaking, and the preservation of the creation tied together. Just as in the story of Adam and Eve, where the consequence of sin is that the ground is cursed and humankind is barred from the Garden of Eden, so here the ground is ruined and Cain must wander where the land is not fertile (see Gen. 3:16–19 and 23f.).

In Greifswald, a beautiful town in the north of East Germany on the Baltic Sea, the smog was so thick it hurt to breathe. In Bitterfeld, half of the speakers in the public rally demanded a stop to the poisonous pollution of air and water by the huge chemical factories nearby. There were no filters on the smokestacks. People were living in apartment buildings next to the factories. Cancer rates were high. The rivers were dead. In Forst, on the eastern border with Poland, the peacemaker group was focusing its main efforts on stopping the ten-story-high strip-mining machines that were gobbling up forests, roads, rivers, and towns. From the Wartburg, perched on a small mountain, where Martin Luther had hidden from the pope and translated the New Testament into German, every direction you could see was thick with smog. The cars had no catalytic converters, and the industries had no antipollution devices. The government was too focused on economic power to pay attention to saving lives and saving the environment.

At Fernald, Ohio, near Cincinnati, seventy-five miles from my home in Louisville, there is a sign saying, "Fernald Feed Materials Plant." The water tower is painted with red and white checkerboard squares. The people who lived nearby thought it was a Ralston Purina plant, making feed for animals. But it was not. It made the fuel for nuclear bombs.

I was once a physicist working with nuclear materials. Realistically, I had expected that a few grams might accidentally leak out from such a plant. I knew that a fleck of radioactive uranium in your lungs slowly causes cancer. I had no expectation of what was finally reported in *Time* and *Newsweek* on October 31, 1988: Since 1951, the Fernald Feed Materials Plant has lost *over 350 tons* of radioactive uranium.

The wind spreads some of the radioactivity around, and the rest flows down into the surrounding aquifer and eventually down the Ohio River. Louisville and other cities draw their drinking water from the Ohio River. According to the Louisville Water Company, the radioactivity in our water sometimes exceeds the law, and then they add water softener to settle it out. According to the Ohio Environmental Protection Agency, the drinking water in towns near Fernald has thirty to fifty times as much radioactivity as the legal maximum allowed. If your body contains one quart of Louisville water, you average ten radioactive emissions per second.

There are similar problems in other parts of the United States—Hanford, Washington; Oak Ridge, Tennessee; Savannah River, South Carolina; Paducah, Kentucky; Denver, Colorado; and so on. And recently, a visiting scientist from the former Soviet Union told me they have the same problems there.

What does it mean to be human?

It means we build so many bombs in order to kill our brothers and sisters over there that we are already killing ourselves and our children and their childrens' children with cancer here. This radioactivity will last for twenty-four thousand years—twelve times as long as the two thousand years from Jesus to us.

It means we are murderers already. We murder our children by wasting our resources getting ready for war instead of getting them ready for life. We murder people with radiation and chemicals and cancer. We murder trees, rivers, the earth, the air with our pollution. The ground has opened its mouth to receive our brothers' and sisters' blood from our hands. And the voice of their blood is crying out to God from the ground.

> What does it mean to be human? The Bible names
>   it realistically:
> It means we have times when things aren't
>   working out.
> When resentment and envy are crouching at the
>   door.
> It means we need to talk and seek to make peace.
> We are our brothers' and our sisters' keepers.
> It means we are murderers already.

"The Lord put a mark on Cain, lest any who came upon him should kill him" (Gen. 4:15).

This is a mark of protection. It means nobody should kill the murderer. It is a mark of grace. Cain is us. We are all sinners. We all need protection. We all need God's grace.

The drama has a surprise ending. The chain of destruction is broken apart—by God who places a mark of grace: Life can begin anew.

Is that not the mission of the Church, too? To place a mark of grace? To offer forgiveness and the community of brotherhood and sisterhood, in spite of our deserving much worse? To help life begin anew? And is that not a much-needed mission? Forgiveness and love and community together? Based on the grace of God, given in Christ, whose blood was spilled on the ground for us.

The East Germans wrote a study book on Cain and Abel. Here is how they concluded:

> Astonishingly God still talks with Cain. He had already said what he needed to say. Who would blame him for shutting Cain out in silence? Cain can justly be sent away with his punishment! What should God do about Cain's fear? Ignore him, give him the cold shoulder? Surely Cain had done just that a few moments before.
>
> But God speaks, answers, does not turn his face away. [God takes a transforming initiative. God talks with Cain.] The cold-blooded murderer remains his creation, his human child. Cain is still a fugitive. But God protects him so he will live on . . . yes, he protects him expressly. In the sign that he places on him, he goes before him. He protects Cain's life from angry vengeance. God's punishment is other than human punishment. Life remains life, even the life of the murderer. God wants the life of a sinner, not his death. Does Cain recognize the opportunity he is being given? Without this chance Cain would already be finished. And so would I.[13]
>
> What does it mean to be human?
> It means we have times when things aren't
>   working out.
> When resentment and envy are crouching at the
>   door.
> It means we need to talk and seek to make peace.

We are our brothers' and our sisters' keepers.
It means we are murderers already.
We are all sinners.
We all need God's protection.
We all live only by forgiveness.

Thank you, God of grace who comes to us—to us with our resentment, our envy, our violence and sin; who comes to us and talks with us and gives us the grace of your presence, the grace of brothers and sisters for whom we are responsible, the grace of our being called to talk and seek to make peace, and the grace to be forgiven and protected when we do not do right. Amen.

NOTES

1. For example, see John Skinner, *A Critical and Exegetical Commentary on Genesis*, 2d ed. (Edinburgh: T & T Clark, 1930 and 1980), 105ff., and Claus Westermann, *Genesis 1–11: A Commentary* (Minneapolis: Augsburg, 1984), 297.

2. Westermann, *Genesis 1–11*, 295, cites Van der Leeuw: This type of offering (or sacrifice) had the purpose of gaining the favor of the God who makes things grow. "The main thing is not that someone or other gets something, but that the stream of life continues to flow." Westermann then says, "The produce of the field and of the flock is, as presumed here, the produce of blessing. There is a power at work in the produce as it comes to fruition that must be acknowledged and respected as something natural and normal. There cannot be the one without the other."

3. Martin Luther King, Jr., *Strength to Love* (Philadelphia: Fortress Press, 1981), 65f. and 85.

4. Gerhard von Rad, *Genesis: A Commentary* (Philadelphia: Westminster Press, 1961), 105.

5. Walter Brueggemann, *Genesis* (Atlanta: John Knox Press, 1982), 62–63.

6. Brueggemann, *Genesis*, pp. 62–63, suggests the connection between Cain and Abel and Jesus' teaching about brothers in the Sermon on the Mount. So do Davies and Allison, *The Gospel According to St. Matthew*, vol. 1 (Edinburgh: T & T Clark, 1988), 510.

7. Kathleen Stassen Berger, *The Developing Person Through the Life Span*, 2d ed. (New York: Worth Publishers, 1988), 406ff.

8. Catharine A. MacKinnon, *Toward a Feminist Theory of the State* (Cambridge, Mass.: Harvard University Press, 1991), 142–43.

9. Karen Lebacqz, "Love Your Enemy: Sex, Power, and Christian Ethics," in *The Annual of the Society of Christian Ethics*, ed. D. M. Yeager (Washington, D.C.: Georgetown University Press, 1990), 4.

10. The story of Cain and Abel is just like the story of Adam and Eve: In both stories God warns us not to do wrong, we do it anyway, God comes and asks what we did, we make up excuses, God sees through the excuses, the land becomes cursed or polluted, and God banishes us to living outside the land where we were meant to be. Both stories portray what it means to be human.

Protestant interpretation of human sin has emphasized the Fall of Adam and Eve and neglected Cain and Abel and the Tower of Babel. And it has interpreted Adam and Eve too individualistically, as the relation of individuals to God, neglecting its implications concerning our drive to make ourselves into gods *and thus to have the knowledge-power to lord it over others.* The Bible gives us three stories of human sin for a reason: They make clear that sin is also social; Cain and Abel clearly concern envy, resentment, domination, and violence among us. The Tower of Babel portrays the urge to make ourselves into gods with the fame and imperialistic power over others of a universal empire as exemplified by the Babylonians with their zigurrats in "the land of Shinar." We would understand ourselves more accurately if we paid attention to all three portrayals of human sin in the prehistory of Genesis 1–11. All three tell us profoundly what it means to be human.

11. Westermann, *Genesis 1–11,* 315ff. I am indebted to the wisdom of Christian Wolf, formerly of the faculty of the Free Church Seminary in Buckow, East Germany, and now the Baptist Theological Seminary in Hamburg, Germany, at this point and others as well.

12. Westermann, *Genesis 1–11,* 317.

13. Veronika Benecke et al., *Kain und Abel und Was es Heisst, ein Mensch zu Sein* (Berlin: Ökumenische Arbeitsgruppe zur Vorbereitung der Friedensdekade, 1989).

38. Someone Said Yes
Michael H. Farris

Luke 1:26–38

She could have said no. I hope you realize that tonight. She could have decided "There are better things to do with my life." She might have said, "No—this is all too much too soon, and besides, isn't there someone better suited to this kind of thing?"

Maybe she should have said no. See it from Mary's point of view. A young girl, fourteen years, sixteen tops. Her very name in Hebrew means "rebellion." Advent begins with a teenager named Rebellion! But even in those wild and distant days, the girl knew children were to be conceived within marriage not without. Everyone knew. What is it we tell teenagers these days? "Just say no, Mary. Just say no." For we are older and wiser people—we're grown up, and we know better.

Mary doesn't, I guess. She said yes. *Yes.* Not like Moses who said, "I have nothing to say." Not an Isaiah who claimed, "I'm not good enough." No Jeremiah who said, "I'm too young." The girl said yes. More than all the prophets, priests, and kings before her—no excuses, no doubts. For once in Holy Scripture someone has it right the first time. "Let it be to me according to your word." Someone said yes, and Advent begins.

Martin Luther saw three miracles in Christ's nativity: God became human, a virgin conceived—and Mary believed. In Luther's

Michael H. Farris is Minister of the First Presbyterian Church in Winnipeg, Canada. A graduate of the University of Toronto and Union Theological Seminary in Virginia, Farris's denomination is the Presbyterian Church of Canada. He is the author of the monthly column "The UnCommon Lectionary." This sermon was first preached for a Nurses Christian Fellowship carol service.

mind the greatest miracle was the last. Think of it this way, Advent begins not on a day—but in a word. Mary said yes.

Annunciation is the name we give it. Have you ever seen those medieval paintings, all gold leaf and lilies? Look at them long enough and you see it is a single moment, sliced so thin it is almost transparent, an instant of absolute silence, even the angel wings lock in stillness. All creation draws a breath and holds it. Look long enough—hold your own breath—then you can see what Annunciation is about: waiting—for Mary, oh yes, waiting for something wondrous to grow, waiting for a child to be born. Advent is waiting. We all know that. Did you know that it is waiting for God, too— waiting for someone at last to say yes? God does not force the child upon anyone—not Mary, not on any of us—and so Advent begins when Mary says yes.

Why and *how* can all this be, you ask? How does such a word come to mortal flesh like ours? To say why is to miss the real moment. To explain how is not to explain at all. It is something more wonderful than the logic we use to build bridges and balance our checkbooks. Maybe when we gather on a night like this to light our candles and huddle against the cold, maybe when we sing carols we only half believe in and hope the rest is true in spite of us—maybe in just that moment—we're close enough to understand with Mary. W. H. Auden talks about that kind of Advent:

> Therefore see without looking, hear without
>   listening, breathe without asking
> The Inevitable is what will seem to happen purely
>   by chance;
> The Real is what will strike you as really absurd;
> Unless you are certain you are dreaming; it is
>   certainly a dream of your own;
> Unless you exclaim—"There must be some
>   mistake"
> —you must be mistaken.[1]

Call it mere poetry, if you wish. This is so often the way Advent is. Call it nonsense, if you want; it is that, too, and better. Advent begins with a new kind of thinking—if it be thinking at all. Call it paradox or call it the gospel—they are one and the same in Advent.

> This is the irrational season
> When love blooms bright and wild

Had Mary been filled with reason
There'd have been no room for the child.[2]

There is no room for the child at the inn of human reason. The child is always born elsewhere. They say the longest distance in the world is between the head and the heart. It's true. Perhaps longer still for us moderns is the distance back from heart to head. After all, it's all uphill.

Please understand, I'm not against rational people or common sense. We are all too sensible for that kind of thing. It is only a plea that Mary's gentle voice be heard among us. Only that some of the holy madness of the season steal upon us.

Maybe it comes upon us like the little advents that brought us here tonight. You could have said no. What made you say yes? No great thing, I guess. You have a friend, a son, or daughter. Perhaps it's just part of the job to sing in the choir. Maybe it's what you do for Christmas. Maybe you didn't want to come at all, and someone made you. Nothing religious really about these little advents. But large or small there is always a moment when you have to say one way or the other, either yes or no; I'll go or I'll stay. No one ever tells you either exactly what to say, only the time has come to answer—just like Mary.

There are so many such moments in this season. When Pavarotti hits the high notes in "O Holy Night" or a child squeals at an opened gift. You know what it's like. Something that begins in the heart and not in the head. A word that wants to answer before our lips move to speak it.

Why and *How,* you say? Those are not the right words for us tonight. Do you explain a baby's smile—or do you give it back? Do you understand a friend's death—or do you weep for them? Do you ask someone why they love you—or do you say, "I love you, too." These are advents, too, "the irrational season when love blooms bright and wild."

You could have said no to so many things, so many people—but you didn't. You said yes, and at least one thing has happened. You are here tonight. Good Christian friends, someone said yes, and to celebrate we are *all* here tonight. I'm talking about Mary, and I'm talking about you, too—all of us. Someone said yes—and something quite amazing begins. What marvelous adventures begin when someone says yes. And the yes is only the beginning. Just ask Mary.

The angel said, "For with God, nothing will be impossible." Nothing will be impossible. Have you ever wondered about the future in the phrase? There is something greater here far beyond Mary's yes. If flesh of our flesh and bone of our bone can say yes like Mary, there is no life in which Christ cannot be born. Nothing is impossible now. With what is done through Mary, nothing will be withheld from God. There is no distance he will not go, no depth to which he cannot stoop in his wild pursuit of humankind.

When does Advent begin this year? And where? It's here in a word. Say yes to God. All creation holds its breath and awaits your answer.

NOTES

1. W. H. Auden, *For the Time Being, A Christmas Oratorio*, (London: Faber and Faber, 1945), 66.
2. Madeleine L'Engle, *The Weather of the Heart* (Wheaton, Ill.: H. Shaw, 1978), 45.

39. Letter to a Child
Stuart G. Collier

Matthew 11:28–30

My Dear Child,

Flesh of my flesh, bone of my bone. Something about the prospect of battle moves me to write you a letter. I'm sitting here in the tent. The flaps are rolled up on the sides, and I can see out across the desert to where the sun is sliding down into the sand. I never knew how beautiful the desert is in the quiet of the evening. The sand is still warm, but the air is cool, and I find my soul refreshed in walking out a little way from the bivouac to where I can feel alone and a part of this great marvel God has made.

I suppose war has a way of helping a person see what is really important in life. Around me here in the tent are some things I used to think were important. There are captain's bars on my uniform. My big shortwave radio is under the bed, and I have my books. I suppose that underneath my cot lies the great field of oil that is more precious than my blood.

It makes me think of you. As if I had never realized it before, I am overwhelmed with the awareness that I helped create you and your beautiful life. I feel in my memory the softness of your cheek and listen to memories of you laughing, and I remember those times I felt your warmth as we hugged. As I think of the gentleness of your spirit, I realize that God has shared with me maybe his greatest gift of all—the creating of a beautiful life.

Stuart Collier is Director of Pastoral Care at the Tri-County Community Hospital in LaGrange, Kentucky. He received his M.Div. and Ph.D. from the Southern Baptist Theological Seminary. A Southern Baptist, Collier has been a pastor in Goshen, Kentucky, and is a former U.S. Army Special Forces officer.

You are my best gift to the world. If I were a millionaire or commanded this whole army or had my name written in all the history books, I couldn't do more than God has graciously allowed me to do in bringing you into the world. I see now that I really need little more from the world.

As the shadows of war lengthen and creep over us, I am more aware than ever that, as I believe General George Patton once quoted the ancient Greeks, "All glory is fleeting." But more than that, all life is fleeting. Dear child of my heart, perhaps I will not see you again. If life and death separate us for a little while, remember that you have been God's gift to me and will be forever. I'll keep this letter with my valuables, and you can have it, if need be.

I am strangely moved to ponder what have I left you. You know there isn't any property to speak of or money or anything to set you up in life. Except one thing. I have given you my example. You have seen me everyday, and you know how weak I am and how often I have failed to live up to what I believe and what I have tried to teach you. But you know, too, that I have tried to live faithfully in God's sight.

Dear child, that is my gift to you. A life lived before God. It is all I have, but what is more than that? And I give it to you, joyfully, with deepest love. Remember me for that, and as you grow up, don't look to the other things I have done or the profession I have chosen—the path you walk must come from within yourself. Make your own place in the world.

But I would give you a few markers for the path you will walk because it won't be too different from mine. I remember that the great Beethoven, when he was feeling his mortality most keenly, wrote a last will and testament to his remaining family. We only write wills for our property these days and not testaments to the spiritual truths that have guided us. How much poorer we are for that. Anyway, Beethoven, beset with deafness at the peak of his musical powers, wrote in his testament to his brothers something to this effect: "Urge your children to follow the path of virtue, as that alone can bring happiness."

Dear child, you are young and have the world before you. You can do almost anything you choose with your life. God made you that way and now trembles to let you choose wisely or foolishly. Maybe you won't understand this for a long time—I didn't, really, and I am just now getting the sense of it—but the highest use of your life and gifts is to give everything in the service of God. I often recall that Albert Schweitzer, when questioned about the validity of his theological beliefs, replied, "My life is my argument." Your life *will* stand for something, whether you want it to or not. You can only choose what it is.

One choice you will make is about Jesus Christ. I am happy to write you about this. To choose him for a master instead of life's other attractions seems to be the hard choice and a loss, but not really. In the long run, Jesus is the only master worthy of your life, and the narrow path doesn't seem more difficult. Or if it is more difficult, the rewards are so satisfying that you won't think much about the hardships.

I want to share with you a few lines of poetry that have meant a lot to me. I keep them in my wallet, though I think I could stand up in class by now and recite them from memory. They are Robert Frost's poem "The Road Not Taken." I read it in high school, but I don't find it in many poetry books anymore. Anyway, the words speak to me of the mystery of life, of irreversible choices, renunciations, adventure, discipleship—all done in the name of someone and something greater than ourselves. There is a daring greatness of spirit here that reminds me of the early Christians:

> Two roads diverged in a yellow wood,
> And sorry I could not travel both
> And be one traveler, long I stood
> And looked down one as far as I could
> To where it bent in the undergrowth;
>
> Then took the other, as just as fair,
> And having perhaps the better claim,
> Because it was grassy and wanted wear;
> Though as for that the passing there
> Had worn them really about the same,
>
> And both that morning equally lay
> In leaves no step had trodden black.
> Oh, I kept the first for another day!
> Yet knowing how way leads on to way,
> I doubted if I should ever come back.
>
> I shall be telling this with a sigh
> Somewhere ages and ages hence:

Two roads diverged in a wood, and I—
I took the one less traveled by,
And that has made all the difference.

Whatever doubts are in your mind now—and believe me, there will always be questions and doubts—these shouldn't stop you from living with the understanding you do have. You will always have questions. There will always be good reasons not to believe that Jesus is the answer to the questions in your life and the source of all lasting meaning. Your life will always have to be based on faith and not sight. That makes life such an adventure. And its conclusion becomes so exciting.

Perhaps I am saying more to you than your age can understand. But I may not have the chance again to tell you the most important things for your life or at least as I have come to believe out of my own life. So be patient with this rambling letter a little longer.

From my heart I want to give you a memory to accompany your life of faith. My own father once told me that his favorite hymn was "Blessed Assurance," and I remember as a boy standing beside him and hearing him sing it in his deep, rich voice. Now when I sing that hymn I feel close to him and to his faith.

I would like to tell you that I was in love with the passages in which Jesus simply says, "Come." Once, two awkward disciples of John wanted to know more about Jesus, and they stumbled around for what to say. Finally, one blurted out, "Where are you staying?" It was enough—he entranced them forever with the words *come and see.* He said come to Simon Peter, and Peter felt the courage and love to walk out on the water. To the rich young man he said, "Give away your treasures, then come and follow me," and the young man couldn't do it, but Jesus looked at him and loved him anyway. Children heard their names called when he said, "Let the children come to me and don't get in their way." How natural to a child it is. Sometimes I have need to dwell on his words "Whoever comes to me, I will no wise cast out."

I have my Bible here. As I have grown older it has become more precious to me. There is one passage in particular that I ask you always to remember. I guess I don't really ask you to remember it as much as to live by it. I have found it true for my life. Jesus is teaching the crowds, and he invites them to come to him and learn from *him*. The words are, as Matthew recalls them,

> Come to me, all who labor and are heavy laden,
> and I will give you rest. Take my yoke upon you,
> and learn from me; for I am gentle and lowly in
> heart, and you will find rest for your souls. For
> my yoke is easy, and my burden is light.

This is Jesus' promise to nurture all those who come to him. You will need that promise. Put it into your backpack with the other treasures you carry.

Of course, Jesus isn't only offering rest. Immature faith looks to God just for relief from burdens. I pray that you will move beyond that stage into the maturity of faith that will make you a productive worker in God's work force. There is no discipleship without a task. Don't settle for welfare and let someone else do your work for you. Don't be a Christian consumer, like the world teaches us to be. You have more in you than that, and you will miss the greatest joy of your faith. Be a productive worker who needs not be ashamed, hearing your share of the hardships and toils it takes to do the work of the kingdom.

Besides that, Jesus said you have to take his yoke to have his rest. Here is the hard part that may make you stumble. The yoke is something that you work with. It helps you bear burdens. Jesus puts it on his followers, if they come to him and ask for it. But that is really no different from the desires of our lives, because they put yokes on us and work us in their service. The difference is that Jesus said his yoke fits and is light, and strangely enough, this yoke and this work don't tire a person out; they refresh.

I hope you come to love the Church and all it stands for and all it does for good. Invest your life in it and give yourself to it, and then, only then, I think, you will come to love the Church. You will find no work more satisfying, if you put your heart into it. When God gives the task, God gives the will and means to accomplish it. You may say that sounds like a line, but I have found it to be reliable in my life.

But enough of this. You can't learn about rest and joy from me and my journey of faith, only from this mysterious one who says, "Come and learn of me." It's your call, but I trust you will find in him what I also have found. That is why I don't have to give you much advice about your life.

Well, the sun has long since set. You know I love you and want the best for you. You are a joy to me. Forever. Choose your teachers well. I will see you when the sun rises.

40. When Blessings Become Commonplace
W. Clyde Tilley

Then the father said to the son, "Son, you are always with me, and all that is mine is yours."

—Luke 15:31

We have here the story of a father and his two sons. The one was a playboy, and the other was a plowboy. The plowboy had stayed home, behaved himself, and enjoyed a good life. The playboy had sought what he thought was a good life, only to end up in a pigpen. Reduced to abject misery, the playboy had swallowed his pride and come home to be welcomed amid a great celebration of joy.

The plowboy was so angry at his father and jealous of his brother that he boycotted the party. Coming late from the field, he heard music coming from his house the likes of which he had never heard before. It was a servant who explained it to him: "Your brother has come home. Your father has killed the fatted calf!"

Boy, was he ever mad! Perhaps he had been fattening that calf for the county fair. But more repulsive than that consideration was the idea that it should be slaughtered for this no-good sibling. Although the dominant mood on the farm that night was one of joy, there were at least two who were unhappy: the fatted calf and the elder brother, the plowboy! So he decided not only to boycott

---

W. Clyde Tilley is Professor of Religion and Philosophy at Lane College, in Jackson, Tennessee. He is also Pastor of Eagle Creek Baptist Church in Holladay, Tennessee. Tilley is a graduate of the Southern Baptist Theological Seminary and has served pastorates in Tennessee and Kentucky. He is the author of numerous articles, sermons, reviews, and poems.

the party but to spill his misery on as many people as he could, to wither the lettuce of their joy with the hot grease of his bitterness.

But thank God, the playboy and the plowboy are not the only two characters in the story. There is also the loving father, a father who loved his two boys with an equal love. Despite his great joy at the playboy's return, he didn't let it eclipse his love for the disgruntled plowboy. So the father came out and reminded his son of the good life they had enjoyed together. The father left the warmth of celebrated joy and went out into the cold dark night of his plowboy son's self-imposed misery. This boy's complaint was that in spite of his accumulated seniority on the farm, there had never been a time when even a lean goat, much less a fatted calf, had been slaughtered for him.

Now it is the father's time to speak. As he does so he counters his son's brokenness and gives us a text for this Thanksgiving season. "Son," he said, "you are always with me, and all that is mine is yours!"

If this text would yield up its treasures to us today, we must remind ourselves that for this boy *the good life had become commonplace*. The thousands of times he had sat at the father's table had taken the edge off his blessings. The plowboy's problem was that, in his resentment about his prize calf roasting on the barbecue, he forgot about his daddy's deep freeze. He forgot all the times he had sat at the family table and nourished himself with the delicious benefits that regularly graced it!

We are all to some degree creatures of habit. It is easy to become so fascinated with the spectacular that we miss out on the ordinary. The tendency is to see God at work at only a few high points in our lives and to give thanks for these. But millions of bite-sized blessings are apt to get overshadowed and overlooked.

God has given us so many blessings that, unless we take special care, some of them will begin to look like reruns. But if this happens, our insensitivity contributes to an optical illusion, for there are no reruns with God. The weeping prophet, who had every reason to weep because his city lay in ruins, had a moment of brilliant insight when he could more easily have yielded to the temptation of oversight. "Thy compassions fail not," he said, "they are new every morning; great is thy faithfulness!" (Lam. 3:22–23).

New every morning! There are no reruns with God! The psalmist captured it equally well when he said, "This is the day [and this can be said of any day] the Lord has made; let us rejoice and be glad in it" (Ps. 118:24). Days do not roll off an assembly line; they come to us, each one especially crafted for us by their Maker, who produces no reruns.

It is easy to know this with our minds and still let the dazzle of the exceptional blind us to what is always with us. The plowboy needed to be reminded that he was ever with his father and that all that belonged to the father belonged to him.

My wife and I often have different philosophies when it comes to travel. She likes to get on the interstate and head straight for the destination. If we have time, I like to take the slower and less-traveled roads and see the countryside on the way, to smell, as we say, the roses. People like to travel at different paces through life. Some like to take the nonstop express and target the destination. Some like to get on the local and stop at every little burg and villa, just to savor the riches of the unpretentious ordinary. If we don't take care, we will miss out on a thousand rich treasures as we bound beyond speed limit to the spectacular.

I often think about the slower-paced years of my youth, although I grant you that everything wasn't hunky-dory then either. When I went to college, I was the first in my family to do so. It cost about seven hundred dollars a year for those four years to attend, and of course, the problem in those days was to get the seven hundred dollars. But there wasn't a day that I didn't feel so fortunate to be there. Missing a class period was out of the question unless it was beyond our power to be there.

But what happens today? College has become ordinary, commonplace. There is so much scholarship money available. So many colleges vie for student recruits. Somehow it takes the edge off. Students miss class going and coming and, from my experience as a classroom instructor, are satisfied to learn little or nothing. Like the plowboy, we often do not know how fortunate we are in this and other arenas.

For a number of years, almost since its beginning, I've been associated with the wonderful ministry of Habitat for Humanity. This ministry works with underhoused people for whom an adequate shelter has not become commonplace. These people are joined in building their own houses, which they then have the privilege of buying at a price they can afford to pay because nobody is making a profit and nobody is charging interest. Hear the testimony of one mother who had recently had the joy of moving her family into a new Habitat home: "I'm so happy," she says, "I could cry. I'm so grateful to God for this house; every morning I start praying in the front bedroom and I go through every room, thanking God for this house!" Maybe she has given us a model for thinking about every day of our lives. Every hour of our day is like a room in the house of our day, a blessing we need to claim and count as we move through them one by one.

Another treasure of insight we need to claim from this text is that of seeing that *the vision of the elder brother was distorted by his ingratitude*. There are some interesting things in this boy's conversation with his father. After his father had left the party to come out to him and the son had begun to file his complaint, he zeroed in upon the focus of his unhappiness: "When this son of yours," he said [he called him "this *son of yours*"], "when this son of yours came back, who has devoured your property with prostitutes, you killed the fatted calf for him!" (v. 30). The amazing thing is that what this elder son said was absolutely true. What he said accords with what the story tells us about the younger son (v. 13) and what he had admitted about himself (v. 21). The problem was not that this boy didn't have his facts straight but that he didn't have his head on straight. It was a matter of perspective, of attitude. His ingratitude had distorted his perspective. Because he had forgotten what the father was about to tell him, he couldn't see his own blessedness and he couldn't see that the same act whereby the father had a son restored meant that he himself had had a brother restored. So that intrusion who had disrupted an otherwise tranquil household was "this son of yours."

But the father could not let this pass. Granted, there is a time to speak of our brothers and sisters as children of their parents. But this was no time for that. This son needed to be reminded that this young man was also his brother. So the conversation was not over until the father had spoken of the playboy as "this brother of yours." "We had to celebrate and rejoice because this brother of yours was dead and has come to life" (v. 32).

It is so difficult at times to see our relational inconsistencies, the denial of brotherhood and sisterhood to those who share a common parentage. There was no way this playboy could be a son of the same father without being his brother. But the plowboy with his distorted perspective was so confused he could not see it. He had to be reminded of it because this was one of the blessings that his ingratitude was obscuring.

This is why the plowboy would not go in to the party. Whether he eventually did, we can never know, but up to that point he had not gone in. His boycott of this grand party tells us volumes about his distorted perspective. It tells us first that, for him, receiving was better than giving. In defiance of a clear teaching of Jesus (Acts 20:35), the boy was perturbed because the brother was receiving at the moment and he was not, and he was letting slip by one of the best opportunities to give he would ever have.

His boycotting of the party tells us also that on the plowboy's scale of values, hoarding was better than sharing. That was his objection to his brother. The plowboy had stayed at home to hoard his share of the estate, which his brother had chosen to waste. But he was not only an advocate of hoarding over wasting; he was an advocate of hoarding over sharing. The time had come to do some sharing, and he still wanted to hoard.

Also, the plowboy would not go in to the party because, for him, calculating was better than lavishing. The time had come in the family to do a little lavishing. But the calculating mentality of the elder brother would not allow him to participate despite a fallen brother's restoration to life and sight. Like the disciples who could not approve the woman's anointment of Jesus on the eve before his arrest because of the dollar marks before their eyes, neither could this brother rejoice at a time that obviously called for joy.

Let us wring one more splash of liquid treasure from this inexhaustible text: *Our God is the source of both the ordinary and the extraordinary.* The reason Jesus told this story in the first place was because some people for whom God's favor had become commonplace could not approve Jesus' receptive demeanor toward those for whom it had not (Luke 15:1–2).

Now that which belonged to the father that the elder son had a share in because he had chosen to stay at home must have looked pretty ordinary alongside that roasted calf. But we need to remind ourselves as he needed to remind himself that both were the gifts of the same parent, each appropriate to its own occasion. The same father had given both the regularly ordinary and the once-in-a-lifetime extraordinary because of the inherent wisdom of each circumstance.

This will likely fall under the category of spiritualizing, but I can't resist it. When the ancient writer set out to write the creation narrative in Genesis 1, he described it this way: "And God made the two great lights, the greater light to rule the day, and the lesser light to rule the night; he made the stars also"—*he made the stars also* (Gen. 1:16). We are still likely to become so enthralled with the great lights that we fail to take proper notice of the stars. But God made them both. If only we could know the profundity implicit in God's ordinary gifts, we would see the cloth that covers our dining table as a star-spangled banner and the roof that covers our heads as a star-studded canopy!

No less than the elder brother, we, too, become victimized by distorted visions. We, too, can come to see God as the source only of the spectacular, the extraordinary. We come to see the routine as something we have a right to, something we have every right to expect. But oh, how great the distortion! Someone asked me if I believed in divine healing. My response was "This is the only kind I do believe in!" Whether healing comes by medicine or by miracle, it is of God, for our God is a God of the ordinary and the extraordinary, of the natural and of the supernatural.

Whatever we have through honest labor, no matter how meager or how massive, we have it because of the smile of God upon us. There are utterly billions in our world who, despite their unavailing efforts, do not have them. When I ask why I do and they do not, I am forced in my best moments to acknowledge that it is not because I deserve them and they don't. For unless God's mercy should somehow exceed our deserts, we are all hopelessly sunk. To be honest, those of us who have these good things deserve them no better than those who do not.

I intimated earlier in this sermon that you should count your blessings. Now let me acknowledge how foolish that was. You can't count your blessings. There is no way most of us can count our blessings. But I'll tell you something else you can't count. You can't count your sins! You can't count those times you disappoint God. You can't count those ways you keep coming up short. Yet God in his mercy continues to bless in mysterious and merciful ways that do not calculatingly take account of our deserts. Thanks be to God, we are ever with God, and the treasures of heaven are ours!

Be thankful, my brother and sister! Celebrate thanksgiving! As you do so, take the second part of this word seriously: *giving*. The father could not be adequately thankful without giving to his destitute son. The plowboy was not adequately thankful and so did not give to his destitute brother. The instability of our economy reminds us how fragile our status is. Let this be a time of expressing gratitude by sharing those blessings that threaten to become commonplace with those who are not faced with that temptation.

Index of Contributors

Index of Sermon Titles

Index of Scriptural Texts